T3-BHM-549

HOW TO
DESIGN & BUILD
YOUR OWN WORKSPACE
with plans

Other TAB books by the author:

No. 1269
$16.95

HOW TO
DESIGN & BUILD
YOUR OWN WORKSPACE
with plans

BY DON GEARY

TAB BOOKS Inc.

BLUE RIDGE SUMMIT, PA. 17214

FIRST EDITION

FIRST PRINTING

MAY 1981

Copyright © 1981 by TAB BOOKS Inc.

Printed in the United States of America

Reproduction or publication of the content in any manner, without express permission of the publisher, is prohibited. No liability is assumed with respect to the use of the information herein.

Library of Congress Cataloging in Publication Data

Geary, Don.
    How to design & build your own workspace—with plans.

    "TAB book #1269."
    Includes index.
    1. Workshops. I. Title.
TT152.G4   643'.58   80-28461
ISBN 0-8306-9638-5
ISBN 0-8306-1269-6 (pbk.)

Cover photo courtesy of Masonite Corp.

Contents

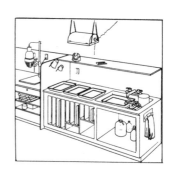

Introduction

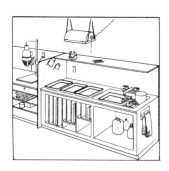

Studios and workshops in the home are special places for accomplishing special tasks. They offer the user a place for expression, creativity and they are set up to take full advantage of available space. The benefit of setting up a studio or workshop includes a highly efficient workspace that can be used and enjoyed for many productive years.

In the ideal situation, you would have a studio or workshop that is large enough for you to pursue your chosen diversion—whether it is woodworking projects or tuning the family automobile. More often than not, however, the reality is one room or area of the home that is more or less set aside for everything from fixing broken toasters to framing pictures.

In many cases, this general work area is part of the basement or garage. There will usually be a workbench of some sort that is piled to eye level with projects in various stages of completion. The first step in any project is usually clearing off part of the workbench so the task can get underway. As you probably know, with the bench piled with who knows what, a project is more likely to get thrown on top of the pile rather than get started.

It is my intention in this book to help you to set up an efficient workshop or studio in your home. This space can vary from a small sewing table to an entire room where clay pots are made and fired. A studio or workshop need not be large if it is well planned and takes the fullest advantage of the alloted space. Planning is the key to success here and at least part of every chapter is devoted to determining your needs and then deciding on how you can best utilize the space you have.

Planning a successful studio or workshop involves a bit of foresight. As you grow your needs for storage and workspace also expand. It is quite important to not only plan for the space you need right now, but to plan for the space you think you will need in the coming years. The end result can only be an efficiently designed workshop or studio that allows you enough freedom to start and finish the projects that you set out to accomplish.

There is enough information in these pages for both the casual hobbyist as well as the professional. For example, in Chapter 3 two types of darkrooms are discussed: the temporary and the permanent darkroom. Similar treatment is given in other chapters. This book is filled with plans for workbenches, storage units and specialized equipment such as a darkroom sink that you can make. There are many different approaches to storage and work areas that can be applied to seemingly different crafts or hobbies.

It is my sincerest hope that you will use this information as a starting point—a warehouse of ideas—to help you set up a personalized workshop or studio in your home. By picking and choosing workbenches, storage units and other projects that apply to your special set of circumstances, you will be able to create a studio or workshop that is tailored to your personal needs. The end result will be a workspace that provides an efficient place to work for many years to come.

Don Geary

Chapter 1
The Home Office

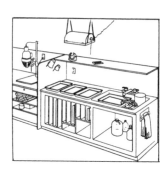

Every home has an office of some type although the area might not be called such. In many cases, this area will be where shopping lists are made out, telephone calls are made and received and bills are kept and paid. At the present time, you probably have some type of file or folder where you keep important papers such as insurance policies, birth certificates and warranties for appliances. More often than not, this home office—if you will permit me to call it such—is in the kitchen. In addition, there might also be other areas in the home which are used as a form of home office such as for childern's school work or study, a table or small writing desk in a bedroom for letter writing away from the usual noise of the household and an area for dad to do a little homework away from the office (Figs. 1-1A and 1-1B).

All of these areas actually are minioffices and each serves at least one specific purpose in the home. A true home office is much more than a place to keep correspondence, bills and other material. In ever increasing numbers, American homes contain a larger area—in many cases an entire room—devoted to office space. From this office, the homeowner might run a sideline business or, in some instances, this office might be used by a professional. Unfortunately, the general rule for a home office is to keep adding material to the room until the user can barely move (let alone work properly).

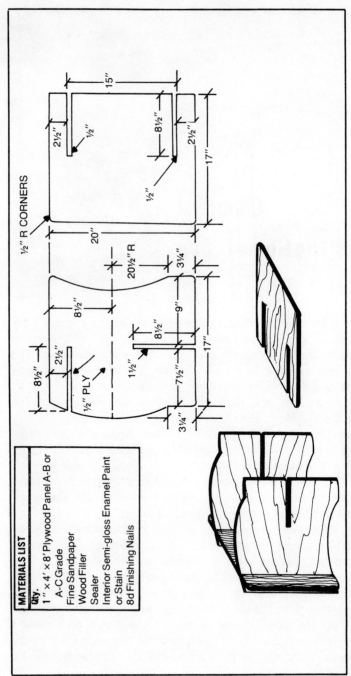

MATERIALS LIST

Qty.

1″ × 4′ × 8′ Plywood Panel A-B or
A-C Grade
Fine Sandpaper
Wood Filler
Sealer
Interior Semi-gloss Enamel Paint
or Stain
8d Finishing Nails

Fig. 1-1A. Plans for a table/rocker/chair (courtesy of Georgia-Pacific).

Fig. 1-1B. Completed table/rocker/chair.

Correspondence gets piled in one area, bills in another, work in progress in another area, completed work in still another area and joining all of these piles are books and magazines. The end result, quite often, is one large pile of paper that easily covers the top of a table. The point is that most home offices suffer from a severe lack of organization. This in turn leads to overall inefficiency and an obvious reduction in productivity.

When an office is organized by a secretary, there will be some type of filing system which insures that everything has a place. Success in a professional office depends in part upon a good organizational system. It will be helpful to discuss how an efficiently organized office is set up. By adapting as many of these practices as possible, your home office will be efficient. In the long run, this will mean that you can accomplish various tasks more easily and, of no small consequence, you will find working in your home office that much more enjoyable. It is not pleasant to spend half an hour searching for a piece of correspondence or information that should be at your fingertips (Fig. 1-2).

Let's take a look at a professional office and see how it is organized. Then you can decide which of these features to include in your own home office to make it as well organized and efficient as possible. Keep in mind that the more time you spend in your home office the greater the need for organization.

FILING CABINET

Probably one of the most important pieces of office equipment is a good filing cabinet. Filing cabinets vary widely in price and it will be to your advantage to learn as much as possible about them before you purchase one. Filing cabinets are available in several different sizes, shapes and basic designs. The most common types are single, double or four drawer models.

Drawer sizes for standard filing cabinets range from letter size—about 12 inches wide—to legal size—about 15 inches in width. The depth of standard filing cabinets is usually in the 28-inch range. However, this size often varies between manufacturers. A standard filing cabinet will pull out so that the files can be viewed vertically (Fig. 1-3). Newer filing cabinet designs are lateral. The entire drawer is exposed when the drawer is pulled out only a few inches. In this case, the files are viewed laterally (Fig. 1-4).

Filing cabinets are made from metal or wood (usually plywood veneer). Generally speaking, a two-drawer wooden filing cabinet will cost as much as a four-drawer metal filing cabinet. The

Fig. 1-2. A perfect example of an office that is suffering from a lack of organization.

Fig. 1-3. Full suspension vertical file features locking security for letter and legal size documents (courtesy of Anderson Desk Inc.).

difference in price is most often a result of the craftmanship involved as well as the cost of materials.

The heart of any filing cabinet is the track system on which the drawers slide. It is this system, in any given file cabinet, that will have a direct bearing on the selling price. The quality of the suspension system will also determine if the filing cabinet will perform under a load. Any file drawer will operate with relative ease when empty. As weight is added—up to 75 pounds is easily possible—the roller system for the drawer becomes more important.

Generally, the more expensive filing cabinets will have a suspension system that will perform well under heavy loads. The best types of suspension systems are called full suspension roller systems and these are easy to spot. Simply pull out the drawer and look to see if the suspension system slides out with the drawer. This will appear as a small track on both sides of the drawer and on which the drawer slides. On lesser quality file cabinets, the drawers themselves will slide on ball bearings or even tiny

Fig. 1-4. Horizontal file drawers feature central locking (courtesy of Anderson Desk Inc.).

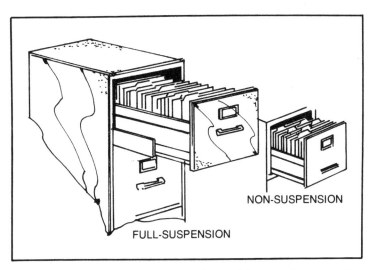

NON-SUSPENSION

FULL-SUSPENSION

Fig. 1-5. Filing cabinet drawers slide on either the full suspension system (the best) or the non-suspension system.

wheels—on older cabinets especially—and these do not work well when a load is added to the drawer (Fig. 1-5).

As I mentioned earlier, prices for filing cabinets vary greatly. It is entirely possible to find a new four-drawer filing cabinet for under $50 but, chances are very good that you will not be satisfied with its performance in the long run. As weight is added, more effort will be required to pull the drawer out. It is a fair assumption that you cannot find a new quality four-drawer filing cabinet for under $100. When shopping for a filing cabinet, the old saying "let the buyer beware" is applicable.

If you cannot afford an expensive filing cabinet, consider buying a used one. Every large city has at least one store that deals in used office equipment. Here you can expect to find a quality filing cabinet for half the new price. Another possibility is to try and find a used filing cabinet at a garage sale or flea market. In some cases, you might have to do a little refinishing. If you have more time than money, you should be able to find a file cabinet within your price range.

Still another possibility, if you are handy with woodworking tools, is to build your own filing cabinet. A material list and diagram is shown in Fig. 1-6.

Of course, a filing cabinet alone will not solve your home office organizational problems unless you use this piece of equipment properly. Obviously, you will not cure your office clutter problems if you simply pile all correspondence and important papers in the file cabinet. You will only be transforming all of the little piles into one great one in a drawer. You must set up and use some type of filing system.

One very real aid to any filing system is a special set of file folders that hang from a metal rack inside the file drawer. One brand is called Pendaflex suspension file folders. Available at any office supply store, these folders are much easier to use than conventional file folders because they hang rather than simply stack inside the drawer (Fig. 1-7).

Because setting up a personal filing system is really beyond the scope of this book, you will have to turn elsewhere for additional information about filing. Generally, all things are filed alphabetically. A letter from John Anderson would logically be filed in the "A" folder. A brochure from Georgia-Pacific on wall paneling could be filed under either "Paneling" or "G". In time, you will work out the filing system that is best for your needs. Then you will have solved the office clutter problem.

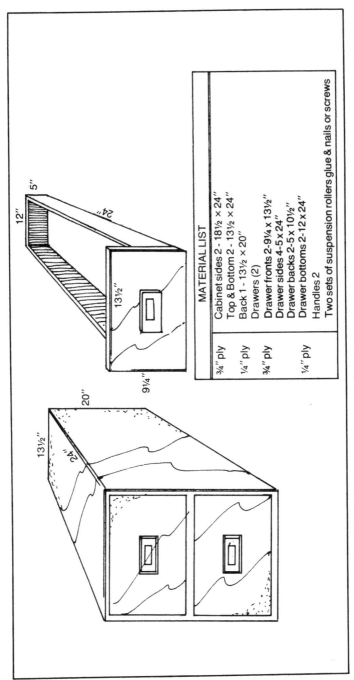

MATERIAL LIST

¾" ply	Cabinet sides 2 - 18½ × 24" Top & Bottom 2 - 13½ × 24"
¼" ply	Back 1 - 13½ × 20" Drawers (2)
¾" ply	Drawer fronts 2-9¼ x 13½" Drawer sides 4-5 x 24" Drawer backs 2-5 x 10½"
¼" ply	Drawer bottoms 2-12 x 24" Handles 2 Two sets of suspension rollers glue & nails or screws

Fig. 1-6. Plans for a two-drawer file cabinet.

17

Fig. 1-7. Files by Pendaflex hang on a special metal rack which makes using the files very simple.

DESKS

Every office needs a desk of some sort. Size, shape, location and cost are all directly related to your needs. The very basic of all desks is a simple table that is large enough for the tasks you have in mind. At the other end of the scale is something along the lines of the desk used by the president of General Motors. Not to be overlooked is the standard knee-hole, flat-top metal office desk used in most offices across the country.

Before you dismiss this type of desk as too impersonal and cold, consider some of the advantages of a desk of this type. The top will be flat and large enough to allow you to work with space to spare. Conventional desks most commonly have several drawers which will prove indispensable in organizing and running your home office. These might include a file drawer which could eliminate the need for a standard filing cabinet. Other drawers can be used for storage of office supplies such as paper, stationary, pencils, etc. Some desks also have a special section that holds a typewriter off to one side. This special arrangement is often designed to "fold" the typewriter into the side of the desk when it is not in use (Fig. 1-8).

New desks are expensive and this is especially true for wooden models. If you shop carefully in used office equipment stores, you should be able to find a second-hand wooden office desk for a fraction of the cost of a new one. You might have to do a bit of refinishing on a used wooden desk, but with a little creativity you will be able to turn the desk into a workable piece of furniture for your home office. Some of the possibilities when refinishing a used office desk include the following.

☐ Entirely remove the finish by hand or have the work done by a furniture stripping service. After stripping, sand all surfaces of the desk until all surface imperfections have been removed.

☐ Refinish the desk by rubbing a wood stain into the surface. After the stain dries, apply several coats of a clear, flat or semigloss finish such as a good polyurethane or varnish.

☐ Spray the desk with a solid color such as white, black or a color that conforms with the surrounding furnishings, walls and floor coverings.

☐ Cover all vertical surfaces of the desk with any of the following: wallpaper, carpeting, paneling, floor tile, cork, or other suitable material.

☐ Recover the top of the desk with solid plastic laminate (such as formica) or with a new wooden covering—either solid

Fig. 1-8. A rather nice knee hole desk (courtesy of Anderson Desk Inc.).

wood or veneer. Keep in mind that the finish on the surface of the desk should be flat rather than glossy. This will reduce glare and make working at the desk easier on your eyes.

Still another possibility for a home office desk is one that you build yourself. Once you start thinking in terms of creating your own working space, unlimited possibilities present themselves. In fact, you will be limited only by your imagination and available space. In addition, adding your personal touch to your home office can be lots of fun. Some of the possibilities for homemade desks include the following.

A hardwood door placed on top of two double-drawer filing cabinets. For this very basic desk, you can use almost any "top" as long as it is wide enough to work on (18 to 24 inches minimum). The top should also be thick enough to offer a sound working surface. Three-quarter inch thick plywood can be used as long as the span is not too great (say 4 feet). For spans greater than this, you can increase the strength of the plywood by attaching reinforcing along the front and back edges of the plywood (see Fig. 1-9).

The desk top described in Fig. 1-9 lends itself to many variations. The basic top can be sanded and then stained a dark wood tone and finally given a few coats of a clear, flat finish. The same top could be primed and painted a solid color using a flat finish rather than a glossy finish.

Another possibility, and one that will produce a desk top that is extremely durable, is to cover the edges and top of the desk with a plastic laminate material (Fig. 1-10).

The base for your home office desk can be two file cabinets. Alternatives to this include wooden cabinets that you can quickly make in your home woodworking shop or simple but sturdy legs fastened to the ends of your desk top. To make simple wooden cabinets that will serve as supports for your homemade desk, it is usually best to work with plywood.

It might be helpful at this time to discuss some of the different types of plywood that are available to the do-it-yourselfer for building simple cabinets. The American Plywood Association recommends that you specify medium density overlaid (MDO) plywood for excellent results when you plan to finish the cabinet with several coats of paint. This grade of plywood has a smooth resin-treated fiber surface that is heat fused to the panel face and will take and hold paint coatings quite well. For any type of cabinet that will be painted, A-A, A-B or A-D interior type sanded plywood

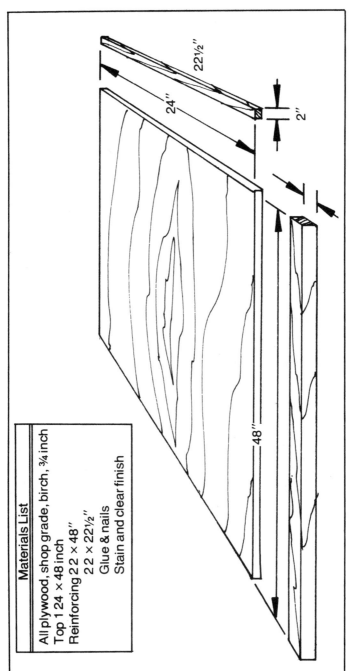

Materials List

All plywood, shop grade, birch, ¾ inch
Top 1 24 × 48 inch
Reinforcing 2 2 × 48''
    2 2 × 22½''
    Glue & nails
    Stain and clear finish

22½''

24''

2''

48''

Fig. 1-9. A plywood desk top.

21

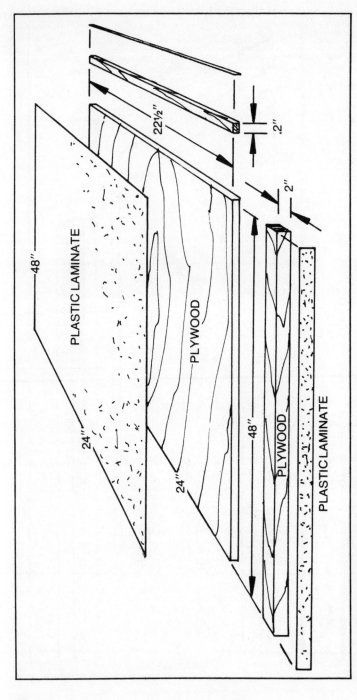

PLASTIC LAMINATE

48"

24"

PLYWOOD

24"

22½"

.2"

2"

48"

PLYWOOD

PLASTIC LAMINATE

Fig. 1-10. A desk top can be covered with plastic laminate.

Table 1-1. Types and Uses of Interior Plywood.

Interior Type

Grade Designation[2]	Description and Most Common Uses	Typical Grade-trademarks	Veneer Grade Face	Veneer Grade Back	Veneer Grade Inner plies solid	Most Common Thicknesses (inch)[3]
N-N, N-A, INT-APA N-B INT-APA	Cabinet quality. For natural finish furniture, cabinet doors, built-ins, etc. Special order items	NN G1 INT APA PS1 74 NA G2 INT APA PS1 74 ND G3 INT APA PS1 74	N	N.A. or B	N.A. or C	3/4
N-D-INT-APA	For natural finish paneling. Special order item.		N	D	D	1/4
A-A INT-APA	For applications with both sides on view. Built-ins, cabinets, furniture and partitions. Smooth face, suitable for painting.	AA G4 INT APA PS1 74	A	A	D	1/4 3/8 1/2 5/8 3/4
A-B INT-APA	Use where appearance of one side is less important but two solid surfaces are necessary.	AB G4 INT APA PS1 74	A	B	D	1/4 3/8 1/2 5/8 3/4
A-D INT-APA	Use where appearance of only one side is important. Paneling, built-ins, shelving, partitions, and flow racks.	A-D GROUP 1 APA INTERIOR PS1 74 000	A	D	D	1/4 3/8 1/2 5/8 3/4
B-B INT-APA	Utility panel with two solid sides. Permits circular plugs.	BB G3 INT APA PS1 74	B	B	D	1/4 3/8 1/2 5/8 3/4
B-D INT-APA	Utility panel with one solid side. Good for backing, sides of built-ins. Industry: shelving, slip sheets, separator boards and bins.	B-D GROUP 3 APA INTERIOR PS1 74 000	B	D	D	1/4 3/8 1/2 5/8 3/4
DECORATIVE PANELS-APA	Rough-sawn, brushed, grooved, or striated faces. For paneling, interior accent walls, built-ins.	DECORATIVE BD G1 INT APA PS1 74	C or btr	D	D	5/16 3/8 1/2 5/8
PLYRON INT-APA	Hardboard face on both sides. For counter tops, shelving, cabinet doors, flooring. Faces tempered, untempered, smooth, or screened.	PLYRON INT APA		D	C & D	1/2 5/8 3/4

is best. Where a quality natural finish will be applied (varnish or clear finish, for example) you should select fine grained panels in A-A, A-B or A-D grades (Table 1-1).

Your first step in building two cabinets as desk supports is to thoroughly plan the project. The best way to do this is to draw a diagram of the cabinets. Carefully determine and indicate the dimensions of the finished cabinet. The height of the cabinet is very important. A desk that is too high or low will not be comfortable to work at.

The standard working height for the top of a desk is 29 inches. To arrive at this finished height, you must take the thickness of the desk top as well as the thickness of the plywood used to build the cabinets into consideration. This is where the diagram comes in handy. If, for example, the top of the desk will be made from one-half inch thick plywood, then the height of each cabinet will be 28 ¼ inches (29 inches minus ¾ inches = 28 ¼). In short, you must subtract the thickness of the desk top from 29 inches to arrive at the proper height for the two cabinets.

The depth of the cabinets will also be directly related to the width of the desk top. If, for example, the desk is 16 to 18 inches wide, then the cabinets should also be this dimension so that they will fit underneath the desk top and provide support. Some leeway is permissible here and especially when the desk top is very wide. In cases when the desk top is wider than 24 inches, you can build the cabinets narrower and then center them under the desk top.

The width of the cabinets is the one area where you have total freedom. The only requirements are that the cabinets should be wide enough to offer adequate support for the top and be wide enough to be useful. But they should not be so wide as to restrict leg room. In Fig. 1-11 the diagram indicates 12 inches for the width and that is a suitable width for most purposes.

One alternative to homemade plywood cabinets is to purchase ready-made cabinets from your local lumber yard or home improvement center. A little shopping will reveal that many kitchen cabinets are quite suitable for desk top supports. Kitchen cabinets are available in a myriad of sizes, shapes, designs and finishes. In most cases you will find that the wall-hung cabinets are better suited to your needs. Cabinets that are used for bases for kitchen counters are generally too high for desk supports.

Still another possibility are simple legs for your desk. A selection of legs suitable for a homemade desk can be found at your local home improvement center. In most cases, these table legs

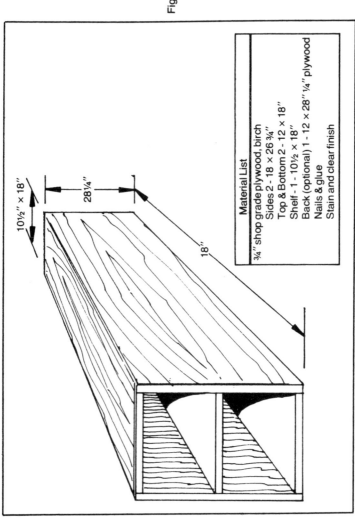

Fig. 1-11. Desk top support cabinet.

10½" × 18"

28¼"

18"

Material List

¾" shop grade plywood, birch
Sides 2 - 18 × 26 ¾"
Top & Bottom 2 - 12 × 18"
Shelf - 1 - 10½ × 18"
Back (optional) 1 - 12 × 28" ¼" plywood
Nails & glue
Stain and clear finish

25

will come with the hardware necessary for installing them under your desk top.

If you are not satisfied with the ready made variety of desk legs, you can easily make ends for your desk that will do the job nicely. One way to support your desk is to use three-fourth inch thick plywood that is cut to the desired height and fastened to both ends of your desk top. Use a good grade woodworking glue and wood screws to fasten the ends. If your desk top is large, it will be to your advantage to reinforce the support system as in Figs. 1-12A and 1-12B.

In addition to a desk for your home office, you will also need a chair. The more time you spend at your desk, the more important the chair becomes. Probably the best bet is an adjustable office chair. With such a chair, you can adjust the height of the seat and angle of the back of the chair so that there is a comfortable balance between desk and chair when in use.

Modern office chairs cost about $100 new, but used models can usually be had for half this amount. It really is false economy to think that you can use just any chair for your home office. Remember that the point of a personal home office is to create an atmosphere that is custom fit to your needs and comfortable to work in (Fig. 1-13).

SHELVING AND STORAGE

In addition to a filing cabinet or some other means of storing correspondence and information, your home office will not be complete unless you have some type of shelving system for the storage of books, magazines and other materials. Because book shelves tend to become part of the home office decoration, you should devote a certain amount of time to planning where the shelves will go, length, height and general appearance. The easiest type of book shelves are those which are ready made of wood, plastic or metal. If you are planning to buy ready-made book shelves, you should shop around because prices will vary widely.

If you are handy with woodworking tools, you will probably be thinking along the lines of constructing custom-made book shelves and cabinets. You might decide that a particular area or even an entire wall in your home office is ideal for book shelves. When you are building your own shelving you are limited only by your woodworking ability. You should build the shelves approximately 9 inches wide for standard books. Larger books and magazines will require a shelf width of approximately 12 inches.

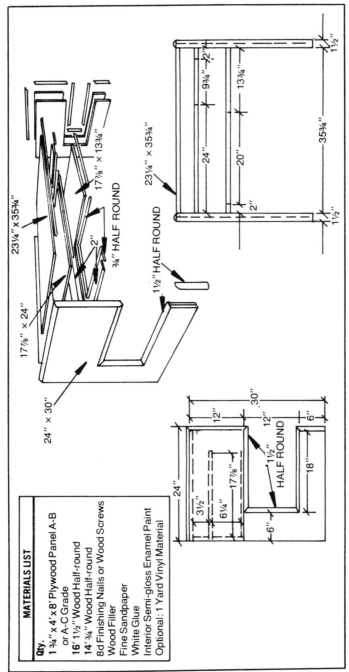

MATERIALS LIST

Qty.

1 ¾″ x 4′ x 8′ Plywood Panel A-B
or A-C Grade

16′ 1½″ Wood Half-round

14′ ¾″ Wood Half-round

8d Finishing Nails or Wood Screws

Wood Filler

Fine Sandpaper

White Glue

Interior Semi-gloss Enamel Paint

Optional: 1 Yard Vinyl Material

23¼″ x 35¾″

17⅞″ x 24″

24″ x 30″

17⅞″ x 13¾″

¾″ HALF ROUND

1½″ HALF ROUND

23¼″ x 35¾″

2″

9¾″

13¾″

24″

20″

35¾″

1½″

1½″

2″

2″

24″

3½″

6¼″

17⅞″

12″

12″

30″

6″

1½″
HALF ROUND

6″

18″

Fig. 1-12A. Plans for a compact desk (courtesy of Georgia-Pacific).

27

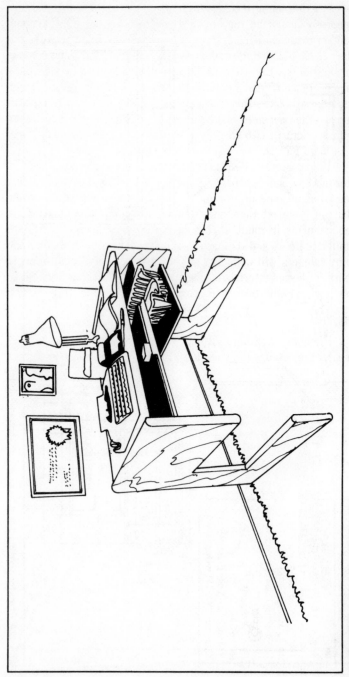

Fig. 1-12B. The completed desk.

Another point to consider is that shelves higher than 6½ feet generally cannot be reached easily. This is about the maximum height for any shelving system or book case. Spacing between the shelves should be large enough to accommodate the highest books in your library. Eleven to 13 inches will be adequate for all but the tallest books. If your home library consists of a large number of paperback books—the trend in publishing is towards smaller books—then consider making most of your shelves 8 inches high with only one or two shelves spaced about 12 inches apart (Figs. 1-14A and 1-14B).

If your storage needs require special characteristics such as storing large sheets of paper or matt board, you will have to custom design some type of storage system for these materials. When planning your storage and shelving system, keep your main requirements in mind. If, for example, your storage needs are limited to books and standard size paper, simple book shelves and filing cabinets will take care of your needs. If you require larger space for large materials or objects, build your storage system so that it will be tailored to your present and future needs (Fig. 1-15).

LIGHTING

Adequate lighting is important for any home office. The greater the detail of the work to be performed, the more important

Fig. 1-13. A good office chair will have a fully adjustable seat and back.

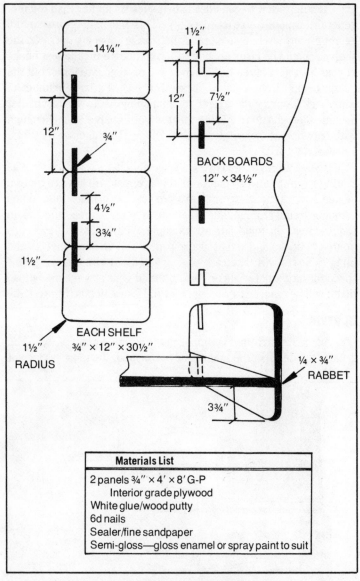

14¼"

1½"

12"

¾"

4½"
3¾"

1½"

EACH SHELF
¾" × 12" × 30½"

1½"
RADIUS

12"

7½"

BACK BOARDS
12" × 34½"

¼ × ¾"
RABBET

3¾"

Materials List
2 panels ¾" × 4' × 8' G-P   Interior grade plywood
White glue/wood putty
6d nails
Sealer/fine sandpaper
Semi-gloss—gloss enamel or spray paint to suit

Fig. 1-14A. Plans for a bookcase (courtesy of Georgia-Pacific).

it becomes to have good lighting. There are many ways to provide good lighting for the home office and I will discuss all of them.

The first and probably the poorest choice of lighting is natural light. During the daylight hours, natural light will vary according to

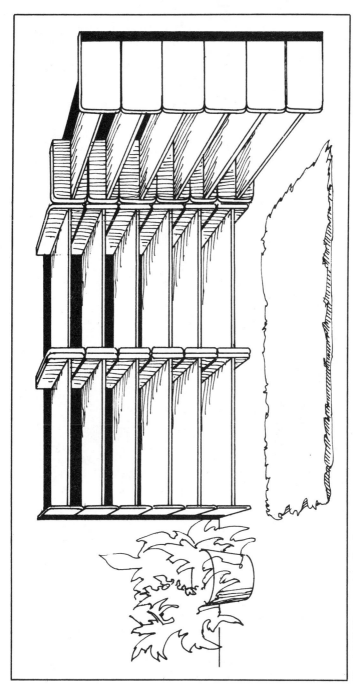

Fig. 1-14B. The completed bookcase.

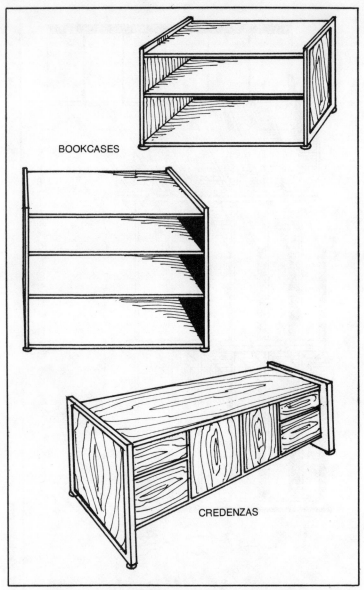

BOOKCASES

CREDENZAS

Fig. 1-15. Bookcases and a Credenzas (courtesy of Anderson Desk Inc.).

time of day, cloud cover and even time of year. In addition, the location of windows will also influence the intensity of natural light. East or west facing windows provide for direct rays of light while north or south facing windows only provide reflected light.

The location of your desk in relation to windows and natural light is very important. Assuming that you are right handed, the natural light should come from your left. This way shadows from your writing hand will not cause distractions while working. This will also mean that your desk will be positioned at a right angle to the window and with the light coming from the left.

The only exception to this is if the windows in the room face north. Then you might want to place the desk so that it faces the window. The light, because it is not direct, will be softer. If the windows in the room face east, west or south, you might want to install window shades or blinds to take the brightness out of the light during the daylight hours. Very bright sunshine can produce a glare.

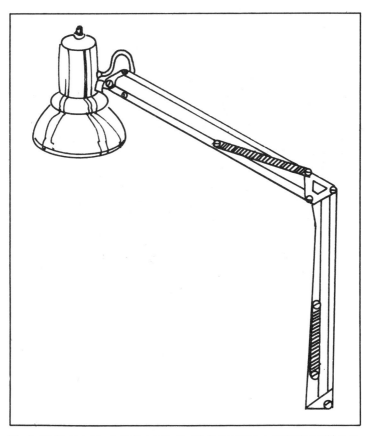

Fig. 1-16. The best type of desk lamp is one that can be pulled into position or moved away with ease.

Probably the best way to provide good lighting in the home office is to use overhead lighting. This is most easily accomplished by using an overhead light fixture. Basically, there are two types: incandescent and fluorescent. There has been a trend over the past few decades to use fluorescent lighting in areas that require good general lighting. This type is your best choice for lighting a home office. As an added bonus, fluorescent lighting uses less electricity while providing at least as much—and often more—light as standard electric light bulbs.

If you find that the work you do in your home office requires more than general lighting, such as accounting or bookkeeping, then you must provide more light over the work area. One good choice is a desk top lamp. There are many types available. You should shop around to find the desk top lamp that is best suited for your needs (Fig. 1-16).

LOCATION OF THE HOME OFFICE

A home office should be located in a room designed or available for the purpose. In many cases, this will turn out to be a spare room in your home or apartment. To think that you can simply set your desk against an unused wall in your living room or other part of your home—that is subject to normal traffic—is to invite distraction from the work at hand.

I can recall an early point in my writing career which might serve to illustrate the necessity of having a special room for your home office. My wife and I had moved from an old brownstone apartment in Manhattan to, of all places—Queens. The old apartment had a spare bedroom that was my office. The new apartment, while being more modern and having more space, nevertheless had fewer rooms. The end result was that I set my desk and files up in a corner of our living room. The room itself was quite large and we found that the space had been wasted because it was not being used.

To make a long and rather sad story short, I never seemed able to work at this desk as long as someone else was in the apartment. Additionally, whenever we had guests there always seemed to be a curiosity about what I was working on and I had a problem with friends and relatives checking out the material on my desk. The end results was that we moved from that apartment to a house about 100 miles north of the city. The house had a spare bedroom that worked very well as an office and I was able to work again.

Fig. 1-17. A telephone in your office can come in very handy, especially if you do any business over the phone.

As an addendum, I should add that we have lived in several houses since then and each had a spare room that I used as an office. Never again will I set up my office in an area that is subject to normal household traffic. A word to the wise is sufficient, I hope.

In addition to having a special place for your home office, there are some other requirements. One is a telephone. If your work requires that you use the telephone, even occasionally for business, then you should consider having an extension phone in your office. In time, this extra cost will be justified if for no other reason than you will have your materials and correspondence close to the phone rather than having them in one place and the telephone in another (Fig. 1-17).

Another requirement to consider when planning a home office is the space. Your special requirements will, of course, be determined by the type of work that you will be doing most of the time in your office. If you are a writer, you will not need too much space unless you also take on projects which require a large flat working surface. One example of this would be laying out artwork and photographs for a book or large magazine article.

Once again, the type of work that you do will give you a very real indication of the basic requirements for the location of your home office. In most cases, you will need at least two electrical outlets in a location that is convenient to where you will be working.

If you plan on dealing with clients in your home office, then you should think along the lines of making your home office more business like. This will mean one or two chairs for clients. If you have enough space, you might want to consider a couch and small coffee table where you can conduct informal business meetings. By all means, add a personal touch to your home office. However, it is important to keep in mind that you want you office to appear professional as well. This makes sense on many levels.

A professional looking office will instill an air of confidence in your clients. The second reason, and one that may not be apparent at first, is that clients will feel comfortable when paying a visit to your office. Logically, if clients feel more at ease in your office, then you will find the same clients coming back with greater frequency. This will be due at least in part to the atmosphere of your office.

A TYPEWRITER & OTHER OFFICE EQUIPMENT

Before you can truly call your home office a professional office, you will need a typewriter. As far as efficiency is concerned,

Fig. 1-18. The IBM ribbon cartridge is a snap to change.

37

the only real choice is an electric typewriter. Even if you are still in the hunt-and-peck stages of typing, an electric typewriter will make any typing job easier and quicker to accomplish.

Additionally, almost any one of the new generation typewriters will help you to turn out correspondence and other material that has a crisp appearance. This is another of those professional traits that I have been detailing throughout this chapter.

At the present time, a professional quality electric typewriter will cost anywhere from $300 to $800. To be sure, a quality electric typewriter will probably be your largest equipment investment for the home office. It is very important to shop carefully because there are many different types of typewriters on the market.

If you haven't been shopping for a typewriter for a few years, you might be surprised at what is currently available. Probably one of the biggest advances in the past decade has been the introduction of a cartridge type ribbon. Gone—hopefully forever—are the days of changing a typewriter ribbon by threading the ribbon through the machine. Now, almost every new typewriter on the market has a ribbon cartridge. To replace the ribbon, you simply lift a lever and the old ribbon can be taken out. To install a new ribbon, you simply drop it into place and push the lever back into position and you are all set to type with a new ribbon (Fig. 1-18).

Another advancement in the past few years was first introduced by IBM (International Business Machines) and it virtually eliminated a moving carriage and character keys. This invention is called a typing element and it is really an example of what American ingenuity can develop.

The IBM typing element is ball shaped and made from plastic. It contains all of the typing characters indicated on the standard keyboard. As you type (in the normal fashion) electrical impulses cause the element to rotate to the desired character and at the same time to strike the page through the typewriter ribbon. The element has the capability of skimming across the page—at a faster rate than anyone can type—typing out characters evenly and rapidly. Type clash—two keys sticking together—is eliminated because the typebars themselves have been eliminated (Fig. 1-19).

In addition, IBM offers a fairly wide selection of typing elements so that you can actually change type styles in seconds by lifting out one element and replacing it with another. This versatility allows you to select a type style best suited for any particular typing project.

Fig. 1-19. The IBM typing element—in an assortment of different type styles—eliminated the moving carriage typewriter.

One last point in favor of a typewriter equipped with a typing element instead of conventional type bars is that because there is no carriage, you need less space for your typewriter. This actually provides more work area around your machine because there is no carriage to slide back and forth. There is also no vibration or machine movement. While IBM has been the pioneer in the typewriter industry, several other companies now offer a machine with similar capabilities.

I purchased an IBM Selectric typewriter in the early '70s and am still using the same machine. It has performed without malfunction and I take the machine for granted at this point. At the time of purchase I paid about $750. Now I am told that the same machine costs about $900 and if I were to sell mine I could probably get $600 for it. As it turns out, I made a sound investment while at the same time having a machine that helps me to turn out professional looking letters and correspondence.

There are several other handy machines to have around the home office. Examples are a pencil sharpener and an electronic

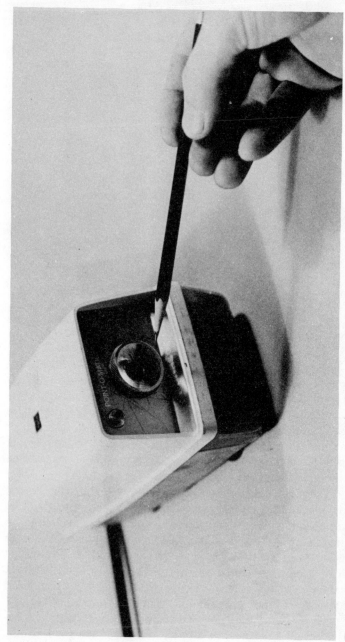

Fig. 1-20. An electric pencil sharpener is one gadget that no office should be without.

calculator. No matter what type of work you plan on doing in your home office, you will always have need of a sharp pencil.

Electric pencil sharpners have been around for several years. When they were first introduced, most people felt that they were a rather frivilous expense that could easily be eliminated. However, you will find one of these handy machines in almost any office in the country. An electric pencil sharpener is the quickest and easiest way to get the job done. If you use pencils at all in your work, buy yourself an electric pencil sharpener and place it close to the area you work. On your desk is probably the best place. Once you start using an electric pencil sharpener, you will wonder how you ever lived without one in the past (Fig. 1-20).

Fig. 1-21. The home office waste basket is almost as handy as a filing cabinet.

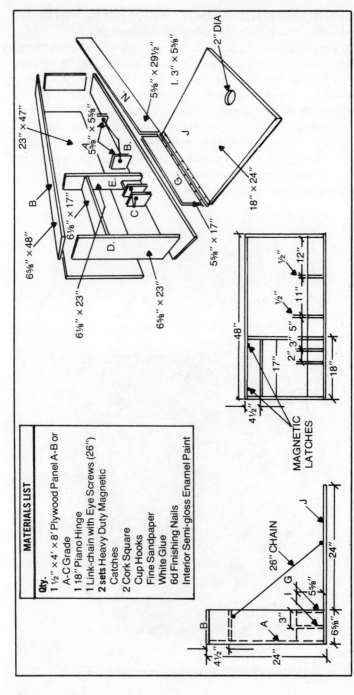

MATERIALS LIST

Qty.
1 ½" × 4' × 8' Plywood Panel A-B or
  A-C Grade
1 18" Piano Hinge
1 Link-chain with Eye Screws (26")
2 sets Heavy Duty Magnetic
  Catches
2 Cork Square
  Cup Hooks
  Fine Sandpaper
  White Glue
  6d Finishing Nails
  Interior Semi-gloss Enamel Paint

Fig. 1-22A. Plans for a message center (courtesy of Georgia-Pacific).

Fig. 1-22B. The completed message center.

43

Another item that is very handy for any home office is an electronic calculator. Ten years ago few people owned one of these little machines. Now you will find one not only in every home, but in classrooms, supermarkets and anywhere else that someone needs to add, subtract, multiply or divide. Hand calculators range in price depending on the function capabilities of any one particular machine. You should be able to find a simple model for about $10 at any variety store. Keep one of these machines on your desk and you will find that you use it for all but the very simplest of calculations.

One last item that no home office should be without is a wastepaper basket. With all of the paperwork that passes through any office, there are only two solutions to the clutter that will result. The first is to respond or file the paper. The second choice is to file the paper in the wastebasket. Buy a wastebasket that is large enough for your needs and make sure that you use it to help you keep some order in your home office (Fig. 1-21).

THE HOME OFFICE AND THE TAX MAN

If you have an office in your home that is used for a business, you might be able to deduct part of your home operating expenses—those which pertain directly to the home office—as a business expense. If your home office occupies one-eighth of your home, you could—if the office meets the Internal Revenue Requirements—deduct one-eighth of your home expenses as a business expense. This would include heat, electricity, insurance, maintenance, and other related business expenses. Not every home office qualifies, however, and you should check with a local office of the IRS before you claim the deduction.

If your home office does qualify for a tax deduction, you would be wise to keep an accurate record of expenses so that you can back up any claims that you make. Probably one of the best ways of keeping track of business expenses is to open a special checking account for your home business and use checks from this account for paying business related bills.

Tax benefits aside, a home office can offer many advantages to those of us who choose to —or must—work at home (Figs. 1-22A and 1-22B). From the start, a home office can be as casual as you want to make it while at the same time offering you a place to turn out professional work. It is important to set up your office according to guidelines that will keep some semblance of order while avoiding the connotations of sterility often attached to the term "office."

Chapter 2
Woodworking Shop

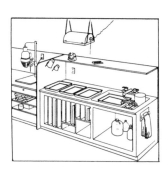

Anyone who works with wood dreams about having the ideal woodworking shop. Imagine, for a moment, what this dream shop would look like. First of all, there would be a room large enough to contain several different woodworking tools such as a table saw, a radial arm saw, a band saw, a drill press, and a jointer/planer. There would be several workbenches which could be used for different projects in progress. Of course, there would be places to hang hammers, screwdrivers, chisels, clamps and other hand tools. In this wonder shop would also have a special place, possibly a closed off area, where you could paint and finish projects away from the dust of the main woodworking shop. Still another area would be used for wood storage. This is where you would stack lumber so that it could dry and cure properly (Fig. 2-1).

Unfortunately, few of us ever get beyond the dreaming stages of a suitable woodworking shop. In fact, the reality of most home woodworking shops is more along the lines of a workbench in the basement piled almost to eye level with tools, broken appliances and other projects that need to be started or finished. With the price of everything rising, American homeowners are realizing that they can no longer afford to have someone else—such as a professional carpenter—come in and remodel or even fix broken things around the home. Except for highly specialized repairs, homeowners are doing the work themselves. But before you can expect to take care of the remodeling and repair projects around your home, you need a place to work (Figs. 2-2 and 2-3).

In this chapter, I will explain how you can set up an efficient home woodworking shop. I will also discuss most of the modern woodworking tools and their uses. The result is that you will be able to create your own home woodworking shop that will be a real aid in performing all of the tasks that are necessary to keep your home in first-class order. The natural extension of a home shop used for repairs is a woodworking shop that can also be used for projects that you enjoy—recreational woodworking, if you will (Fig. 2-4).

The backbone of any woodworking shop is a workbench. In the most basic sense, a workbench is simply a strong table to work on. In reality, a workbench must be much more. When you think about some of the tasks that are commonly done on a workbench, the design of the bench itself becomes clearer. Some of the functions include hammering and sawing wood. Therefore, the surface must be sound and the bench itself must be sturdy.

Fig. 2-1. The home woodworking shop is a place for learning and creativity (courtesy of Shopsmith Inc.).

Fig. 2-2. A woodworking shop (courtesy of Masonite Corporation).

Fig. 2-3. A small workshop fits easily into this special cabinet (courtesy of Masonite Corporation).

Fig. 2-4. A workbench (courtesy of Georgia-Pacific).

The actual location of the workbench will have a direct bearing on how the bench itself must or should be constructed. If, for example, the workbench will be attached to an existing wall, then it need not be as sturdy as if the bench were free standing in the center of the workshop. Nevertheless, a workbench base should be strong enough to withstand the kinds of stress normally associated with woodworking projects.

The base of your workbench can be made from a variety of materials. These include three-fourth inch thick plywood, 2 x 4 or even 4 x 4 inch dimensional lumber. Several different plans for workbenches are given in Figs. 2-5A, 2-5B, 2-6 and 2-7. You should choose the type that is best suited for your needs. Alternate workbench bases can be fashioned from discarded kitchen counter bases. If you are more proficient at woodworking projects, you could make your own base.

The top of your workbench must be constructed so that it will be able to stand up well to impact from hammering. One good material for this is three-fourth inch thick plywood. An alternative is to construct the workbench top from 2 x 2 or 2 x 4 inch dimensional lumber fastened together as shown in Fig. 2-8. A top such as this will be very strong and permit you to accomplish almost any woodworking task.

HAND TOOLS FOR THE WOODWORKING SHOP

The tools most commonly used around any woodworking shop are simple hand tools. In most cases, these are the same tools that

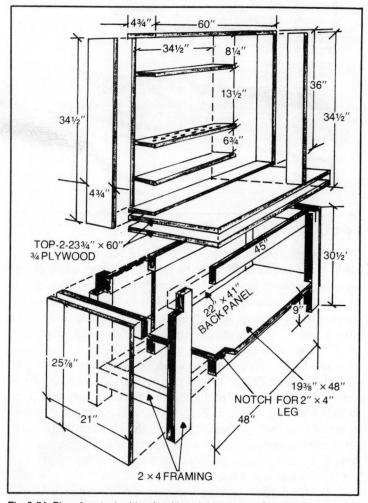

Fig. 2-5A. Plans for a tool cabinet/workbench (courtesy of Georgia-Pacific).

Fig. 2-5B. The completed tool cabinet.

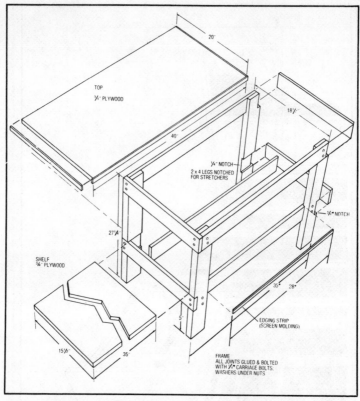

Fig. 2-6. Light-duty workbench plans.

we all initially buy. If you have invested wisely, these tools will last a lifetime. As a basis for your home woodworking shop, it will be helpful to list and discuss these common and useful tools. With a list such as this you will be able to judge if your workshop is equipped well enough to handle most types of woodworking projects. For convenience, I have grouped these tools into general categories and, while many tools are listed, there might be a few of your favorites that are not included.

Measuring Tools

You will find at least three types of measuring tools invaluable around your home woodworking shop. These include a yardstick, a folding ruler and a tape measure. Each has specific uses for measuring and laying out projects. A yardstick is handy for small projects that require precise measurements and your yardstick will

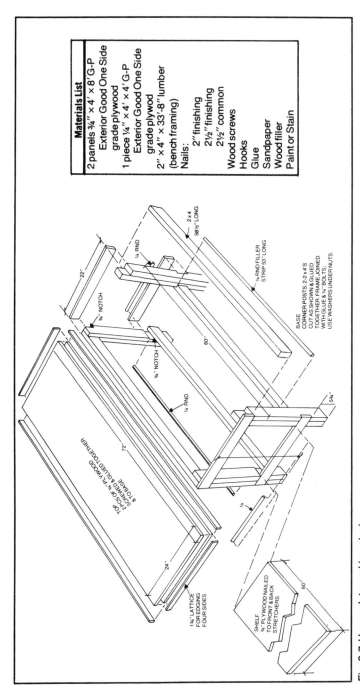

Materials List

2 panels ¾'' × 4' × 8' G-P
  Exterior Good One Side
  grade plywood
1 piece ¼'' × 4' × 4' G-P
  Exterior Good One Side
  grade plywod
2'' × 4'' × 33 -8'' lumber
  (bench framing)
Nails:
  2'' finishing
  2½'' finishing
  2½'' common
Wood screws
Hooks
Glue
Sandpaper
Wood filler
Paint or Stain

2 × 4
58½'' LONG

¼ RND

¾'' NOTCH

¾'' NOTCH

¼ RND FILLER
STRIP 53' LONG

¼ RND

60''

BASE
CORNER POSTS 2-2 × 4'S
CUT AS SHOWN & GLUED
TOGETHER. FRAME JOINED
WITH GLUE & ¼'' BOLTS;
USE WASHERS UNDER NUTS.

5¾''

22''

72''

TOP
2 PCS OF ¾'' PLYWOOD
SCREWED & GLUED TOGETHER
& TO BASE.

24''

1¾'' LATTICE
FOR EDGING
FOUR SIDES

SHELF
¾'' PLYWOOD NAILED
TO FRONT & BACK
STRETCHERS

60''

Fig. 2-7. Heavy-duty workbench plans.

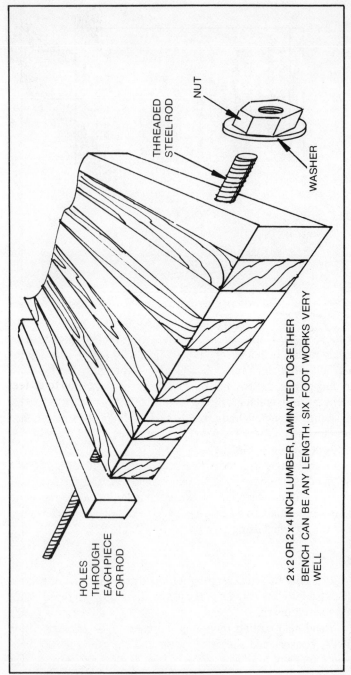

NUT

THREADED
STEEL ROD

WASHER

2 x 2 OR 2 x 4 INCH LUMBER, LAMINATED TOGETHER
BENCH CAN BE ANY LENGTH. SIX FOOT WORKS VERY
WELL

HOLES
THROUGH
EACH PIECE
FOR ROD

Fig. 2-8. A diagram of a workbench top.

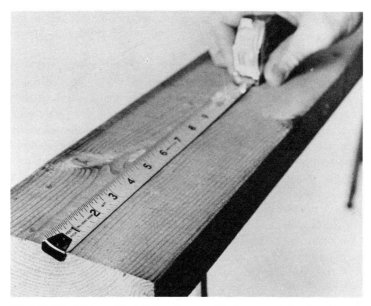

Fig. 2-9. A tape measure is quite handy around the home workshop (courtesy of The Stanley Works).

be most useful if it is marked off in thirty-seconds of an inch. A folding ruler 6 or 8 feet long is very handy for laying out projects that fall within its range. A cabinet or other similiar furniture building project are two examples. A tape measure—up to 25 feet in length—is useful for large projects. While most commonly used for laying out remodeling projects such as floor coverings, other uses for this type of ruler can easily be found around the woodworking shop (Fig. 2-9).

In addition to the rulers mentioned above, you will also find a try square extremely handy around the shop. The try square is invaluable for drawing lines which are at a perfect 90 degree angle or 45 degree angle to a board's edge. You should not mark a board for cutting without using a try square (Fig. 2-10).

Cutting Tools

Probably the largest group of woodworking tools are those which fall into this category. Basically, there are two types: hand held and stationary.

Hand held cutting tools include many types of saws, razor knives, scissors and shears. Every home workshop should have several types of hand saws (Fig. 2-11) to help tackle the various types of cutting tasks. All saws are described according to the number of teeth per inch along the blade as well as the general uses of the particular saw in hand.

For example, a crosscut saw—as the name suggests— is designed for making cuts across the grain of a board. Teeth on a crosscut saw are shaped like tiny knives that face alternately outward. The distance or angle of these teeth results in a cut which is wider than the saw blade itself. This kerf reduces the chances of the saw blade binding in the cut while sawing. The standard crosscut saw is the most frequently used of all saws and, as a result, is available in lengths from 16 inches to 26 inches. The number of teeth per inch along the blade can be from seven to 12.

A rip saw is designed for cutting with the grain of a board. Special chisel-shaped teeth allow the user to cut in the direction of the wood fibers with little effort. A good ripsaw will generally have around four teeth per inch.

It is important to keep in mind that there is a vast difference between a crosscut saw and a ripsaw. Until this day, I still remember when I first learned the difference between these two saws. I was working with my father in his woodworking shop and he

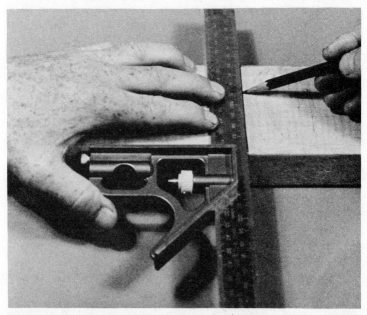

Fig. 2-10. A try square should always be used for marking lumber for a straight cut.

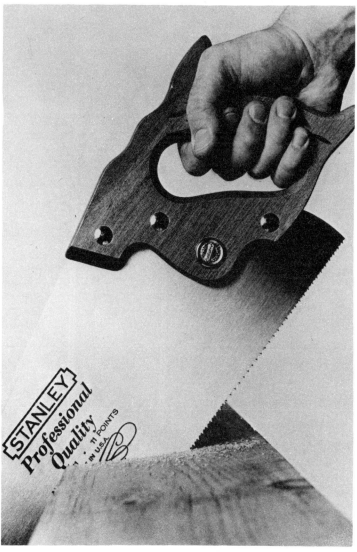

Fig. 2-11. A hand-held saw (courtesy of The Stanley Works).

was teaching me how to use a hand saw to cut a piece of lumber. I
was probably 12 years old at the time. We stopped for lunch and
after eating my father had to tend to some other chores. I elected to
continue practicing my wood cutting.

Back in the shop, I picked up the first saw that came to hand
and began sawing a board along the cut line. After about 20 minutes

of laboring with the cut, my father walked into the shop to check on my progress. As soon as he saw the handsaw I was using, he asked me to stop and try another type of saw.

I remember that my arm was killing me and I couldn't understand why it was taking me so much time and energy to do something that before lunch seemed so easy. I tried the saw offered by my father and much to my surprise I found that cutting was once again relatively easy. The difference, my father pointed out, was that I was attempting to make a rip cut (with the grain of the board) with a crosscut saw.

The results were that the cutting was very difficult and the finished cut was very ragged. If you ever want to commit the difference between a crosscut saw and a ripsaw to memory, simply try using a crosscut saw for making a rip cut or a ripping saw for crosscutting. The difference will become very apparent after a few strokes.

Most home workshops will also have a few other saws. The most common are a coping saw, a backsaw and a hacksaw. Coping saws (Fig. 2-12) are very handy for cutting irregular shapes such as curves or complete circles rather than straight cuts. Blades are easily replaced and they are available in several different points per inch designations.

Coping saws work their best with relatively thin pieces of lumber such as one-fourth inch thick stock up to about three-fourth inch thick stock. For thicker material as well as faster cutting, an electric sabre saw is a better choice. More on this electric saw later in the chapter.

A backsaw is a cutting tool designed to be used in a miter box and for cutting straight lines in lumber. Because a backsaw is considered a finish saw, in that the final cut will have a clean appearance, backsaws are never longer than about 14 inches and they are mainly used for cutting lumber up to about 12 inches in width.

A hacksaw is primarily designed for cutting metal and it is therefore not generally used for cutting wood. However, there are often a number of metal items that need to be cut around the shop. Hacksaw blades, which are very easy to replace, are available in a wide variety of teeth-per-inch designations. As a rule, the more teeth per inch the finer the finished cut will be. This holds true for hacksaw blades as well as for crosscut saw blades.

Until this point, I have only been discussing hand held cutting tools that are powered by muscle. There is a continuing debate

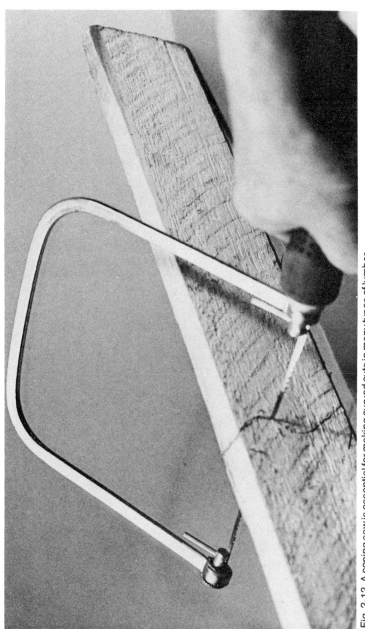

Fig. 2-12. A coping saw is essential for making curved cuts in many types of lumber.

between purists and do-it-yourself woodworkers (not necessarily implying that the two cannot also be one) that the only way to turn out a quality piece of woodwork is with hand-powered tools. The other side of the argument is that the same work can be accomplished with electrically powered cutting tools—with speed the added advantage.

Whichever side of the argument you subscribe to, the fact remains that there are quite a number of electrically powered wood cutting tools that can make woodworking easier and less time consuming to accomplish. For this reason, I will cover some of the more common electrical cutting tools for the home woodworking hobbyist.

Probably the most common cutting tool is a hand-held circular saw. The biggest seller, according to industry sources, is the 7½-inch blade model. At the present time, you can easily find a circular saw in almost any price category from $20 to $200. Differences in price are determined by the horsepower of the unit as well as some of the amenities such as ripping guide, tilt adjustment and depth of cut adjustment (Fig. 2-13).

While a circular saw was originally designed for speeding up the lumber cutting in a house framing operation, reasonable

Fig. 2-13. A hand-held saw (courtesy of Black & Decker).

Table 2-1. Circular Saw Blades.

Combination
Chisel tooth configuration means this blade is the fastest cutting blade in our line. Specifically designed for general-purpose ripping and cross cutting where the finish of the cut is not the most desired effect.

Framing/Rip
An all-purpose blade for smooth, fast cutting in any direction. Rips, cross-cuts, miters, etc. One of the most popular all-purpose blades available. Gives especially fast, smooth finishes when cutting with the grain of both soft and hard woods.

Metal Cutting
Teeth shaped and set specifically for cutting aluminum, copper, lead and other soft metals.

Hollow Ground Planer
Specifically hollow ground fro stain-smooth finish cuts (cross-cuts, rips and miters) in all solid woods. A professional quality blade for use in cabinet work, furniture, etc. Specifically designed to make extremely smooth cuts in wood 1″ thick and thicker. Eliminates need for sanding.

Carbide Tipper (8 tooth)
Specifically designed for cutting tough-to-cut materials such as wallboard, Cemesto Board, asbestos, Formica and Masonite. Will also cut wood where speed and finish are not critical. Each blade has tungsten carbide permanently brazed on each tooth for up to 15 times the cutting life without sharpening.

Carbide Tipped (18 & 20 tooth)
Chisel tooth combination blade for fast general-purpose cutting in all types of woods. Tips are of tungsten carbide material which outlasts regular steel blades up to 10 to 1. Teeth are accurately set for ease of cutting. This all adds up to a blade which gives you the fastest cutting, longest life of any blade available.

Hollow Ground Plywood
Special hollow grinding on the sides of this thin rim blade gives an absolutely smooth cut in plywood, veneers and laminates, etc. Can be used in cross-cutting and mitering for a professional finish on all types of cabinet work. Eliminates need for sanding.

Steel Cutting Friction
Designed for cutting corrugated or sheet roofing, black iron, furnace pipe or thin bar stock. Cuts faster with less filings than abrasive blades. Cuts by friction action.

Cross-Cut
Specifically designed for smooth, fast cutting across the grain of both hard and soft woods where finish is an important factor. May also be used for rip and crosscuts on extremely hard woods.

Flooring
For use where nails or other metal objects may be encountered, such as cutting reclaimed lumber, flooring, opening crates. Allows cross-cuts as well as miters.

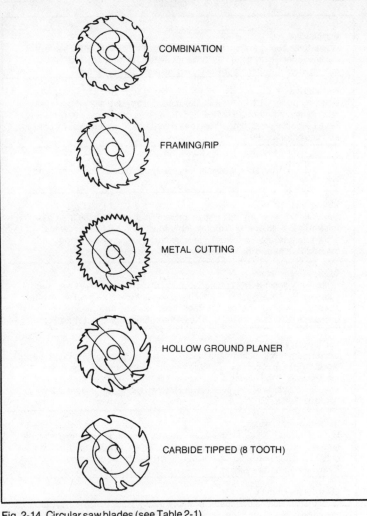

COMBINATION

FRAMING/RIP

METAL CUTTING

HOLLOW GROUND PLANER

CARBIDE TIPPED (8 TOOTH)

Fig. 2-14. Circular saw blades (see Table 2-1).

accuracy can be achieved with a little care and using an edge guide for the saw. Because of the popularity of the hand-held circular saw, many different types of blades are available (see Fig. 2-14 and Table 2-1).

It is important that you choose the right saw blade for the particular cutting job at hand. It is equally important that the blade you are using be kept sharp. This will result in clean cuts and long saw life.

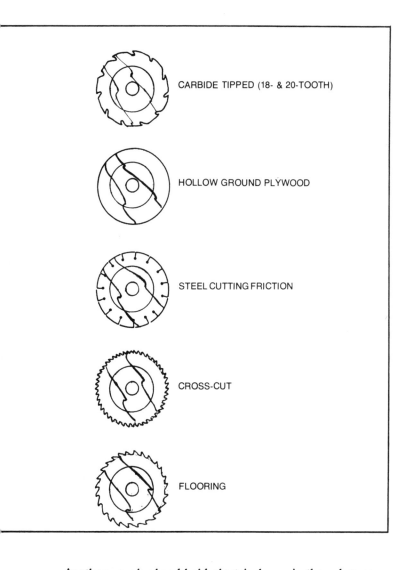

CARBIDE TIPPED (18- & 20-TOOTH)

HOLLOW GROUND PLYWOOD

STEEL CUTTING FRICTION

CROSS-CUT

FLOORING

Another popular hand-held electrical saw is the sabre saw. This tool is used primarily for making other than straight cuts in lumber (Fig. 2-15). This is the electrical version of a coping saw and it is capable of doing the same type of cutting with the added advantage of speed. There are a number of different types of sabre saw blades available and you should choose the proper blade for the type of cutting you are doing (see Fig. 2-16 and Table 2-2).

In addition to the hand-held electric saws, there are also

Table 2-2. Jigsaw Blades.

Blade Type	Description of Blade and Use	Type of Cut	Speed of Cut	Blade Length	Teeth per in.
Set Tooth	Cuts soft wood ¾" and thicker. Canted shank for fast cutting action. High carbon steel. Twin pack of two U1350 jig saw blades	Rough	Fast	33	5
Set Tooth	Cuts soft wood under ¾" thick. Canted shank for fast cutting action. High carbon steel. Twin Pack of two U1351 jig saw blades	Medium	Medium	3"	7
Set Tooth	Twin Pack assortment of 1 U1351 and 1 U1355 jig saw blades. Cuts most wood and fiber materials. Design allows cutting in both directions for ease in pocket cutting. High carbon steel.	Rough	Fast	3"	7
Double Cutting	Cuts most wood and fiber materials. Design allows cutting in both directions for ease in pocket cutting. High carbon steel.	Medium	Medium	3"	10
	Cuts wood up to 1" thick and leaves smooth finish High carbon steel.	Medium	Medium / Fast	3"	5
Hollow Ground	Cuts wood up to ¾" thick and leaves smooth finish. High carbon steel.	Smooth	Medium	3"	7
	Cuts wood up to ¾" thick and leaves smooth finish. Canted shank for fast cutting. High carbon steel.	Smooth	Medium	3"	7
	Cuts wood up to ½" thick and leaves smooth finish. High carbon steel. Twin Pack of two U1362 jig saw blades.	Fine	Medium	3"	10
Fleam Ground	Cuts wood ⅜" to 2½" thick. Special grinding cuts wet and green woods best. High carbon steel.	Rough	Fast	4"	6
	Cuts wood ¼" to 2" thick. Special grinding cuts wet and green wood best. High carbon steel.	Medium	Medium	4"	10
	Cuts wood up to 1" thick. Best combination for fast cutting and smooth finish. High carbon steel.	Smooth	Medium	4"	6
Fleam Ground Hollow Ground	Cuts wood up to 2" thick. Best combination for fast cutting and smooth finish. Wider blade for extra strength. High carbon steel.	Smooth	Medium	4"	6
	Cuts wood up to ¾" thick. Best combination for fast cutting and smooth finishing. High carbon steel.	Extra Fine	Medium	4"	10

Type	Description	Cut	Speed	Length	Teeth
Metal Cutting	Cuts steel 1/16" to 1/8", aluminum and copper 3/32" to 3/16", plastic sheets 1/2" to 3/4" thick. High carbon steel. Twin pack of two U1354 jig saw blades.	Medium	Medium	3"	14
	Cuts steel 1/8" to 1/43, aluminum and copper 1/16" to 1/8", pipe 3/64" to 1/8" wall thickness. High speed steel.	Smooth	Medium	3"	18
	Cuts steel 1/16" to 3/16", aluminum and copper under 1/16", pipe under 3/64" wall thickness. High speed steel.	Fine	Slow	3	24
	Cuts steel 1/64" to 3/32", aluminum and copper under 3/32", pipe with thin walls, plastic sheets up to 1/2" thick. High speed steel. Twin Pack of two U1355 jig saw blades.	Very Fine	Slow	3"	32
Skip Tooth	Cuts most plastics and woods. Special tooth design gives extra chip clearance. High carbon steel.	Rough	Fast	3"	5
Set Tooth	Cuts wood up to 4" thick. Special tooth design gives extra chip clearance. High carbon steel.	Rough	Fast	6"	7
	Cuts wood up to 4" thick. Wider blade for strength during scroll cutting. High carbon steel.	Medium	Medium	6"	7
Plaster Cutting	Special V-tooth design for cutting plaster and high density plastics. High carbon steel.	Rough	Fast	3-5/8"	9
Scroll Cutting	Cuts plastic and wood 1/4" to 1" thick. Thin blade construction allows radii as small as 1/8". High carbon steel.	Smooth	Medium	2-1/2"	10
Knife Blade	Cuts leather, rubber, composition tile, cardboard, etc. High carbon steel.	Smooth	Medium	2-1/2"	Knife Edge
Flush Cutting	Cuts wood over 1/4" thick. Offset teeth allow flush cutting up to wall. High carbon steel.	Rough	Fast	3"	7
Coarse Carbide Coated	Cuts most tough to cut materials like ceramics, fiberglass, plaster, tile, slate, Masonite, etc. Carbides resist wear.	Rough	Fast	3"	Carbide Edge
Medium Carbide Coated	Cuts most tough to cut materials like ceramics, fiberglass, plaster, tile, slate, Masonite etc. Carbides resist wear.	Medium	Medium	3"	Carbide Edge
Fine Carbide Coated	Cuts most tough to cut materials like ceramics, fiberglass, plaster, tile, slate, Masonite etc. Carbides resist wear.	Smooth	Slow	3"	Carbide Edge

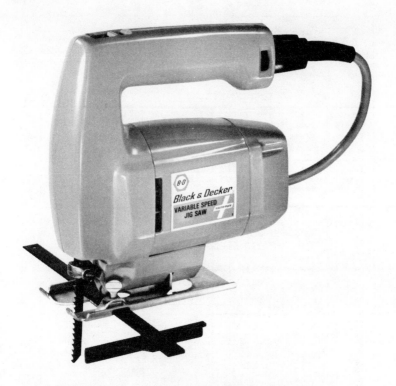

Fig. 2-15. A variable speed jig saw (courtesy of Black & Decker).

stationary electric saws. You really cannot call your woodworking shop complete unless you have at least one of them.

A 10-inch table saw is probably the most versatile saw to have around the home workshop. With it, you can cut most types of lumber—up to about 4 inches thick—and you can be reasonably certain of straight, smooth cuts. In addition, a good table saw will have several other capabilities such as any or all of the following: a ripping fence, depth of cut adjustment, table slanting ability, mitre gauge and various safety features. Table saws range in price from about $200 to $800 for a professional unit. (Fig. 2-17).

Another stationary power cutting tool that is common in woodworking shops is a radial arm saw. Part of the popularity of this tool is the versatility of the machine. Most radial arm saws are not suitable for making long ripping type cuts. Their real value is in making angle cuts, straight crosscuts and bevel cuts. In addition, most radial arm saws can also be adjusted and used as a power

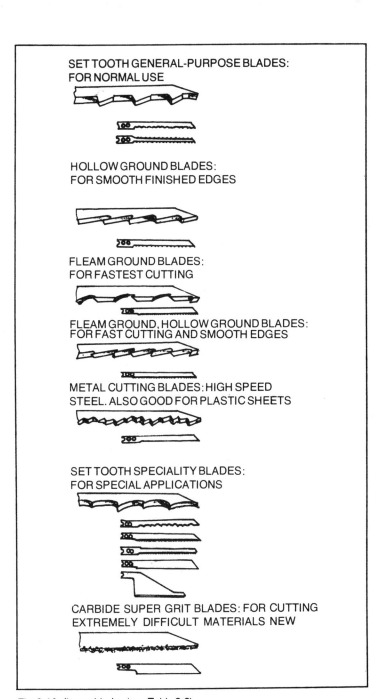

SET TOOTH GENERAL-PURPOSE BLADES:
FOR NORMAL USE

HOLLOW GROUND BLADES:
FOR SMOOTH FINISHED EDGES

FLEAM GROUND BLADES:
FOR FASTEST CUTTING

FLEAM GROUND, HOLLOW GROUND BLADES:
FOR FAST CUTTING AND SMOOTH EDGES

METAL CUTTING BLADES: HIGH SPEED
STEEL. ALSO GOOD FOR PLASTIC SHEETS

SET TOOTH SPECIALITY BLADES:
FOR SPECIAL APPLICATIONS

CARBIDE SUPER GRIT BLADES: FOR CUTTING
EXTREMELY DIFFICULT MATERIALS NEW

Fig. 2-16. Jigsaw blades (see Table 2-2).

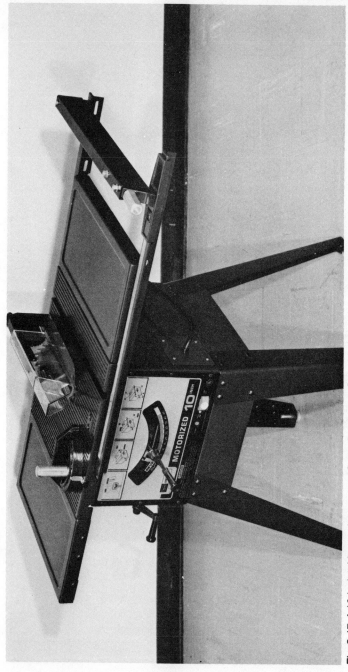

Fig. 2-17. A 10-inch table saw (courtesy of Sears Roebuck & Co.).

Fig. 2-18. A radial saw (courtesy of Sears Roebuck & Co.).

router. This is a real aid when you are making furniture and cabinets (Figs. 2-18 and 2-19).

Still another type of woodworking shop machine is a bandsaw and anyone that builds cabinets and furniture will surely have one in the shop. A bandsaw is similar to a jigsaw with the exception of having greater capabilities and enabling the user to establish more control on cuts. Some of these capabilities include making cuts in lumber up to 6 inches thick, cutting curves, intricately shaped contours and even scrollwork. There are a number of different cutting bands available for band saws. Some models even have a special sanding belt that can be used for sanding the edges of intricately shaped contours (Fig. 2-20).

At the tail end of the cutting tools category, we find several useful and often taken-for-granted cutting tools. These include a razor knife or utility knife, shears and even scissors. A utility knife has countless uses around the woodworking shop. Part of the versatility of such a tool is that the blade can be changed quickly

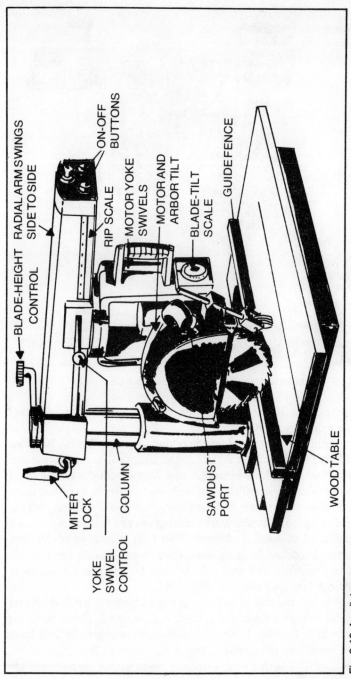

BLADE-HEIGHT CONTROL

RADIAL ARM SWINGS SIDE TO SIDE

ON-OFF BUTTONS

RIP SCALE

MOTOR YOKE SWIVELS

MOTOR AND ARBOR TILT

BLADE-TILT SCALE

GUIDE FENCE

MITER LOCK

YOKE SWIVEL CONTROL

COLUMN

SAWDUST PORT

WOOD TABLE

Fig. 2-19. A radial arm saw.

70

when it becomes dull. A supply of new and sharp razor blades will insure that you always have a sharp cutting tool at your disposal (Fig. 2-21).

Fig. 2-20. A band saw (courtesy of Shopsmith Inc.).

A sturdy pair of shears or tin snips and a strong pair of scissors have many uses around the home shop. The former is useful for cutting templates out of light gauge sheet metal and the latter will come in handy for many different types of light cutting tasks (Fig. 2-22).

SANDING AND SHAPING TOOLS

There are a number of simple, but very useful sanding and shaping type tools that are a necessary part of any woodworking shop. Examples are wood finishing tools such as planes and rasps, for the earlier stages of a project, as well as sandpaper for the final surface preparation. For some modern woodworkers, it is almost inconceivable that any woodworking project can be attempted without the use of electrically operated tools.

Craftsmen have been working with muscle powered tools for centuries with long lasting results (to say the least).

Consider for a moment the furniture that Louis XIV had built for Versailles. To be sure, there are a number of useful and—from the standpoint of time saving capability—necessary modern tools which will be touched upon later in this section. The first half of the section, however, will be devoted to those tools which help to shape and smooth wood during the various stages of construction of a project.

Probably one of the most useful hand-smoothing tools in any shop is a plane and there are many types. The longest plane of all,

Fig. 2-21. A utility knife has many uses around the woodworking shop. Blades are very easy to replace so you can always have a sharp cutting tool (courtesy of The Stanley Works).

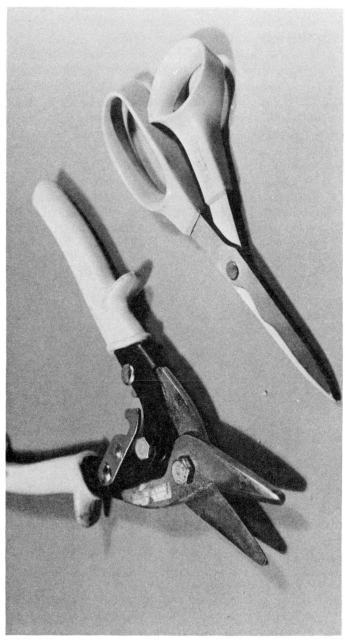

Fig. 2-22. Tin snips (left) and scissors have many uses around the home shop.

73

24 or more inches in length, is called a jointer plane. With such a plane, you can smooth the edges of boards so that they fit together perfectly. Moving down the sizes of hand planes, we find the fore plane which can measure up to about 18 inches. Then comes the jack plane that is up to abut 15 inches in length.

All of these planes are used for smoothing and flattening the ends, edges and faces of boards which will later be joined to give the final appearance of a smooth flat surface composed of more than one board—a table top for example. A hand plane measuring about 9 inches in length is called a bench plane. With such a tool you can handle most types of shop work. You can flatten and smooth the surfaces of boards, for example, or even taking off the bottom or edges of a door so that it closes properly.

A small plane—up to about 6 inches in length—is called a block plane. This tool is especially suited for planing the end grain of boards. Because the blade angle on a block plane is especially designed to be low, this is the best type of plane for end grain work.

Fig. 2-23. Blade adjustment or removal is simple with this plane (courtesy of The Stanley Works).

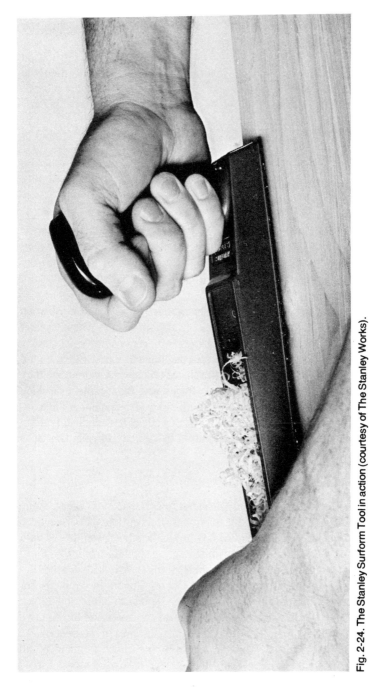

Fig. 2-24. The Stanley Surform Tool in action (courtesy of The Stanley Works).

One last type of plane is called a trimming or pocket plane and it is easy to identify because of its size. It is less than 4 inches and generally has a blade less than 1 inch wide (Fig. 2-23).

A new generation of plane type hand tools was first introduced by the Stanley Company several years ago and since then has revolutionized the planing and shaping process. They are a set of tools that combine all of the best features of conventional planes, rasps and files into one easy to use tool. They are called Surform Tools and no woodworking shop or tool box should be without at least one type.

One of the outstanding features about Surform tools is the blade. Each blade has many teeth and each is shaped like a tiny plane blade. The tool itself never needs any adjustment, as conventional planes do, because the blade exposure is predetermined during the manufacturing. Sharpening is also eliminated. When the blade becomes dull, simply replace it with a new one. Surform Tools are suitable for all types of woodworking projects and their low cost makes them quite attractive to woodworkers (Fig. 2-24).

Your woodworking shop should have an assortment of wood rasps and files to help you to smooth surfaces where a plane cannot work. Rasps, because of their large teeth, remove material quickly and are therefore quite handy for roughing out work. Files, on the other hand, are used later in the smoothing operation because they tend to remove less material. Rasps and files come in a wide variety of length, shapes and tooth sizes and shapes. A "four-in-hand" combination rasp/file is probably one of the handiest types of shaping tools because it combines both flat and half-round surfaces in one tool (Fig. 2-25).

ABRASIVES

Abrasives, commonly referred to as sandpaper, have a value that is hard to estimate for the home woodworker. No project can be considered finished until the surface has been smothered with some type of abrasive and a finish coating applied. Ironically, there is no sand in sandpaper. Nevertheless, the term is widely used.

There are four types of abrasives generally available for woodworking projects: flint, garnet, aluminum oxide and silicon carbide. The first two types are natural abrasives and the last two are totally man-made. I will discuss all four types in this section.

Flint Paper. This is probably the most familiar of all abrasives sold in home improvement and hardware stores across

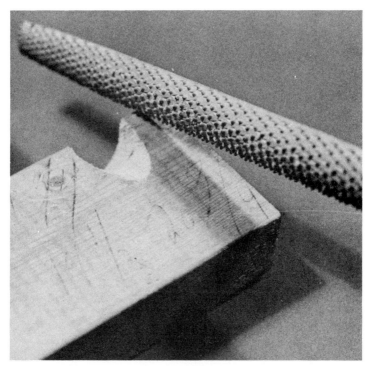

Fig. 2-25. A rasp is very handy for removing sections of wood quickly.

the country. It has an off-white color. Although it is almost universally sold, flint paper is probably the poorest choice for wood finishing because it is not as durable as the other types of abrasives.

Garnet. This is harder than flint and therefore a better choice for sanding woodworking projects. Garnet abrasive paper is the most popular type for finish sanding in industry and among non-professionals. Garnet abrasive paper is easy to identify because of the reddish-brown appearance. This type of abrasive is available in all forms from 8 x 10 sheets to sanding belts for power sanders.

Aluminum Oxide. This is the third hardest abrasive available and it is excellent for sanding the harder type woods such as oak. Aluminum oxide is a byproduct of aluminum ore to which are added small amounts of other materials to create a brownish colored abrasive that is fast cutting and durable.

Silicon Carbide. This is the hardest and sharpest of all abrasives. It is suitable for all types of sanding from rough sanding to the final sanding prior to finishing. Silicon carbide abrasives are related to the same carbide used for sharpening stones and grinding wheels. Silicone carbide is dark—almost black—in appearance and one of the best choices for sanding materials.

Abrasive papers for woodworking projects are available in 9 x 12 inch sheets for hand sanding and smaller sheets for orbital or finish sanders, belts and disks. Generally, if you have a portable or stationary sander, you can find abrasive belts, disks or pads to fit it. Different grades of abrasives are used for different sanding tasks. Therefore, it is important that you keep a good selection of various grits handy in your home woodworking shop. Table 2-3 lists the various grits and uses of different types of abrasive papers.

For small sanding jobs, you can use a small block of wood with abrasive paper attached to it or a small hand-sander with the addition of a piece of felt between the paper and the sander. For

Fig. 2-26. The table top disk/belt sander is a real aid for finishing woodworking projects (courtesy of Dremel).

Table 2-3. Grit Sizes and Uses for Common Abrasive Papers.

	Grit#	Grade	General Uses
Very Fine	400	10/0	Polishing, finishing after stain, varnish or glossy paint has been applied. For finish sanding.
	360	-	
	320	9/0	
	280	8/0	
	240	7/0	
	220	6/0	
Fine	180	5/0	For finish sanding prior to staining or sealing.
	150	4/0	
	120	3/0	
Medium	100	2/0	For final removal of rough texture.
	80	1/0	
	60	1/2	
Coarse	50	1	For sanding after rough sanding has been done.
	40	1 1/2	
	36	2	
Very Coarse	30	2 1/2	For sanding very rough textured wood surfaces.
	24	3	
	20	3 1/2	
	16	4	

larger sanding needs, you will find the work much easier to accomplish if you use an electric type sander such as a belt, disk or other type of tool (Fig. 2-26).

The final part of this section on shaping tools covers three power machines that are quite useful for woodworking projects and especially for furniture and cabinetmaking. These are the router, jointer/planer and wood lathe. I will discuss each of these machines and point out the functions of each.

A popular do-it-yourself magazine pointed out recently that the most popular electric tool in American home workshops is the router. This handy tool is almost indispensable for many different types of woodworking projects. Basically, a router consists of a high-speed motor (generally about 25,000 rpm), a chuck for holding the cutting bit and an adjustable base.

Routers are hand held except that a radial arm saw often has a router chuck on one side of the motor. There are many different types of cutting bits for routers (as Fig. 2-27 shows). Some cutting bits have pilot bearings for guiding the cutter around the edge of the work while other bits do not (Fig. 2-28). With the later, some type of guidance system must be used to keep the router in position during use.

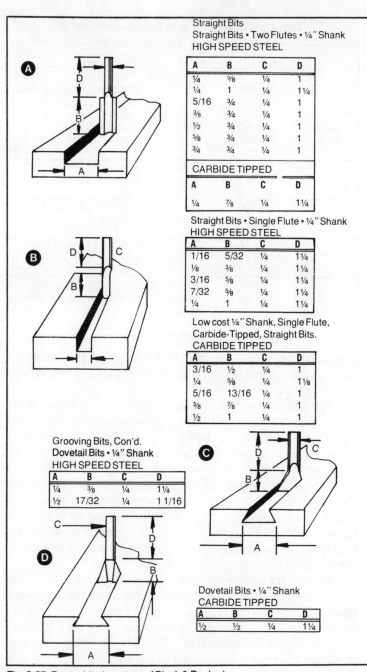

Straight Bits
Straight Bits • Two Flutes • ¼″ Shank
HIGH SPEED STEEL

A	B	C	D
¼	⅝	¼	1
¼	1	¼	1¼
5/16	¾	¼	1
⅜	¾	¼	1
½	¾	¼	1
⅝	¾	¼	1
¾	¾	¼	1

CARBIDE TIPPED

A	B	C	D
¼	⅞	¼	1¼

Straight Bits • Single Flute • ¼″ Shank
HIGH SPEED STEEL

A	B	C	D
1/16	5/32	¼	1¼
⅛	⅜	¼	1¼
3/16	⅝	¼	1¼
7/32	⅝	¼	1¼
¼	1	¼	1¼

Low cost ¼″ Shank, Single Flute,
Carbide-Tipped, Straight Bits.
CARBIDE TIPPED

A	B	C	D
3/16	½	¼	1
¼	⅝	¼	1⅛
5/16	13/16	¼	1
⅜	⅞	¼	1
½	1	¼	1

Grooving Bits, Con'd.
Dovetail Bits • ¼″ Shank
HIGH SPEED STEEL

A	B	C	D
¼	⅜	¼	1¼
½	17/32	¼	1 1/16

Dovetail Bits • ¼″ Shank
CARBIDE TIPPED

A	B	C	D
½	½	¼	1¼

Fig. 2-27. Router bits (courtesy of Black & Decker).

80

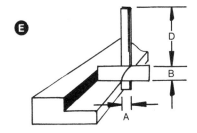

(E)

Rabbeting Bits
¼" Shank
HIGH SPEED STEEL

A	B	C	D
¼	7/16	¼	1
⅜	9/16	¼	1

CARBIDE TIPPED

A	B	C	D
⅜	⅝	¼	1

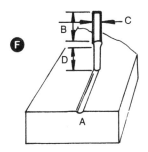

(F)

Grooving Bits
Veining Bits • ¼" Shank
HIGH SPEED STEEL

A	B	C	D
1/16	3/16	¼	1
⅛	5/16	¼	1
3/16	7/16	¼	1
7/32	7/16	¼	1

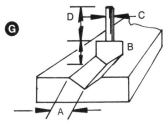

(G)

"V" Grooving Bits • ¼" Shank
HIGH SPEED STEEL

A	B	C	D
⅜	7/16	¼	1
⅞	15/16	¼	1

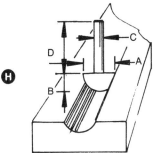

(H)

Core Box Bits • ¼" Shank
HIGH SPEED STEEL

A	B	C	D
¼	¼	¼	1
⅜	¼	¼	1
½	11/32	¼	1
¾	15/32	¼	1

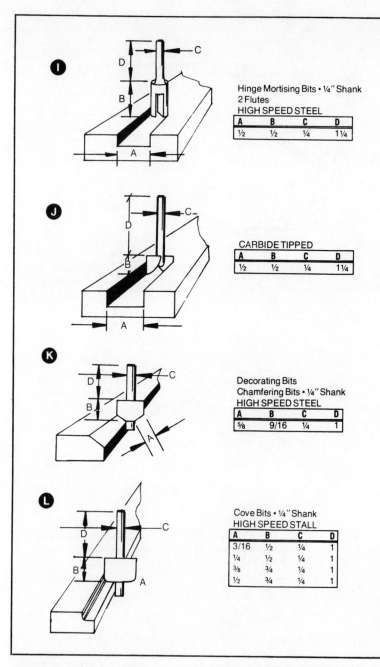

I

Hinge Mortising Bits • ¼″ Shank
2 Flutes
HIGH SPEED STEEL

A	B	C	D
½	½	¼	1¼

J

CARBIDE TIPPED

A	B	C	D
½	½	¼	1¼

K

Decorating Bits
Chamfering Bits • ¼″ Shank
HIGH SPEED STEEL

A	B	C	D
⅝	9/16	¼	1

L

Cove Bits • ¼″ Shank
HIGH SPEED STALL

A	B	C	D
3/16	½	¼	1
¼	½	¼	1
⅜	¾	¼	1
½	¾	¼	1

Fig. 2-27. Router bits (courtesy of Black & Decker) (continued from page 81).

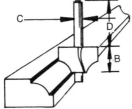

Beading Bits • ¼" Shank
HIGH SPEED STEEL

A	B	C	D
⅛	⅜	¼	1
¼	½	¼	
⅜	¾	¼	1

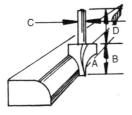

Cornder Round Bits • ¼" Shank
HIGH SPEED STEEL

A	B	C	D
3/16	⅜	¼	1
¼	½	¼	1
5/16	½	¼	1
⅜	⅝	¼	1
½	13/16	¼	1

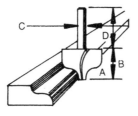

Ogee Bits • ¼" Shank
HIGH SPEED STEEL

A	B	C	D
3/16	⅝	¼	1
9/32	29/32	¼	1

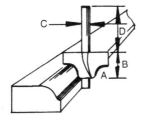

Roman Ogee Bits • " Shank
HIGH SPEED STEEL

A	B	C	D
5/32	½	¼	1
¼	¾	¼	1

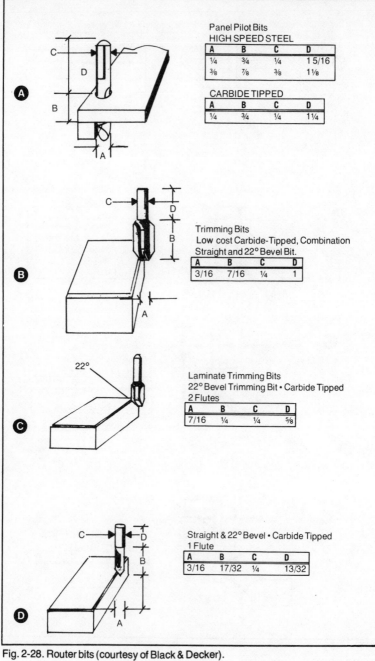

Panel Pilot Bits
HIGH SPEED STEEL

A	B	C	D
¼	¾	¼	1 5/16
⅜	⅞	⅜	1⅛

CARBIDE TIPPED

A	B	C	D
¼	¾	¼	1¼

Trimming Bits
Low cost Carbide-Tipped, Combination
Straight and 22° Bevel Bit.

A	B	C	D
3/16	7/16	¼	1

Laminate Trimming Bits
22° Bevel Trimming Bit • Carbide Tipped
2 Flutes

A	B	C	D
7/16	¼	¼	⅝

Straight & 22° Bevel • Carbide Tipped
1 Flute

A	B	C	D
3/16	17/32	¼	13/32

Fig. 2-28. Router bits (courtesy of Black & Decker).

84

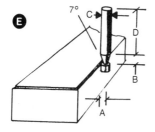

E

7°

7° Bevel • Solid Carbide

A	B	C	D
3/16	3/8	1/4	1

Flush Trim • Solid Carbide

A	B	C	D
1/4	3/8	1/4	1

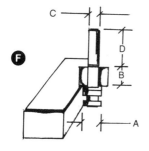

F

Trimming Cutters
Low cost 1/2″, 2 Flute, Carbide-Tipped,
Veneer Flush Cutter with Screw,
Washer & Ball Bearing.

A	B	C	D
1/2	1/2	1/4	1 1/4

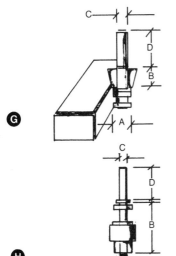

G

Low-cost 1/2″, 2 Flute, Carbide-Tipped,
22° Bevel Cutter with Screw, Washer
and Ball-Bearing

A	B	C	D
11/16	1/2	1/4	1 1/8

H

Veneer Trimmer Arbor

A	B	C	D
5/8	1-3/32	1/4	1

85

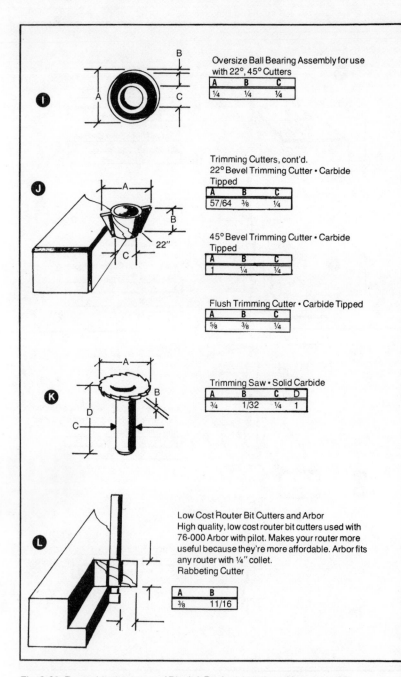

I   Oversize Ball Bearing Assembly for use with 22°, 45° Cutters

A	B	C
¼	¼	¼

J   Trimming Cutters, cont'd.
22° Bevel Trimming Cutter • Carbide Tipped

A	B	C
57/64	⅜	¼

45° Bevel Trimming Cutter • Carbide Tipped

A	B	C
1	¼	¼

Flush Trimming Cutter • Carbide Tipped

A	B	C
⅝	⅜	¼

K   Trimming Saw • Solid Carbide

A	B	C	D
¾	1/32	¼	1

L   Low Cost Router Bit Cutters and Arbor
High quality, low cost router bit cutters used with 76-000 Arbor with pilot. Makes your router more useful because they're more affordable. Arbor fits any router with ¼" collet.
Rabbeting Cutter

A	B
⅜	11/16

Fig. 2-28. Router bits (courtesy of Black & Decker) (continued from page 85).

86

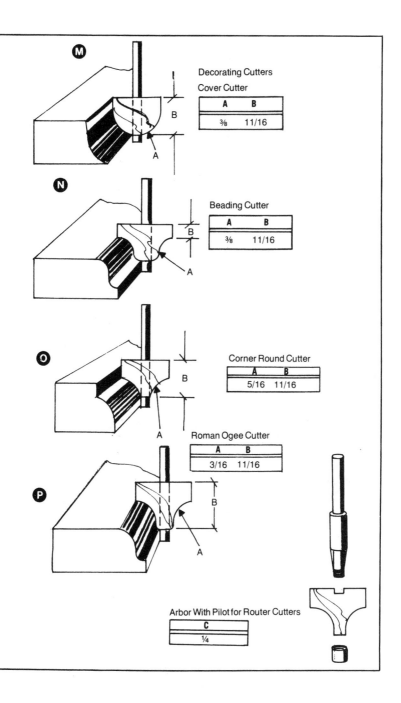

M

Decorating Cutters

Cover Cutter

A	B
3/8	11/16

B

A

N

Beading Cutter

A	B
3/8	11/16

B

A

O

Corner Round Cutter

A	B
5/16	11/16

B

A

Roman Ogee Cutter

A	B
3/16	11/16

P

B

A

Arbor With Pilot for Router Cutters

C
1/4

87

Some of the woodworking tasks that are made possible by using a router include the following: decorative edges on moldings and furniture, special wood joints such as tongue and groove, lap and dovetail, trimming plastic laminate and veneer, and many types of dado trough like cuts. Because routers are so popular with woodworkers, there are a large number of different type cutting bits and accessories available for them (Fig. 2-29).

A jointer/planer is another electric machine that is very useful for woodworking projects. This is especially true for those projects where more than one board is joined to form a flat surface such as a table, cabinet and other furniture making. With a jointer/planer, you can trim to size and smooth, plane, square or bevel angle joint edges for a tight, flush fit. You can also bevel or chamfer a decorative edge and plane certain size surface areas to help alleviate imperfections. A jointer/planer will enable you to do various finishing tasks that would be nearly impossible with any other tool.

A wood lathe is necessary for several specialized woodworking projects such as making table legs and shaping symmetrical

Fig. 2-29. A hand-held router.

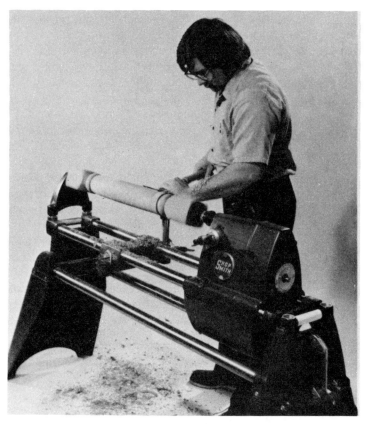

Fig. 2-30. A wood lathe is just one of five different machines contained in the basic Shopsmith Mark V system (courtesy of Shopsmith Inc.).

objects such as planters and bowls. To be sure, there is a certain skill required to manipulate the turning tools effectively and this can be gained only through practice and a fair share of time. Once these skills have been mastered, you can apply them to turning out anything from a fluted table leg to a miniature goblet for a doll house (Fig. 2-30).

HOLE MAKING TOOLS

Hole making is one necessary function of many woodworking projects. In this section, I will cover those tools and accessories that have the sole function of helping you make holes in wood for such things as a screw, a nail or a bolt. Primarily, I will discuss both hand-operated and electric tools and the bits that are used in them.

The most basic of all tools that make holes, and probably the oldest, is the simple brace. A brace is often overlooked by the modern woodworker because of the availability of electric drills. Nevertheless, a brace has many uses. With a brace, you can drive a bit of any size from more than 1 inch to less than one-fourth inch. More importantly, it is slow working but produces a lot of torque which is essential when twisting stress is great. Additionally, a brace and bit will often be the only tool that can be used in certain situations such as when electrical power is not available (Fig. 2-31).

Electric hand drills are one of the most common and popular tools in America. At the present time, the bottom of the price range is about $10 and runs to over $100. Some of the features that can be included are variable speed, reversing, battery powered (no electrical source is required, but the drill must be recharged periodically) different size chucks from one-fourth to one-half inch, and lightweight construction.

To be sure, the addition of any of these features increases the selling price. But they also increase the versatility of the drill. For example, a variable speed drill allows you to adjust the speed of the

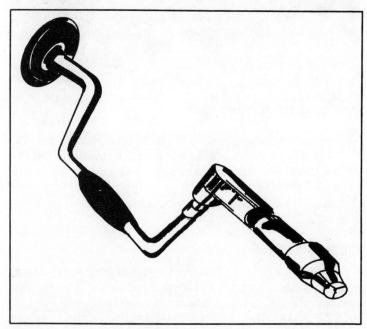

Fig. 2-31. A brace is handy for boring large holes.

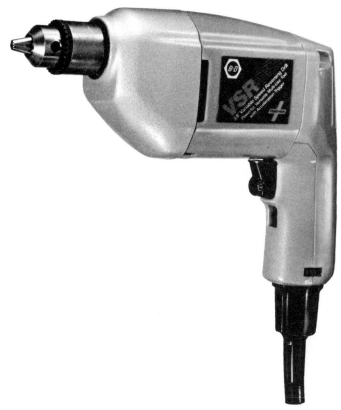

Fig. 2-32. A variable speed, reversing drill (courtesy of Black & Decker).

drill to a particular drilling situation and a reversing feature allows you to reverse the bit out of a tight, deep hole where you could not possibly pull the drill itself out (Fig. 2-32).

A push drill is primarily intended for drilling small holes and works very much like a ratchet type screwdriver. The greatest value of a push drill is for making holes from one-sixteenth to one-sixty-fourth of an inch. Larger holes are easier to make with a brace and a bit or electric drill.

A drill press—that is a stationary drill mounted on a vertical shaft—is the tool to use for drilling perfectly vertical holes exactly where you want them. For your information, the drill press was originally invented for drilling holes in metal. Later it became useful for precision drilling in wood as well. In addition to standard drill presses, there is a new generation of drill presses that can be

Fig. 2-33. The drill press on the right of the workbench is very handy for many woodworking projects (courtesy of Masonite Corporation).

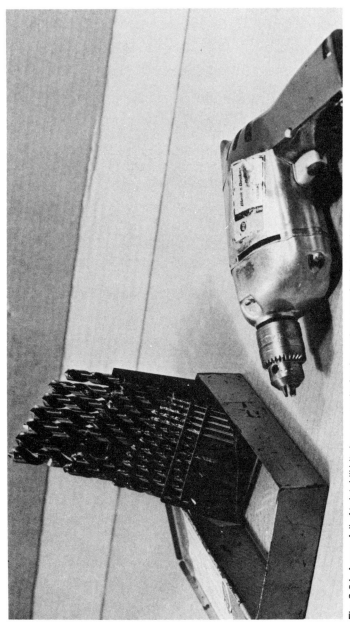

Fig. 2-34. A case full of twist drill bits is a necessity for the serious woodworker and craftsman.

used with the standard hand-held electric drill. There is some sacrifice in accuracy with this setup, but most woodworkers find that the portable drill press meets most of their needs (Fig. 2-33).

Any drill is useless without some sort of bit and there are many different types. These include the common twist drill bits, spade bits, auger, counter sink bits, rim cutting bits and hole or circle cutting bits.

Twist Drill Bits. These are the most common of all drill bits and the most widely used. Ironically, twist drills were originally invented for drilling holes in metal, but they are now used just as much for making holes in wood, plastic and similar materials. These bits have chisel-like cutting edges and a pair of spiral channels that twist up the shank of the bit and help to carry away the cut material. Twist drill bits range in size from one-sixteenth to one-half of an inch. A special carrying case, with a full selection of twist drills, should be part of every home workshop. As you break or wear out the bits, replace them as soon as possible (Fig. 2-34).

Spade Bits. These are simply a shaft of steel with a flattened end (the spade) which is beveled so that it scrapes more than cuts as it passes through the work. Spade bits are designed primarily for use with an electric drill, but they can be used with a brace. The real value of spade bits is in making larger holes—up to about 1 inch (Fig. 2-35).

Auger Bits. These are the most common type of bit used with a brace. An auger bit is simply a steel spiral that has a cutting end, a tip to guide the hole and a cutting edge or edges that do the cutting of the circle. At the same time, it floats the cut material out of the hole. These bits are designed for use with a brace. This means slow rotation and lots of torque. An auger bit is used for large holes that are from one-fourth to about 1½ inches in diameter (Fig. 2-36).

A Counter Sink Bit. This is a rather specialized woodworking drill bit. It not only makes a hole in wood, for a screw, but makes the top of the hole slightly wider so that the screw head can be turned below the surface. When you want to secure a woodworking project with wood screws, then conceal the heads, the countersink drill bit is the best way to achieve this. Countersink drill bits are available in sizes that are quite compatible with standard wood screws that have countersink type heads (Fig. 2-37).

Rim Cutting Drill Bits. These make the smoothest and truest hole of all. The bit itself has a thin steel rim with teeth that

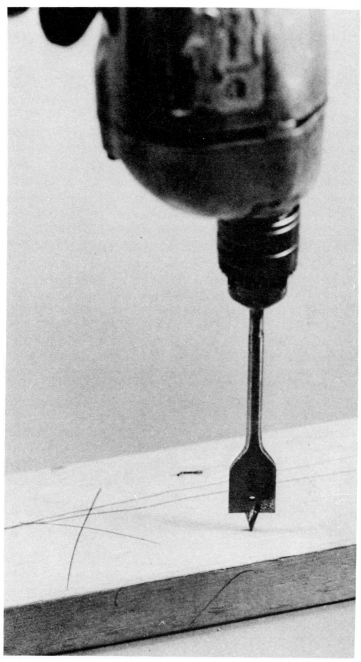

Fig. 2-35. A spade drill bit in use.

Fig. 2-36. An auger drill bit is designed for use with a muscle powered brace.

cut through the wood. Inside the rim of the bit are sharp, chisel-like cutters that peel away wood after it has been rim cut. These bits are designed for rather slow speed woodworking and they are very useful when joining pieces of a project with dowels (Fig. 2-38).

A Hole Or Circle Cutting Drill Bit. This type is used when a large hole is required in a project. Generally, these bits are used for holes larger than 1 inch in diameter—such as the hole in a door for the knob hardware—and they are designed for use in an electric drill.

FASTENING TOOLS

In this broad category of tools, we find those which are used to join pieces of material by some type of fastening aid such as nail,

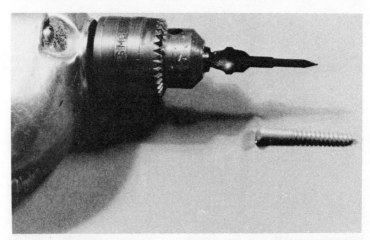

Fig. 2-37. A counter-sink drill bit both drills a hole for the screw and indents the top of the hole to help conceal the screw head.

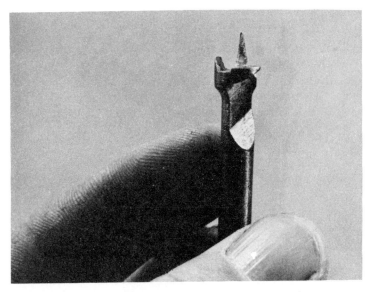

Fig. 2-38. A rim cut drill bit makes a perfect hole in any wooden surface.

screw or staple. The obvious tools in this category are hammers, screwdrivers and staplers.

Every home woodworking shop should have a selection of hammers. There is no such thing as an all-purpose hammer. Instead there are several different types and weights of hammers designed for specific applications and tasks. For example, a woodworker might have need of wire brads to hold tiny mouldings in place, finish nails or box nails to build a cabinet, or 10- to 16-penny common nails for framing. Each of these different types of nails is best driven with a hammer of the weight and size that is suitable for the job at hand. You would not, for example, drive tiny wire brads with a 20-ounce framing hammer any more than you would drive 16-penny nails with a tack hammer (Fig. 2-39).

A good selection of hammers for the average home woodworking shop should include the following: a tack hammer for light-duty work, a 10-ounce ball pein hammer for light nailing (if you are not pulling nails what do you need a claw hammer for?), a 16-ounce claw hammer for medium duty hammering and light framing, and a 20-ounce ripping or framing hammer for serious carpentry. In addition, the home craftsman might find occasional use for a small sledge hammer (up to about 2 pounds). With an assortment of hammers such as this, the home woodworker will be able to choose the right hammer for the particular job at hand (Fig. 2-40).

Even if you are just beginning to set up a woodworking shop in your home, you undoubtedly own several screwdrivers. In fact screwdrivers are the most common of all hand tools in existance. There is no such thing as an all-purpose screwdriver and you might be surprised to learn that there are many different types. For example, a quick glance at a catalog which offers fine woodworking tools reveals screwdrivers described as: cabinet, London, Scotch, spindle-bladed, gentlemen's, gunmakers, model makers, military

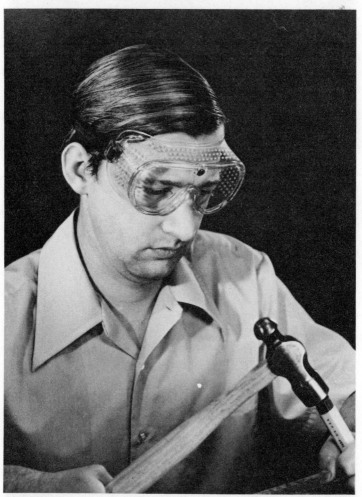

Fig. 2-39. Always wear eye protection when hammering metal (courtesy of The Stanley Works).

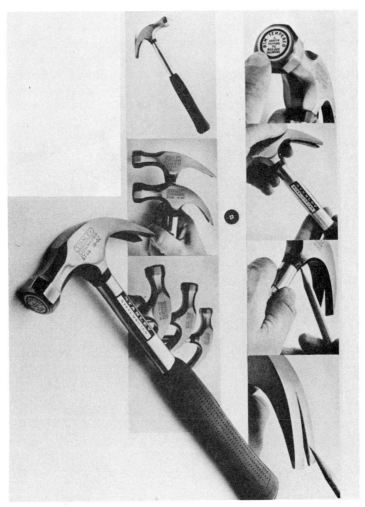

Fig. 2-40. A 16-ounce claw hammer (courtesy of The Stanley Works).

and even undertaker's. There are also Phillips, Allen head and miniature types of screwdrivers in several varieties.

With such a vast selection of screwdrivers available, the casual user might be a bit confused. The result is that when a screw needs to be driven or removed, the first screwdriver that comes to hand is the one used. As often as not, the blade of the chosen screwdriver slides off the screw head and mars the workpiece or screw slot or both. Just as there is a right hammer or saw for a particular project or task, there is also always a right screwdriver.

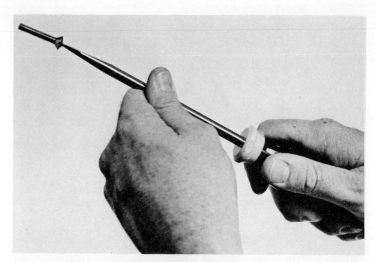

Fig. 2-41. The blade should fit snuggly into the slot.

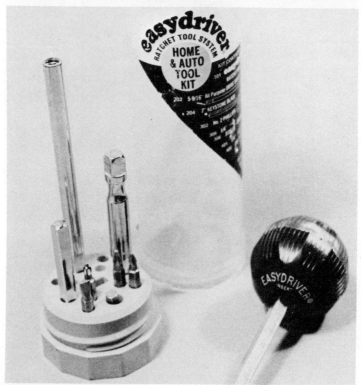

Fig. 2-42. One of the more modern versions of the ratchet screwdriver.

One of the most important considerations about proper screwdriver use is that the blade of the tool must fit snugly into the slot in the head of the screw. It must not be either too wide or too short and the bottom edge of the blade should be square for best results (Fig. 2-41).

A good selection of screwdrivers for the average home woodworking shop should include one each of the following screwdrivers: 3, 4, 5, 6, 8, and 10-inch standard, a small, medium and large Phillips and one ratchet type screwdriver with an assortment of tips for both standard and Phillips screws (Fig. 2-42).

Every home workshop should have a stapler to help with special or temporary fastening projects such as upholstery or fastening the backs to cabinets. Basically, there are two types of

Fig. 2-43. A hand-powered stapler has many uses around the home and installing ceiling tile is one example.

hand staplers for the home craftsman: hand powered and electrical powered. The standard hand powered stapler has been around for many years and is widely used for many projects around the home and workshop. A typical model (Fig. 2-43) will drive staples from one-fourth inch to nine-sixteenth of an inch long.

A relatively new addition to homeowners has been the electric stapler. The obvious advantage over a hand powered unit is the ability to effortlessly drive staples with the touch of a button (Fig. 2-44).

MISCELLANEOUS TOOLS AND EQUIPMENT

In addition to the above mentioned categories of necessary tools for the home woodworking shop, there are a number of other items that fall into the general category. Tools described in this section, while not always necessary, can save you hours of time and in many cases help you to turn out more professional looking projects. In addition, there are also tools and accessories that help you to do a better job.

Clamps are often quite handy for joining pieces of a project while the glue dries and hardens. There are many different types of clamps such as C-clamps, pipe and bar clamps, spring clip clamps and wooden hand screws, to name just a few. Someone once said that you can never have enough clamps around the woodworking shop and I quite agree.

Clamps are indispensable for holding parts of a project together as the glue sets and this is their primary function. Every home woodworking shop should have a selection of various size clamps. Newer clamps, if you have not shopped for them lately, now come mostly with plastic covered jaws to protect the surfaces being clamped. Older clamps require that you slip a piece of cardboard or scrap lumber between the clamp jaws to protect the surfaces being clamped. A good assortment of clamps for the home shop should include several small C-type clamps for small projects and some larger, bar type clamps for the bigger projects (Fig. 2-45).

Right along with clamps in the home workshop, the woodworker will need at least one vise. Preferably you should get one of the newer designs that can easily hold a 6-inch wide board. In a pinch, a machinist vise can be used to hold lumber, but the surfaces of the piece must be protected from the metal bit of the vise's jaw.

Another possibility for both clamping and a bench vise is a handy little portable workbench type affair introduced by the Black

Fig. 2-44. An electric staple gun (courtesy of Duo-Fast).

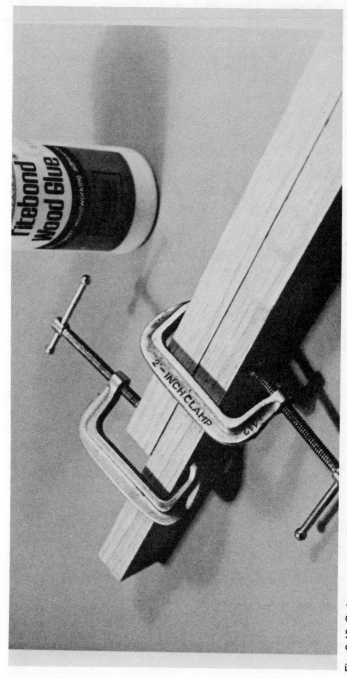

Fig. 2-45. C-clamps are very handy around the home woodworking shop for holding work together while the glue hardens.

104

& Decker Company several years ago—The Workmate. This portable unit combines several useful functions in one collapsible storage unit. The original Workmate had two working heights, a double screw vise—which opened the two top sections of the bench—and several holes in the top which could be used for holding special dogs or bench stops. Now I notice that there are several different types of Workmates available. These include a small unit that mounts on top of your present workbench (Fig. 2-46 and 2-47).

Still another useful accessory to have around the home woodworking shop is a vacuum cleaner. Some people might say that a shop vacuum cleaner is not an accessory but a necessity and I know my wife would agree with that. There are several different types of heavy-duty vacuum cleaners designed for the workshop. Some are portable and roll around on special wheeled canisters. Others are stationary units that are centrally located in the shop and from which run rigid plastic pipe that is usually 2 inches in diameter. Some units pick up only dry material while others, usually newer units, have both wet and dry vacuuming capabilities.

Fig. 2-46. The Workmate (courtesy of Black & Decker).

Fig. 2-47. A bench top Workmate (courtesy of Black & Decker).

A quick survey among woodworking companions reveals that for the money the stationary vacuum systems are hard to beat. All of the good units have much more power than any portable vacuum and are therefore much more useful around the shop. In addition, special plumbing type plastic pipe can be run to stationary machines around the shop—such as the table saw—and they will quickly remove the sawdust as it is made by the machine. There are several types of both portable and stationary vacuum units designed for the home shop. It is wise to investigate several before making a purchase (Fig. 2-48).

A bench grinder is very handy around the home workshop. With even a small unit, you will be able to keep your woodworking tools razor sharp. A good bench grinder is also necessary for most types of metal work. A point to consider when shopping for a bench grinding unit is the rated horsepower—one-half to three-fourth horsepower will handle most projects that you will encounter. You should also look for adjustable tool rests, special light attachment, removable wheel covers and a stand for the unit. When you buy a bench grinder you should also buy a clear plastic face shield and keep it next to the machine. When ever you use the machine, make sure you have your face mask on to protect your eyes from flying bits of ground metal (Fig. 2-49).

MINIATURE AND SPECIALTY POWER EQUIPMENT

The last decade has seen the introduction of two new items for the home craftsman worth mentioning. The first is miniature woodworking machinery and the second is the Shopsmith. I will briefly discuss both of these items (Fig. 2-50).

The introduction of miniature woodworking machinery has been brought about by the Dremel Company. You might already be familiar with their line of engraving tools that are used for marking metal tools with an identification number or other identifying

Fig. 2-48. A portable wet/dry vacuum cleaner (courtesy of Black & Decker).

Fig. 2-49. A bench grinder has many uses around the home shop.

Fig. 2-50. The Shopsmith Mark V (courtesy of Shopsmith Inc.).

marks. This hand-held machine comes with many different attachments which enable the user to grind, cut, drill, sharpen, carve and polish—as well as engrave—most types of surfaces (Fig. 2-51).

A relatively short time ago, Dremel introduced a line of miniature woodworking tools designed for light duty woodwork such as cutting moulding, plywood, turning wooden dowels and sanding. The first miniature tool is a table saw that measures 13 x 12 x 9 inches. This saw can cut up to 1-inch stock at a 90-degree angle and three-fourth inch stock at a 45-degree angle. Because most woodworking projects use lumber in these sizes, this little saw can be used for many cutting tasks. The 4-inch table saw was designed for the do-it-yourselfer, hobbyist and craftsperson for home or shop repairs, picture framing, models, hobby and crafts work, and general purpose sawing of wood and plastics. And the saw does all of these things well.

At first glance, it is hard to keep in mind that this saw is not a toy. But with an electric motor that is rated at 9800 rpm, this saw is far from the toy category. Several types of saw blades are available

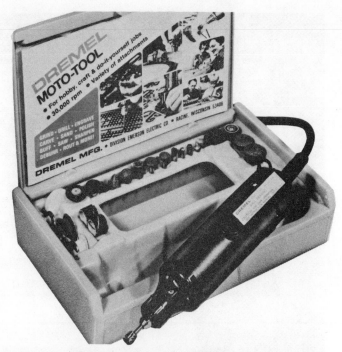

Fig. 2-51. The Dremel Moto-Tool (courtesy of Dremel).

Fig. 2-52. The Dremel 4-inch table saw is not a toy (courtesy of Dremel).

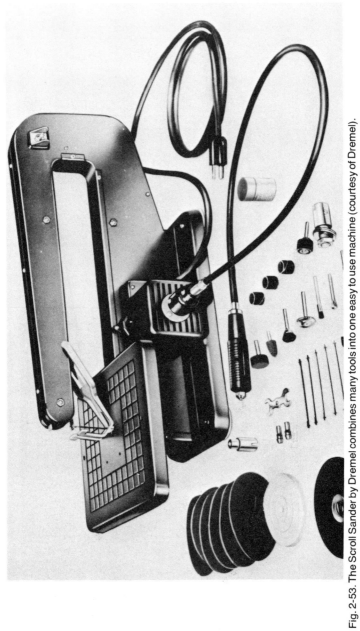

Fig. 2-53. The Scroll Sander by Dremel combines many tools into one easy to use machine (courtesy of Dremel).

Fig. 2-54. The Shopsmith Mark V and accessories can be stored in a very small area (courtesy of Shopsmith Inc.).

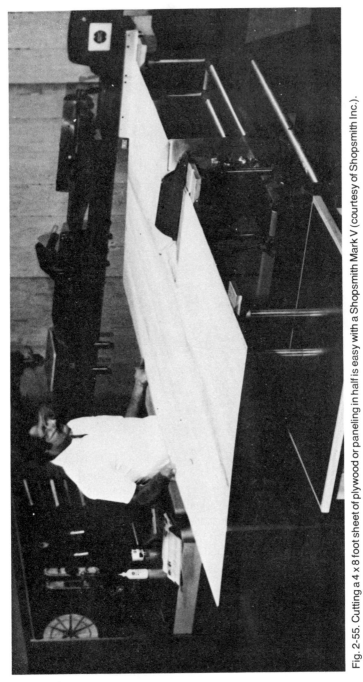

Fig. 2-55. Cutting a 4 x 8 foot sheet of plywood or paneling in half is easy with a Shopsmith Mark V (courtesy of Shopsmith Inc.).

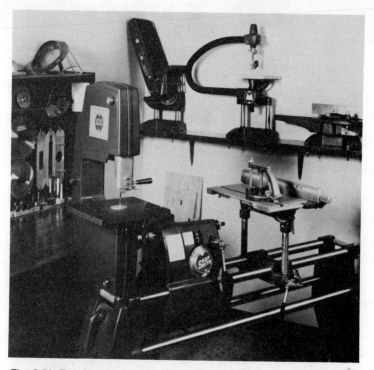

Fig. 2-56. The Shopsmith Mark V with several accessories: Bandsaw, belt sander, jigsaw, and jointer (courtesy of Shopsmith Inc.).

for this 4-inch table saw. Included are an all-purpose blade and a 100-tooth, fine work blade for smooth finish cuts in all types of wood (Fig. 2-52).

Another introduction by Dremel is a combination machine called a Scroll Saw/Sander. This miniature machine (Fig. 2-53) can perform many different functions around the home workshop . It can make all types of cuts in lumber up to 2 inches thick, sanding, polishing, drilling, shaping, and making bevel cuts. A number of accessories are available for the Scroll Saw/Sander which make it quite versatile around the home shop.

Dremel also offers a new disc and belt combination sander that stands only 15 inches high. Any do-it-yourselfer who does any kind of finish sanding will appreciate the capabilities of this machine. It can be used to sand and even shape almost any wooden surface that you can create in your woodworking shop.

Disc sanding sheets are available in three grits—coarse, medium and fine. The 1-inch wide by 30-inch long belts come in six

Fig. 2-57. A nice setup for a small general purpose shop (courtesy of Masonite Corporation).

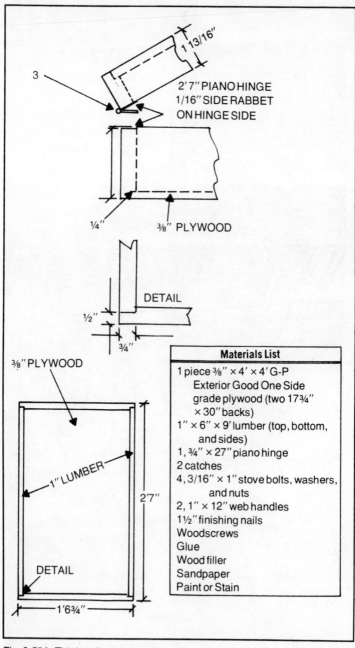

1 13/16"

3

2' 7" PIANO HINGE
1/16" SIDE RABBET
ON HINGE SIDE

1/4"

3/8" PLYWOOD

DETAIL

1/2"

3/4"

3/8" PLYWOOD

1" LUMBER

2'7"

DETAIL

1'6¾"

Materials List
1 piece 3/8" × 4' × 4' G-P Exterior Good One Side grade plywood (two 17¾" × 30" backs)
1" × 6" × 9' lumber (top, bottom, and sides)
1, ¾" × 27" piano hinge
2 catches
4, 3/16" × 1" stove bolts, washers, and nuts
2, 1" × 12" web handles
1½" finishing nails
Woodscrews
Glue
Wood filler
Sandpaper
Paint or Stain

Fig. 2-58A. This handy carrying case will save you a lot of leg work (courtesy of Georgia-Pacific).

116

Fig. 2-58B. The completed carrying case.

grits which will enable you to produce a glass-like surface on any woodworking project that you can lift up to the machine. If ever there could be considered an all-around sanding machine, the Disc-Belt sander by Dremel would be the most likely candidate (Fig. 2-26).

In addition to the three miniature tools mentioned above, Dremel also offers several other tools which you might want to consider for your woodworking shop. These include a router, drill press, wood lathe, and a wide assortment of blades, grinding wheels, cutters, and other useful tools for the do-it-yourself woodworker. Most of these tools are very affordable. Because of their size, they can be easily stowed in even the smallest of workshops.

If you do not own very much in the way of stationary woodworking power equipment, you should know about one of the most versatile of all woodworking machines in existence today: The Shopsmith Mark V. The Shopsmith Mark V, as the name suggests, combines five of the most commonly used woodworking tools into one machine. It combines a 10-inch table saw, a 34-inch wood lathe, a horizontal boring machine, a 12-inch disc sander and a 16½ -inch vertical drill press. This same machine employs a single table, spindle, stand and motor that requires less storage space than a bicycle (Fig. 2-54).

Each of these five machines is a full scale, professional quality woodworking tool. The 10-inch table saw, for example, offers a 3¼-inch depth of cut that enables you to rip or crosscut all but the most unusually large pieces of lumber stock. The huge 48-inch ripping capacity helps you to accurately halve 4 x 8 foot sheets of plywood or paneling with precision and convenience. There is a special speed control dial on the saw motor that also allows you to lower the normal speed for easier sawing of hardwoods. The other four basic parts of the machine are equally professional in performance (Fig. 2-55).

In addition to the basic Shopsmith Mark V, Shopsmith offers an extensive line of accessories that fit the unit. These include: a 11-inch bandsaw, a 4-inch jointer, a 6-inch belt sander and an 18-inch jigsaw (Fig. 2-56).

The Shopsmith Mark V and accessories offer an alternative to anyone wanting to set up a quality woodworking shop for a fraction of the cost if each of these machines were purchased seperately. Shopsmith offers an extensive manual with their system that is very easy to follow and in almost no time you will be doing advanced woodworking projects you only dreamed about in the past.

As you can see in this chapter, the bulk of any woodworking shop is composed of hand tools and electrically operated tools. Of course, the type of woodworking projects that you mainly do will help you to determine the selection of tools that you need to have on hand in the shop. It is important to keep in mind that your woodworking shop need be only as large as the projects that you do. A fair sized shop is shown in Fig. 2-57. A shop of this size has many capabilities and should suit the average woodworker. For those just getting started or if you have limited space, the tool box shown in Figs. 2-58A and 2-58B might be more up your alley.

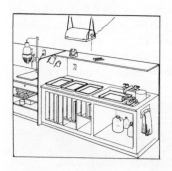

Chapter 3
The Home Darkroom

If you are a photographer, one of the greatest joys is the sight of a perfect print that you have made in your own darkroom. All of us that push a shutter give occasional thought to what happens to the film after it has been properly exposed and removed from the camera. For some, it is sufficient that all of the processing is done by the local lab. But for others, there is a need for more control of picture taking and printing. If you are serious about photography, sooner or later you will spend some time in a darkroom processing your own film and making your own prints.

There are several ways of doing this such as enrollment in a photography workshop that offers darkroom time. If you are short of funds, this is probably the best way to get introduced to darkroom work. In time, however, you will long for your own workspace and if you are determined enough you will find the money, place and time for your own processing equipment (Fig. 3-1).

To begin with, a very serviceable home darkroom can be set up on a shoestring budget. For the price you would normally pay to have five rolls of black and white film developed, you can set up your own darkroom with the capabilities of developing black and white film. All you really need are some chemicals, a thermometer, a clock, a developing tank and a dark room for loading the tank. Once you have developed the negatives, you can then pick out the best ones and have them printed by your local lab (Fig. 3-2).

Fig. 3-1. A home darkroom (courtesy of Eastman Kodak Co.).

If you decide that you would like to do your own printing—and you will once you start processing your own negatives—you will need more space and more equipment. You will need a darkroom with hot and cold running water, a sink and counter space, trays, electrical outlets and an enlarger (in addition to a developing tank and other equipment mentioned above). In short, you will need a basic darkroom as opposed to a closet for loading the film tank.

If you are very serious about your photographic work, you can take the basic darkroom a few steps further by adding professional equipment. Generally, this will mean that your space requirements will be greater and the darkroom itself will be much more than a bathroom.

In this chapter, I will discuss three different types of darkrooms for the home. Each is aimed at providing the photographer with the space and equipment required for specific parts of the processing task—developing film, printing and enlarging, and developing papers. While these three functions are different in procedure, there are several parts of each process that are common to the other types of work. In the beginning of this chapter, I must mention that I will make no attempt to discuss darkroom techniques. The amount of space needed for this information would easily fill all of the pages in this book. There are a number of quality

Fig. 3-2. A daylight developing tank (courtesy of Eastman Kodak Co.).

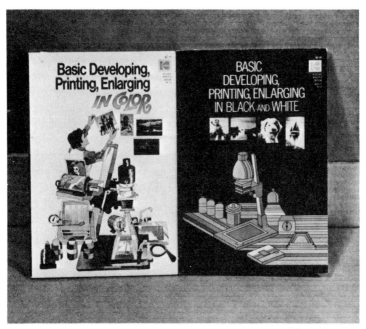

Fig. 3-3. Two good books which no serious home darkroom should be without.

books on the subject. One of which is *Basic Developing, Printing, Enlarging in Black and White* and another is *Basic Developing, Printing, Enlarging in Color*. Both are published by Eastman Kodak and they are available in most photographic equipment stores or directly from Kodak (Fig. 3-3).

There are a number of important questions that need to be answered by anyone contemplating a home darkroom. The first question is what type of work will be done in your darkroom now. You might be thinking about simply developing your own black and white negatives. For this type of work, you will need only a few pieces of equipment. But if you are planning to pursue darkroom work in the future, you will have to consider investing in equipment and materials that will enable you to enlarge and develop prints as well. The point is that you should take your present and anticipated needs into consideration during the planning stages of your darkroom.

There are several features that are essential to any darkroom. These include hot and cold running water, drains, electrical outlets, counterspace, areas for wet work and areas for dry work, and of no small consequence, the room must be "light safe"—that is you must be able to make it completely dark. When you are considering a space for your home darkroom, you must determine if all of these things are present or if they can be easily created.

One last question that you must ask yourself is whether or not you really need a full fledged darkroom with running water, counterspace and specialized equipment. As I mentioned earlier, there are many different facets to darkroom work and to accomplish basic film developing you will not require much space at all. Basically, there are two types of darkrooms—temporary and permanent. If you are a casual picture taker, the first type might be more than adequate for your needs. On the other hand, if you are running over five rolls of film through your camera a week, then you will probably be in the market for a darkroom with more capabilities that is set up in such a way as to permit you to accomplish your darkroom work efficiently.

TEMPORARY DARKROOMS

A temporary darkroom is the type of space where you can perform printing and developing tasks that need to be done now. For the hobbyist, this is the most common type of darkroom. It has many advantages in its favor, but also a few disadvantages. On the plus side, you do not have to commit part of the space in your apartment or home to the pursuit of photographic excellence. Instead, you simply convert an area, such as a bathroom or kitchen, into the darkroom for a few hours at a time. Assuming that you limit your darkroom time to the evening and night hours, a temporary darkroom is almost a snap to set up and use. There are a few precautions that you should keep in the back of your mind. These include testing the space, each time you use it, to make certain that it is light tight.

If you are considering doing some darkroom work, it should come as no surprise to you that film and prints must be handled in either a totally dark or in a specially safe-lighted situation. As a rule, undeveloped film must be handled only in total darkness. There is a simple test that you can do to determine if your space is truly dark. Begin by attaching a piece of white paper to a dark background in the room where you are planning to load your film into a developing tank. Make sure before you begin the test that you have closed the door or doors into the room and, if windows are present, you have hung some type of material over the window to prevent the entrance of light from the outside.

Just because you are working at night does not mean that light cannot come in through your windows. Considering that automobiles have headlights and streetlights might also be present, you should cover windows in your darkroom. Even the moon and stars can throw enough light to expose your undeveloped film.

After the room has been sealed for light, turn off the light in the room and sit in the dark for at least five minutes. If, after that time, you still cannot see the sheet of white paper that you put up before starting the test, it is a safe assumption that the room is light tight. If you can see the white page, the room is not light tight and you should discover where the light is coming from.

Some areas that you might not think to check are the cracks around window jambs and door frames and all edges of doors and vents to the outside.

One thing to keep in mind about darkrooms that must be light tight is that generally the smaller the room, the easier it will be to achieve darkness. A closet, for example, is much easier to make light tight than a kitchen. Some other good choices for a temporary darkroom include a room in your basement and your bathroom. Basements are usually dark as a result of being below ground level. Bathrooms are usually easy to make dark because they are generally located in the center of the house rather than on an exterior wall.

Many photographers that do their own processing have two darkrooms. One is light tight and used for loading exposed film into a developing tank. The other darkroom is light safe rather than being light tight. The difference is that a light safe room, in addition to being light tight, also has working lights by which you can see what you are doing. Working lights are special safelights designed for use during the developing of prints (Fig. 3-4).

The term *safelight* is used to describe special darkroom illumination that will not fog a light sensitive material—paper, for example. The thing to keep in mind is that there are different safelights for different types of photographic materials. The Eastman Kodak Company produces a line of safelights with different types of filters for use with specific materials (Table 3-1). Never, for a moment, think that you can simply buy a colored light bulb and use it as a safelight. Even though the bulb might appear to be the right color and intensity, these bulbs will transmit light that fogs a photographic emulsion.

For the temporary darkroom you will need, in addition to a light tight room for loading film into a developing tank, another

Fig. 3-4. A safelight (courtesy of Eastman Kodak Co.).

room for the actual processing. In most cases, for simple developing in a daylight tank, you will only require running water. Because the developing tank is light tight, you can develop, rinse and fix in daylight. That means, of course, that you can process in your kitchen or bathroom with the lights on as long as you keep the tank closed until the processing has been completed (Fig. 3-5).

The most basic of all darkrooms can be as simple as a closet where you load exposed film into a daylight developing tank. All processing can then take place in your kitchen or bathroom. If you want to do more in the film processing field, such as making contact sheets, enlarging and developing, you will require a darkroom that has electricity, a safelight and a little space in addition to hot and cold running water.

Probably the most popular temporary darkroom is the home bathroom. A few years ago, one famous photographer mentioned that he had developed and printed more photographs in bathrooms than any other place. Most photographers begin working in a bathroom as a temporary darkroom and, as needs get greater, eventually set up a permanent darkroom.

Temporary and permanent darkrooms have one point in common. There is a place for dry work such as contact sheets and enlarging and a place for wet work such as developing film and prints. It is important that the functions of each area do not overlap into the other area.

A dry work area is where the exposure tasks such as printing and enlarging take place. For the temporary bathroom darkroom, probably the best place for the dry area is the top of the bathtub. A sheet of plywood cut to fit over the tub makes a very serviceable

Table 3-1. Safelight Recommendations (courtesy of Eastman Kodak Co.).

KODAK Filter	Color	KODAK Material	Direct Illumination (not less than 4 ft [1.2 m])	Indirect Illumination*
			Bulb Wattage (110-130 volts)	
		NOTE: Always refer to the carton or the instruction sheet packaged with the product for complete safelight recommendations.		
OA	Greenish Yellow	Black-and-white contact and duplicating materials, projection films.	15-watt	25-watt
OC	Light Amber	Contact and enlarging papers, High Resolution Plate, TRANSLITE Film 5561, and OPALURE Print Film 5552.	15-watt	25-watt
OO	Light Yellow	Used for flashing halftones made through a KODAK Contact Screen.	7 1/2-watt 1.8 m (6 ft)	Not Applicable
No. 1	Red	Blue-sensitive materials, KODAGRAPH Projection, and some LINAGRAPH Papers.	15-watt	25-watt
No. 1A	Light Red	KODALITH and KODAGRAPH Orthochromatic Materials.	15-watt	25-watt
No. 2	Dark Red	Orthochromatic materials, green-sensitive x-ray films, EKTALINE Papers, and orthochromatic LINAGRAPH Papers.	15-watt	25-watt
No. 3†	Dark Green	Panchromatic materials.	15-watt	25-watt
No. 6B	Brown	Blue-sensitive x-ray films.	15-watt	25-watt
		KODAK SB Film.	7 1/2-watt	15-watt
No. 7	Green	Some black-and-white infrared materials.	15-watt	25-watt
No. 8	Dark Yellow	Some EASTMAN Color Print and Intermediate films.	15-watt	25-watt
No. 10	Dark Amber	EKTACOLOR 37 RC, PANALURE, and PANALURE Portrait Papers.	7 1/2-watt	15-watt
		EKTACOLOR Slide Film 5028, EKTACOLOR Print Film 4109 (ESTAR Thick Base), and RESISTO Rapid Pan Paper. (Not recommended for EKTACHROME RC Paper, Type 1993 or EKTACOLOR 74 RC Paper.)	15-watt	25-watt
No. 11	Appears Opaque, Transmits Infra-red Radiation	For use with infrared scopes.	15-watt	Not Applicable
No. 13‡	Amber	EKTACOLOR 37 RC, EKTACOLOR 74 RC, PANALURE, PANALURE Portrait, and RESISTO Rapid Pan Papers. § DO NOT USE with EKTACOLOR Slide Film 5028, EKTACOLOR Print Film 4109 (ESTAR Thick Base), and EKTACHROME RC Paper, Type 1993.	15-watt 7 1/2-watt‖	25-watt 7 1/2-watt‖
Type ML-2	Light Orange	Dental x-ray films.	15-watt	25-watt

CAUTION: Refer to particular product instruction sheets about time limitations on exposure to safelight illumi-nation. This is particularly important with Safelight Filters No. 3, No. 7, No. 10, and No. 13.

*Data in this column refer only to use of the KODAK Utility Safelight Lamp, Model D.

†Follow instructions for use of the No. 3 filter when processing panchromatic films.

‡The No. 13 Safelight Filter is generally preferable to the No. 10 Safelight Filter for use with products that are listed under both filters because, with the 15-watt bulb for direct illumination, it provides brighter illumination

§Use intermittently only to locate apparatus when using RESISTO Rapid Pan Paper.

‖For EKTACOLOR 74 RC Paper.

Fig. 3-5. Proper washing of developed film is important for predictable results in the home darkroom (courtesy of Eastman Kodak Co.).

work surface for enlarging or making contact sheets. The only drawback to using this arrangement for a dry area is that you might find the work height too low. Usually a small foot stool or milk crate will allow you to sit comfortably while printing.

The wet area in the temporary darkroom is quite important because this is where you will be doing your developing of prints. If you are using a bathroom, you might find that there is a general lack of space. There are a number of things that you can do to most effectively use what little space you have. The first and probably the most important task is to build a sink that fits over the existing sink that will be adequate for your needs. A special sink is also one very good way of insuring that the existing surfaces are protected from damage by processing chemicals.

Plans for a simple but quite effective temporary darkroom sink are shown in Fig. 3-6. This sink is made from one-half inch thick exterior plywood. After the sink has been built, you can make it

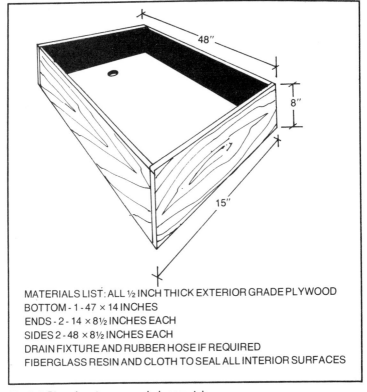

MATERIALS LIST: ALL ½ INCH THICK EXTERIOR GRADE PLYWOOD
BOTTOM - 1 - 47 × 14 INCHES
ENDS - 2 - 14 × 8½ INCHES EACH
SIDES 2 - 48 × 8½ INCHES EACH
DRAIN FIXTURE AND RUBBER HOSE IF REQUIRED
FIBERGLASS RESIN AND CLOTH TO SEAL ALL INTERIOR SURFACES

Fig. 3-6. Plans for a temporary darkroom sink.

totally waterproof and impervious to processing chemicals by covering all interior surfaces with a coat of fiberglass resin. A visit to any automobile parts store should uncover a fiberglass fender repair kit.

Every one of these kits that I have ever seen has a quart of fiberglass resin, hardener, fiberglass cloth and some mixing tools. Simply follow the directions on the package and you almost cannot come out wrong. It is also a good idea to use the fiberglass cloth for all interior seams where the sides join the bottom of the sink and around the drain. After the fiberglass hardens—usually within 24 hours—the sink will be waterproof and ready to be pressed into service.

If you decide to make a temporary darkroom sink, you should give careful consideration to the place where you will place your sink. Figure 3-6 plans call for a sink that is about 4 feet long and about 15 inches wide. If your bathroom or kitchen sink area is other than normal in dimensions, you should custom make your sink so that it will suit your purposes exactly. It is important that the sink be long and wide enough to accommodate at least four 8 x 10 inch developing trays. Other than that, you should feel free to make any modifications for your own custom purposes.

The wet area in your temporary darkroom will be where most of your processing will take place and that means you will need hot and cold running water and at least one electrical outlet. Because this is a temporary darkroom, you can get by quite nicely with an extension cord, but a certain amount of care must be exercised here because of the close proximity of water to the electrical connection. One very good way to protect yourself from the hazards of electrical shock is to install a Ground Fault Interrupter (GFI) in the circuit that will be used over the wet area.

A Ground Fault Interrupter, in case you are not familiar with this life saving circuit breaker, is simply a special unit that looks at first like a conventional electrical outlet. A GFI is a special circuit breaker that will turn off the circuit if there is a faulty connection or if the circuit is shorted out.

Keep in mind that it is very easy to short out an electrical circuit if you have wet hands or if you are standing on a wet floor. Without a GFI, you reduce your chances to zero. For several years, modern building codes have required that a special GFI outlet be installed in any area of a new home where water is present. This obviously includes the kitchen and bathroom and around swimming pools. If your home is new, you might already have a GFI in the line

130

in your temporary darkroom. If your home is an older one, chances are good that you will have to install one for your safety.

Other than those items already mentioned for the dry area and the wet area, there is little else that you will need for a temporary darkroom. Keep in mind that a temporary darkroom, by its very nature, is not really set up to be convenient or efficient. It is simply used to get a particular processing project completed. For this you will need only the most basic of equipment. But if you reach a point where you feel that your temporary darkroom facilities are sorely inadequate—and you will reach this point—then you should consider setting up and equipping a permanent darkroom.

Such a place will enable you to efficiently process your work with ease and it will be an aid in turning out professional looking work. When you and your family finally get tired of you tying up the bathroom or kitchen for hours at a time, when you get tired of moving equipment out of storage and setting it up, you are probably at the point where you need a permanent darkroom.

PERMANENT HOME DARKROOMS

A home darkroom is the dream of every photographer interested in expanding and improving the quality of his or her photography. And there are several things that can be said in favor of such a place. A home darkroom will, at the very least, save you time, money and help you to turn out professional looking work. The home darkroom is also an experimentation laboratory where you can explore the possibilities of photography. As you become more serious about your photographs, you will get closer to setting up your own permanent home darkroom. When you finally reach this stage in your photo work, there are a number of things that you should make sure are certain. If features such as electrical outlets are not present, you will be better off in the long run if you install them or if you have them installed by a qualified professional while the darkroom in under construction.

The first thing to consider when planning a permanent home darkroom is the location. Depending on how serious you are about photography, there is a necessary trade off between the ideal location and one that is workable from the standpoint of not having to rearrange your household around your photographic pursuits.

When all things are considered, the basement (or part of it) is probably the best choice for darkroom location. To begin with, basements are naturally darker than other rooms in the home. If windows are present, they are usually small enough to permit easy covering. The humidity of your basement is another factor that might be in your favor. Ideal humidity for a darkroom is between 45 and 50 percent. Basements are generally within this range so you will be starting in the right direction.

If your basement is drier or wetter than normal, consider installing a humidifier or dehumidifier to achieve the proper humidity in your darkroom. This is no small consideration because if the basement is generally too damp, you will have a problem with mildew and possibly rust on supplies and equipment. In addition, dampness causes deterioration of films and papers. The end result will be weak, mottled prints.

Another good reason for choosing a basement is that you can usually frame out a suitable size section for the darkroom and include such features as plumbing and electrical outlets where you need them. While the size of your darkroom will, at least in part, be determined by the amount of available space you have to spare, your darkroom will be most effective if it is at least 6 x 8 feet and no larger than 10 x 12 feet. If you are planning to build a darkroom in an unfinished basement, the larger size room will meet your present and future needs quite nicely.

It makes sense to partition off your darkroom for several reasons. The first is that the air and dust in the sealed off room will be much easier to control. This is especially true if your furnace is located in the basement and it is either coal-fired or forced-air. By making a special place for your darkroom, you should be able to almost eliminate any dust problems and this will save you untold headaches.

One other good reason for sealing off a special place for your darkroom is that other members of the household will be able to use the basement without disturbing or interfering with your darkroom work. There are a number of good books about how to finish off a basement by framing interior walls and then covering them with gypsum board.

Ventilation is very important in the permanent darkroom. A supply of fresh air is needed when you are working around chemicals. Even though they are not generally toxic, they can be unpleasant to work around for long periods of time. The best type of system will keep the air temperature between 65 to 75 degrees. There will be a vent to bring in fresh air and another to remove fumes. The incoming vent should have some type of filter to prevent the entrance of dust and air born particles. Incoming air will also increase the air pressure in the room and help to keep dust down. The exhaust vent should lead directly to the outside of the home and not into another room. Keep in mind that both intake and exhaust vents should be made light tight in some manner.

Electricity is necessary in the darkroom for the enlarger, safelights, the timing light, normal lighting and possibly other equipment such as a print drier. Outlets should be located over counter and work areas so that they are always within convenient reach. The probablility of electrical shock increases around wet areas and in the dark. Some type of safety device such as the GFI should be in the electrical circuit. At the very least, you should provide electrical fixtures such as the safelight with a pull chain or cord for safe on/off control.

If wall switches are present (or planned) in the darkroom, consider locating the switch for the normal lighting about 18 inches above the switch for the safelights. With the normal light switch located at this height, the chances of turning on a white light are reduced greatly. Another possibility is to install a special switch cover over the normal light switch such as shown in Fig. 3-7.

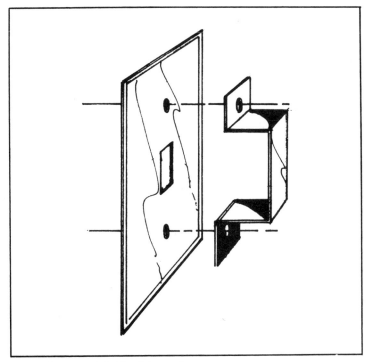

Fig. 3-7. Diagram of a light switch guard.

133

One of the features that both the temporary and permanent darkrooms have in common is that there must be areas for specific tasks or functions such as wet areas and dry areas. The major difference between a temporary and a permanent darkroom is that you can plan the layout of the wet and dry areas for a permanent darkroom.

It will be helpful to discuss the functions or tasks that are normally carried out in both the dry and wet area of the home darkroom. Then you can plan and build the required counters and cabinets that are best suited to your needs.

In the dry area of your permanent home darkroom, you will be enlarging and printing, making contact sheets, storing unexposed papers, cutting or trimming prints, storing dry chemicals, and possibly viewing slides and negatives prior to enlarging or printing. For all of these dry type operations, you will need counter space and cabinets for storage. For efficient operation, your enlarger should be mounted on one section of the counter separated from the rest of the counter by a small partition. With the enlarger segregated in this way, you can paint the wall and background around it in flat black to eliminate the possibility of fogged prints caused by light being reflected off white surfaces.

As a side note, all other surfaces in the home darkroom should be painted flat white so they will reflect the safelight illumination and give good overall lighting.

Around the enlarger should be a timer or some type of automatic timing device that is hooked into the enlarger circuit. A safelight will also be helpful in this area but it is not necessary. An electrical outlet should be located within the range of the enlarger cord as well. There should be a minimum of 12 inches on either side of the enlarger for placement of materials and enlarging aids.

Below the enlarger should be a special drawer for storing unexposed photographic papers. A dark drawer is shown in Fig. 3-8. One alternative to a dark drawer, if you have the space, is a lightweight safe for paper storage. These paper safes are generally available in any large photographic store. In any event, you must have some means of protecting unexposed papers. At the very least, paper can be stored in the package it came in.

The area below the enlarger bench can be used for storage. Cabinets with doors or a series of drawers are very handy and you will have little problem filling them as you accumulate darkroom equipment. For efficiency, it is a good idea to only store under this

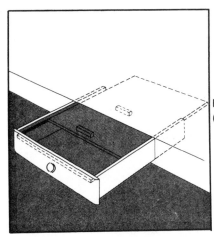

Fig. 3-8. A special light-tight drawer (courtesy of Eastman Kodak Co.).

bench those materials and accessories that are used in the enlarging process.

Next to the enlarging bench and separated by a partition, there should be more counter space for other dry type tasks. These tasks include making contact sheets, cutting or trimming prints, viewing negatives and slides, dry mounting prints, and other dry darkroom work. Electrical outlets should be present as should be a safelight. Shelves can be handy above the counter as well. Below the counter can be some type of storage. Cabinets with doors—that slide rather than open outward—are preferred.

In this area you can also provide a space for drying negatives. One way to do this is to string clothespins (the spring type) or film clips from a galvanized wire that is suspended between a wall and the partition seperating the two dry work areas. Use these clips to hold developed films while they dry.

The surfaces of the counters for the dry area should be covered with a material that will not absorb moisture. Even though this area is for dry work only, the possibility of something becoming wet still exists. Probably the best material for counter tops is plastic laminate. Formica is one popular and commonly available brand.

The working height of your dry area counter tops should be comfortable for you. Remember that your home darkroom is being custom built for you and among other things that means counter heights that are tailored for comfortable and efficient use. In order for you to determine a good counter top working height, you will have to experiment a bit. If you plan on working while standing up,

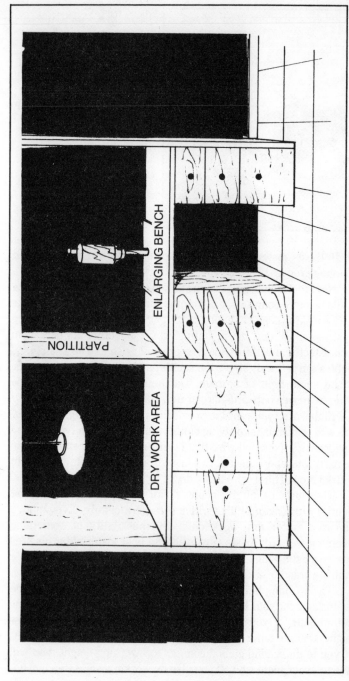

Fig. 3-9. Dry work areas in home darkroom.

the height will be different than if you sit on a stool or chair. Try working at your kitchen counter to see if this height is about right for your darkroom counters.

You might want to heighten or lower the dimensions. Generally, a working height of between 30 to 35 inches is usable by someone who is about 6 feet tall. Needless to say, if you are taller or shorter than 6 feet, you will have to make suitable adjustments to your darkroom counter height (Fig. 3-9).

The wet area of your darkroom consists of a sink that is large enough to hold at least four of your largest developing trays. You should have a drain, hot and cold running water, electrical outlets (suitably grounded), counter space, storage areas, shelves and a safelight (or more than one if the area is large). The set up should be at a height that permits efficient and speedy processing of work.

Adequate sink space is quite important in the wet area of your darkroom for obvious reasons. While it is entirely possible to do all of your tray developing on top of a counter (next to the sink), you will save yourself considerable grief if you buy or construct a large

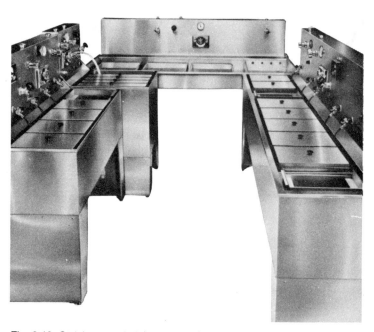

Fig. 3-10. Stainless steel sinks are used in all commercial processing labs because they last and they are easy to clean.

137

Fig. 3-11. A large stainless steel sink (courtesy of Eastman Kodak Co.).

sink in which to place your trays and work. This will virtually eliminate spilling processing chemicals and water on the floor. You can also use this large sink for mixing chemicals as well as for processing (Fig. 3-10).

As you probably have already guessed, there are a number of quality sinks manufactured specifically for use in the darkroom. Sizes range from 18 inches on up. One very good argument in favor of buying a ready-made sink is that they are made from materials which are impervious to the corrosive effects of processing chemicals. These materials include stainless steel (probably the most long-lived sink material), fiberglass or molded plastic. Most of these ready-made sinks include special fittings for faucet and drain connections.

Check current photographic orientated magazines for advertisements about special sinks designed for the home darkroom.

Your photo dealer will also sell sinks. About the only two problems with ready-made darkroom sinks are that they are expensive in the larger sizes, and they might not be available in a size that fits your needs. One alternative is to custom make your own darkroom sink. The cost will be considerably less and you can be certain that it will fit in with your planning (Figs. 3-11 and 3-12).

A sink for your permanent home darkroom can be made from three-fourth inch thick exterior plywood and covered with fiberglass cloth and resin. Earlier in this chapter, I mentioned building a portable sink (see Fig. 3-6) for the temporary darkroom

Fig. 3-12. An in-line therometer (courtesy of Eastman Kodak Co.).

this sink is simply an extension of that one. The difference between the two is that the permanent darkroom sink can be larger and better suited to your needs.

Plans for a darkroom sink are given in Fig. 3-13. Because the sink is simply a rectangular box, you should have little problem tailoring these plans for your own needs. The depth should be a minimum of 12 inches and the width should be wider than your largest developing tray. Length and height of the overall sink can be dictated by your special requirements in the darkroom.

If you decide to build your own custom darkroom sink, remember that the fiberglassing is the most important part of the project. Special attention must be given to all joints and the area around the drain. It is false economy to skimp on the fiberglass resin or cloth. There are materials that will make your custom sink watertight.

Probably the best approach is to build the sink in place with drain and plumbing connections installed. Then glass all interior surfaces. Be careful not to seal the drain. Apply cloth and at least two coats of resin to all joint areas and around the edge of the drain. Fiberglass resin cures within a short period of time. Therefore, the sink could be built and sealed in a single day.

If you are not familiar with working with fiberglass materials, there are a number of good publications on the subject. A few manufacturers of fiberglass materials also supply pamphlets for the beginner. As I mentioned earlier, automobile fiberglass repair kits—containing both resin and cloth—are very useful for this type of project. Follow the directions carefully and in a short period of time you should be able to build and seal a custom darkroom sink that will give you years of efficient service.

One alternative to fiberglassing your custom darkroom sink is to build the basic sink from plywood. Then have a sheetmetal fabricator custom make a stainless steel liner. Then simply set the liner in place and make the plumbing connections. While a custom sink lined with stainless steel will be more expensive than the same sink covered with fiberglass, the steel sink should last for a lifetime.

While I am on the subject of a darkroom sink, I want to comment on the plumbing for the darkroom. Photo processing, by its very nature, requires an adequate supply of both hot and cold running water. More often than not, a specific temperature of water is required for various processes. One way to achieve a required water temperature is to install a special automatic water

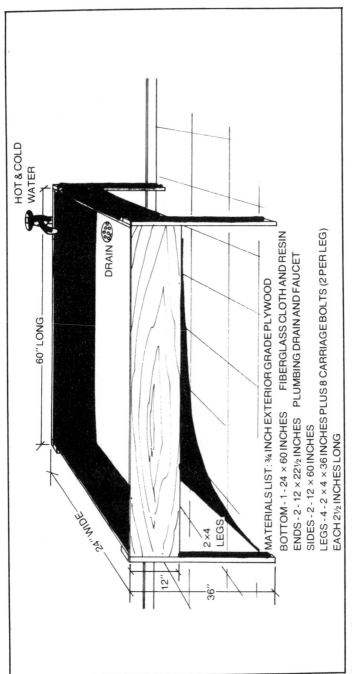

HOT & COLD WATER

DRAIN

60" LONG

24" WIDE

12"

36"

2 × 4 LEGS

MATERIALS LIST: ¾ INCH EXTERIOR GRADE PLYWOOD   FIBERGLASS CLOTH AND RESIN
BOTTOM - 1 - 24 × 60 INCHES   PLUMBING DRAIN AND FAUCET
ENDS - 2 - 12 × 22½ INCHES
SIDES - 2 - 12 × 60 INCHES
LEGS - 4 - 2 × 4 × 36 INCHES PLUS 8 CARRIAGE BOLTS (2 PER LEG)
EACH 2½ INCHES LONG

Fig. 3-13. Plans for a permanent darkroom sink.

mixing or blending valve at the faucet. One type is the Calumet Temperature Controller. This model is generally available and there are other types as well.

Special consideration should be given to an adequate supply of hot water. This is particularly important for those areas of the country where during the winter months the temperature of the normal tap water goes below 60 degrees. Keep in mind that some types of color processing require large quantities of hot water. Actually, the amount of processing you are planning to do will help you determine if you can use your present household hot water heater or if you should install a separate unit for the home darkroom (Fig. 3-12).

The water itself in your home darkroom is important and it must be clean and free of impurities. If your water contains

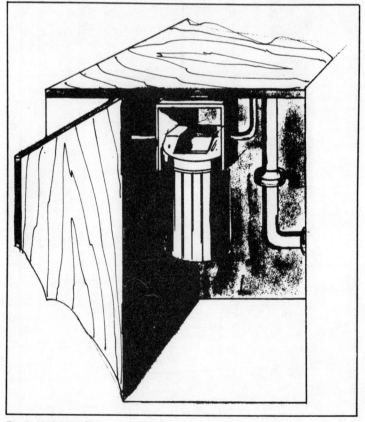

Fig. 3-14. A water filter.

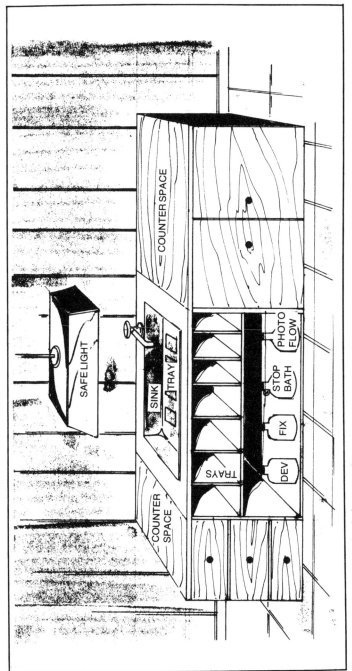

Fig. 3-15. Suggested set up for darkroom wet area.

143

additives such as chlorine, flouride or salts, you should install a water filtration system in the line (Fig. 3-14).

The drain for your darkroom sink is another consideration. Generally, the drain line should be at least 2 inches in diameter and at a pitch steep enough to permit quick exhaust of water and chemicals. Keep in mind that it is always a good practice to flush the drain with rapidly flowing water after old processing solutions have been dumped. This will minimize corrosion and it helps to wash away any sludge or gelatin that might be present.

You should also give some consideration to where your drains lead. If a septic tank is in the system, its activity might by impaired temporarily by an excessive amount of photographic chemicals. Generally, any septic tank can handle up to about 35 gallons of chemicals a day without adverse effects. Needless to say, your existing drain lines must be in sound condition to reduce the possibility of contaminating the water table in your vicinity.

Underneath the sink is a good place to store processing trays while they are not in use. Some type of rack system or partition walls will aid in storing this type of equipment. On one side of the sink—usually the left side—should be counter space. Make the counter as wide and as long as space permits. This will ensure ample working space as you expand your darkroom capabilities and knowledge. As with the dry work area, the wet work area counter top should be covered with a material that will resist chemicals and water. Plastic laminate material or stainless steel are the best choices. Back splashes on the back of the counter top will help to keep accidental spills from flowing behind the counter. The area underneath this counter can also be used for storage of materials and equipment used for wet darkroom work. (Fig. 3-15).

Shelves are important in the darkroom because there are many things that need to be stored within easy reach. Over the sink area, a shelf can be used for storing bottles of chemicals that have been mixed and are ready for use. Shelves in the darkroom must be built with weight holding capability in mind. When you consider that a gallon bottle of developer weighs at least 6 pounds, a shelf full of such bottles can be quite heavy. Plan accordingly and avoid an unfortunate and possibly disastrous experience (Fig. 3-16).

There should be a safelight over the sink area so that you can see as prints are placed into the various processing chemicals. The light should be suitably grounded and be activated with a pull cord rather than a switch. This will help to reduce the possibility of an electrical shock. A timer should also be present so that you can time the various processing steps.

Fig. 3-16. Shelves for the home darkroom must be strong because bottles of developing chemicals are heavy.

The floor in your home darkroom also bears consideration during the planning stages. There are several requirements for a good floor. It must be waterproof and resistant to chemicals used in the processing of films and papers. The floor must not become slippery when wet, it must be easy to keep clean and it must be comfortable to stand on (resilient, as the flooring makers say).

The best choices for darkroom floor coverings are those known as resilient floor coverings. These include asphalt tile, vinyl asbestos tile, vinyl tile, and sheet vinyl floors. Generally, all of these floor covering materials hold up very well to the abuses normally encountered in the home darkroom. A brief description of each follows.

Asphalt Tile. This is probably the least expensive floor covering of the group. It has been used in commercial photographic processing rooms for many years. As with all flooring materials used in the darkroom, proper installation is crucial for a long life. Special adhesives are available (and should be used) which resist the action of photographic chemicals and water. Other than special adhesive, only care during installation is required for a darkroom floor that will provide years of silent service.

Vinyl Asbestos Tile. This is an excellent all-purpose floor covering material. It is more expensive than asphalt tile, but it is easier to maintain.

Vinyl Tile. This is probably the most expensive of all tile type floor coverings. This is largely because of the base material. It is also probably the easiest of all floor tiles to maintain. There are several grades of vinyl tile, but only the better types (price is the best indication here) are suitable for home darkroom floor coverings. Another reason for the high price for vinyl tile is that it is generally available in a wide range of colors and design patterns.

Because aesthetics in floor covering is not really a prime consideration for the home darkroom, I suggest that you use either asphalt or vinyl asbestos tile instead of vinyl tile. The price of the materials will be much less and the durability satisfactory for your purposes (Fig. 3-17).

Sheet Vinyl Floor Material. This is a floor covering of vinyl which has no apparent seams and it has a lot of appeal for the home darkroom. Because there are no seams, there is little chance of water or chemicals undermining the floor covering. Sheet vinyl floors are also available with a special cushion backing that is very easy underfoot. This is an important quality in a floor covering if you spend long hours standing in the darkroom.

Also, sheet vinyl floors can be turned up around the edges to form a cove around the perimeter of the floor. This will virtually eliminate dust collecting corners and angles. As you may have guessed, a sheet vinyl floor is the most expensive of all floors that you can install in your home darkroom.

ARRANGEMENT OF DARKROOM AREAS

Your permanent home darkroom should be arranged and set up to offer the most efficient use of space and to aid you in performing the various darkroom tasks with the greatest speed. This holds true for both the temporary and permanent darkroom. By setting up your darkroom in sections—a wet area and a dry area—you will be on the road to taking full advantage of the space you have allowed for the darkroom.

However, there are other considerations as well. For example, where will you put the dry area, the wet area, and how much storage space do you really need. You must ask yourself how you can best put the available space to good use and this requires more than a casual approach. Once cabinets and counters are built or installed and plumbing connections are made, it will not be an easy task to rearrange things. In order to avoid having to live with a mistake, you must plan the darkroom layout very carefully.

146

Fig. 3-17. A good floor is easy to clean (courtesy of Armstrong Cork Company).

147

Some suggestions for effective home darkroom layout are as follows. Locate dry and wet areas or units on opposite sides of the darkroom with ample space between them. Then when you are enlarging, for example, you can simply turn around, take a step or two and be at the sink or wet area. With this set up, there is little chance of spilling water or processing chemicals on the dry work area.

An alternative to opposing work areas is to locate your wet and dry work areas side by side. The areas must be separated by some type of partition (Figs. 3-18A and 3-18B) to avoid mishap in the event of an accidental spill.

Locate a safelight over each specific work area such as the enlarging bench, the sink area, etc. Generally, the safelight should be no less than 4 feet above the counter top. A larger safelight should be over the wet processing area than over the enlarging bench.

During the planning stages of your permanent home darkroom, you should try to determine how you can most effectively set up your work areas. As an aid, Fig. 3-18 offers some simple yet very workable suggestions.

To increase your knowledge of how an effective darkroom is set up, find other photographers that have their own darkrooms and ask for a tour. Someone once said that a darkroom is a personal thing which should be acquired on the basis of need and only after trial of various arrangements. By visiting other darkrooms, you will be better able to judge what type of set up is best suited for your needs. Simply pick the best parts from other working darkrooms and apply them to your own.

Another possibility is to rent a darkroom for a few hours or a day and see how particular setups feel for the way you work. Most

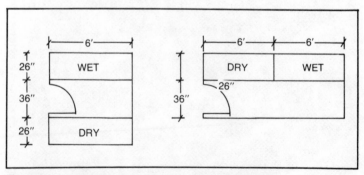

Fig. 3-18A. A darkroom layout (courtesy of Eastman Kodak Co.).

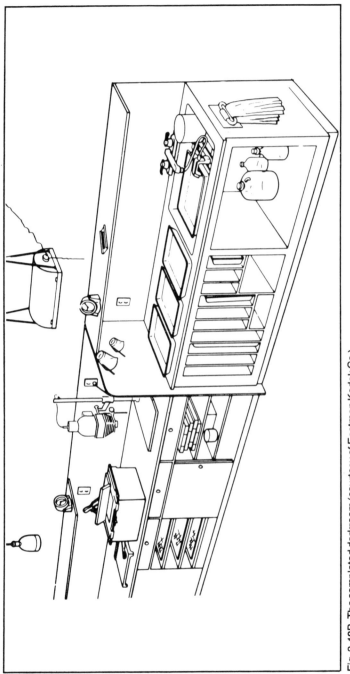

Fig. 3-18B. The completed darkroom (courtesy of Eastman Kodak Co.).

large cities have such darkrooms for rent. Public libraries are another possibility. It is not uncommon for them to offer darkrooms for rent by the hour or free of charge. Still another way to find out how to set up a home darkroom is to enroll in a basic developing and photography course offered by a local college or continuing education program. While classroom darkrooms will be much larger than you will ever need, you will nevertheless gain an important insight into how a darkroom can function when it is set up properly.

In short, you must gain as much information about how working darkrooms are set up and then, based on your needs, draw a diagram of your own darkroom. The space you have available, amount of funds available and your enthusiasm are all important factors in determining the type of darkroom you will create.

Most experts agree that the costs of setting up a home darkroom can run into a considerable sum. But once set up, operating costs are reasonable. Additionally, a home darkroom can provide years of enjoyment for anyone willing to invest some time to learn and master the basics of film finishing.

Chapter 4
Light Studio

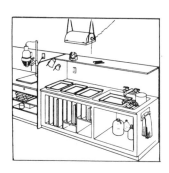

This chapter is primarily aimed at the photographer interested in creating a place in the home where he or she has complete control of lighting. While a photographic light studio might seem a bit specialized, you might be surprised to learn that there are thousands of light studios around the country. The control of light, for photographic purposes, enables the photographer to achieve predictable results for a specific photograph. Every day we see photographs in magazines, newspapers and even on television that were created in a special light studio. The typical light studio is used by professional photographers for commercial purposes and the amateur or hobbyist photographer can learn much from what is presently being done in the industry (Fig. 4-1).

There are few secrets in controlling light for photographic purposes. Actually, the basic underlying principles are quite simple. Quality of light is the key to achieving photographs that are interesting and professional looking. This holds true whether the photographer is working indoors or out. The big difference, however, is that in the studio the photographer has complete control of the light and can therefore produce predictable results each and every time. You might never plan to take photographs for commercial purposes, but knowing how the pros accomplish various lighting techniques will help to make you a more versatile amateur photographer. The end result is that you will develop a better understanding of what light does for the photographer and your photographs will begin to take on professional characteristics.

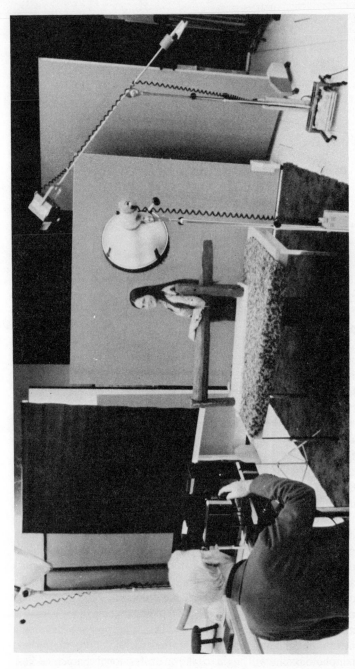

Fig. 4-1. Using artificial light and special backgrounds (courtesy of Eastman Kodak Co.).

Fig. 4-2. A professional large format camera (courtesy of Calumet).

It is important to discuss how professional photographers set up and operate a light studio. A discussion of cameras, lighting equipment and related accessories will prove helpful in the long run to the amateur photographer. In many cases it is possible to build or jury-rig lighting equipment that does very much the same job as professional lighting equipment. The major difference, of course, is that the homemade lighting equipment can be had for a fraction of the cost of the real thing. And it will do very much the same job for you.

CAMERAS

Professional studio cameras can be lumped into three rather broad categories: large format, medium format and 35-millimeter cameras. While most amateur photographers only use the 35mm camera, it will be helpful to discuss the other two groups of cameras as well.

153

The large format view camera is the standard tool of the commercial photographer and it has remained virtually unchanged for over a century. You have no doubt seen pictures or movies showing old time photographers. They have a large camera with a drape over the back end. This same type of camera, with a few modifications to be sure, is the large format view camera.

The large format camera is just a few steps up from the camera obscura. One end has a lens and the other end has some means of holding the film. Usually this is a film holder containing one sheet of 8 x 10 film. And there is also a ground glass viewing screen. Between the lens and the film is a bellows which can be adjusted up, down, left, right, and at just about any imaginable configuration.

As you might have guessed, the manipulation of the bellows relative to the lens and film plane is the key to using a large format view camera. It is possible to completely control the end result by adjusting the bellows. This is practically an art in itself (Fig. 4-2).

The standard size large format view camera is 8 x 10 inches. Smaller cameras such as 5 x 7 and 4 x 5 are also used but it depends on the assignment. Large format cameras can produce very high quality negatives because the print does not have to be enlarged very much for reproduction (as a print from a 35mm negative does, for example). Obviously, a large format view camera cannot be handheld. Instead it is mounted on a tripod. The end result is a camera that can consistently produce crystal clear negatives. This is a must for commercial work. There is little doubt that the large format view camera is far superior to all other types of cameras in the hands of a professional (Fig. 4-3).

The second category of cameras are those which use 120-size roll film rather than the larger sheet films. Cameras in this group produce a negative that is in the neighborhood of 2¼ inches square in size. The advantage of cameras in this category, over those in the large format group, is the increased portability and quicker shooting capabilities. Medium format view cameras can be handheld. This frees the photographer from the rigidity that is common with the use of a tripod.

Undoubtedly the most popular and spectacular medium format view camera is the Swedish made Hasselblad. It is equipped with interchangeable lenses and film magazines and a vast array of other accessories such as a film magazine that holds standard Polaroid film. The price of a new Hasselblad—or a used one for that matter—is rather steep for amateur photographers. Nevertheless

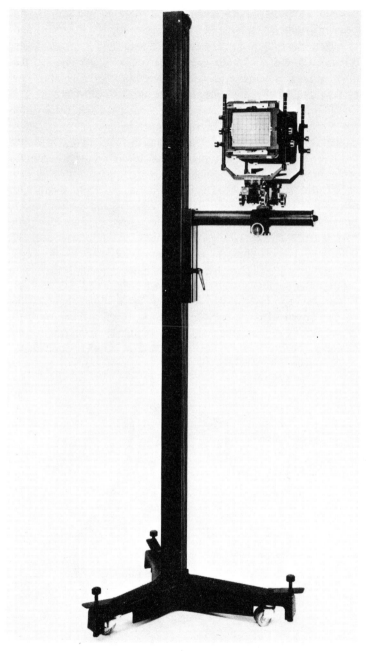

Fig. 4-3. The only way to use a large format camera is on a tripod or modern stand such as this (courtesy of Calumet).

this is a quality piece of photographic equipment that many feel is more than well worth the price (Fig. 4-4).

The last category of cameras for the serious photographer is the small format or 35mm single lens reflex (SLR) camera. The development of this type of camera put the capabilities of professional looking photographs in the hands of the amateurs. The first 35mm camera was introduced in about 1914 and it was called the Leica. Since then, there have been a vast number of improvements and refinements resulting in a camera that is simple to operate and has the capability of turning out consistently professional looking photographs (Fig. 4-5).

There are many fine 35mm cameras available today with names like Nikon, Minolta, Cannon, Yashica, and the originator, Leica. Almost all have interchangeable lenses, light meters and a vast assortment of accessories. Nikon alone offers over 75 different lenses. Other camera makers offer similar selections. The end result is that the amateur photographer can own a professional quality camera for just a few hundred dollars. This same camera will enable you to do many of the things that cameras costing three and four times as much can do (Figs. 4-6A and 4-6B).

There are basically two types of 35mm or small format cameras: the single lens reflect (SLR) and the range finder camera.

Fig. 4-4. A medium format camera (courtesy of Eastman Kodak Co.).

Fig. 4-5. The first 35mm camera, Leica Model A (courtesy of E. Leitz Inc.).

Fig. 4-6A. A modern 35mm SLR camera with motor winder (courtesy of E. Leitz, Inc.).

The major difference between the two is that the SLR uses the same lens to view the subject as well as record it. The range finder camera uses a split image or overlapping field focusing system. Most professionals prefer the SLR over the range finder camera largely because there is no difference between what is seen and the final photograph. There can be a difference when the range finder camera is used for the same shot.

Professional or commercial photographers will most often use a large format view camera for their work. Chances are very good, however, that the do-it-yourself photographer will not have access to such a camera, but will rely on a 35mm camera for all photographs. While there will be some sacrifice in overall quality with the 35mm, the amateur photographer can produce highly acceptable photographs with this system. Part of the key to success lies in controlling the lighting in the studio and using some other aids—such as a tripod and time exposures—to help you achieve professional looking photographs.

LIGHTING EQUIPMENT

All photographs require a sufficient amount of light on the subject to permit exposure of the film. In the past, most of your photographs might have been taken outdoors or possibly indoors with the aid of a flash attachment for your camera.

In a photographic studio, you can control light so that you can achieve a desired effect. This is accomplished, at least in part, by

Fig. 4-6B. A 35mm camera (courtesy of Eastman Kodak Co.).

159

using several different types of lights. These include spotlights, floodlights, scooplights and bounced lights. Because each of these pieces of lighting equipment has certain uses, it will be helpful to discuss each type as well as their intended uses.

Spotlights, as their name suggests, offer the capability of specialized light for the subject. Spotlights are quite common in commercial photography largely because they can be used at any range and they deliver light of a reasonably high quality. More often than not, a spotlight will have a special Fresnel lens over the business end of the lamp. This lens helps to sharply chisel the highlight areas away from the shadows. The end result is a subject with clean, crisp lines.

The light given off by a conventional spotlight is highly controllable and is often used to highlight a special part of the subject. There are several different sizes of spotlights that are used for specific applications—lighting the subject, or as accent lights, or as localized fill lights. Because the beam of light is so controllable, spotlights can be directly on the subject or at a low level to enhance texture. Spotlights also make excellent fill lights.

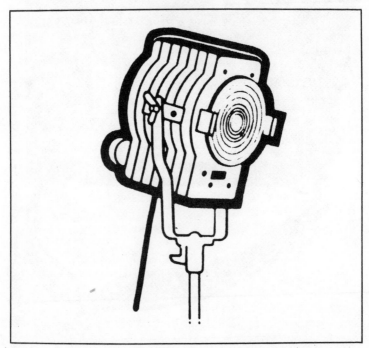

Fig. 4-7. A spotlight with a Fresnel lens (courtesy of Eastman Kodak Co.).

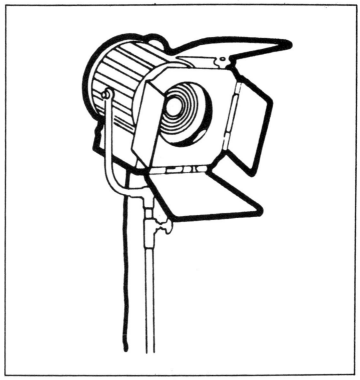

Fig. 4-8. A spotlight with a set of flaps (courtesy of Eastman Kodak Co.).

They provide light only where it is needed and therefore you can avoid unwanted shadows (Fig. 4-7).

There are a number of accessories commonly used in conjunction with spotlights such as snoots and barndoors. These accessories help the user to achieve a very high degree of control of the spotlight beam. In the case of spotlights, the various accessories can be used to good advantage (Fig. 4-8).

Floodlights can cover a large area with a reasonably even light. The quality of this light is entirely another matter. It depends on the type of bulb and reflector being used. One thing that all floodlights have in common is that they are generally hot to work under for both the subject and the photographer. The three most common types of floodlights are: sealed beam, high-intensity miniature floods and parabolic reflectors.

Sealed Beam Flood Bulbs. These are designed to be miniature sources of light. Each bulb has a built in internal reflector which effectively spreads light over a fairly large area (about 120 degrees from the point of origin). Sealed beam flood lights are primarily intended for use at a fairly close range—up to about 5 feet. If the lights are placed much further away, the end result is a spotlight effect with sharp shadows as well as floodlight spread. For distances greater than 5 feet, the light from sealed beam floodlights are most commonly bounced off a large surface or covered with a diffusion material such as a large scrim (a loosely woven cotton or linen cloth curtain, for example). Either of these two methods will result in floodlighting that is soft, diffused and indirect (Fig. 4-9).

High-Intensity Miniature Floodlights. These most commonly use a quartz-iodine type bulb. The light produced by

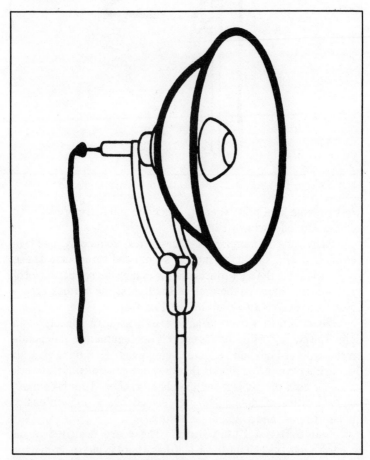

Fig. 4-9. A sealed beam floodlight (courtesy of Eastman Kodak Co.).

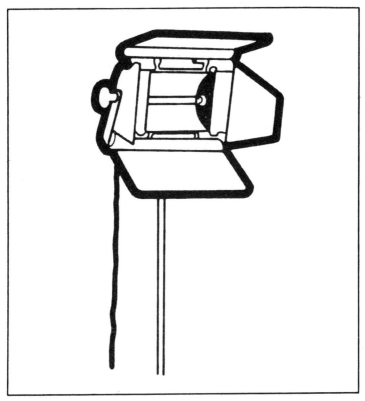

Fig. 4-10. High-intensity miniature light source (courtesy of Eastman Kodak Co.).

these floodlights is extremely high in intensity and yet they draw a relatively low amperage. They are very hot to work under and because of the traditionally small reflectors tend to produce sharp shadows, harsh highlights, and (at great distances) almost a spotlight quality. High-intensity miniature floodlights are remarkable in that they are very efficient at spreading light over a large area. The light will be harsh unless the light is altered by bouncing off a surface or by using some type of diffuser for each lamp (Fig. 4-10).

Parabolic Reflector Type Floodlights. These are actually a two part light made up of the bulb and a reflector specifically designed for that particular bulb. There are several different size parabolic reflector type floodlights ranging in size from 9 inches to about 16 inches in diameter. It is obviously important that the reflector and bulb be matched for maximum light delivery.

163

Additionally, each size reflector has a certain range in which it will perform with excellence. More or less than this specific distance and the parabolic floodlight will leave a lot to be desired and the result will be hot spots on the subject. The larger the diameter of the reflector and the closer that reflector is to the subject, the more diffuse in quality the light will be (Fig. 4-11).

Parabolic floodlight quality is also directly related to the surface type in the reflector itself. For example, if the inside of the reflector is brushed or matte-silver (one of the most common types) the resulting floodlight will be rather soft in quality. On the other hand, if the interior surface is chrome plated, the light will be specular and sparkling in quality.

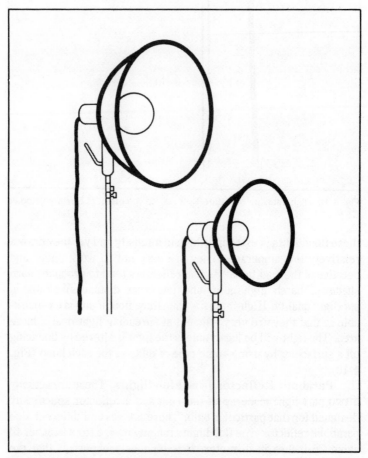

Fig. 4-11. Parabolic reflectors (courtesy of Eastman Kodak Co.).

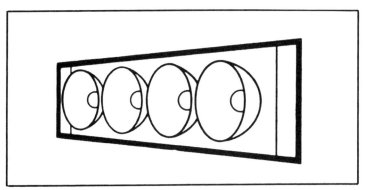

Fig. 4-12. Large lighting boards (courtesy of Eastman Kodak Co.).

As you might have guessed, the bulb itself used in the reflector will also have an effect on the quality of light. A clear glass bulb, for example, will tend to create a specular highlight and rather sharp edged shadows. A frosted bulb will result in more diffused overall lighting. In short, it will be softer than a clear glass bulb.

Scooplights or lightboards are, most often, a group of lights mounted in series that produce general or overall lighting. These lighting units can cover a rather large area with plenty of light. On the whole, lightboards tend to produce a softer quality light than the previously mentioned lighting sources. More often than not, a lightboard is simply a group of parabolic reflectors mounted in series. Obviously, each reflector must be designed for a particular bulb for best results. If the unit is not balanced in such a manner, the overall effect will be closer to several spotlights rather than good general lighting (Fig. 4-12).

Bounce lighting is more of a technique than a particular type of lighting fixture. To accomplish this, the photographer must provide something such as a white surface, a special reflector umbrella or a foil covered reflector close to the subject off which some type of light is bounced.

A spotlight is commonly used as a light source and bounced off a surface onto the subject. The end result is known as *ambient light*. The term describes a good quality light coming from a general direction, but with no obvious point of source. This type of lighting has become quite popular in the past decade or so because the overall effect is one of softness. I will discuss the various means of bouncing light later in this chapter. For now, just keep in in mind that probably the softest of all lighting is ambient lighting and to achieve this some type of light must be bounced off a surface that will do the job (Fig. 4-13).

BACKDROPS, REFLECTORS AND OTHER ACCESSORIES

After the camera and the suitable lighting of the subject, the next thing to consider is the background of the subject. This is no small consideration because the wrong type of background can be distracting from the subject and the result is a photograph that is too busy or cluttered or not interesting enough.

The type of background will, at least in part, be determined by the subject itself. You must ask yourself if you think the background should be part of the final picture or seemingly non-existent. In many cases, the best type of background is a simple white background. In others, a colored background will do the trick better (Figs. 4-14 and 4-15).

Professional photographers often use a special paper for backgrounds. This paper is called seamless background paper and is commonly sold in the larger photo shops and through photographic magazines. Most often, a roll will measure 107 inches in

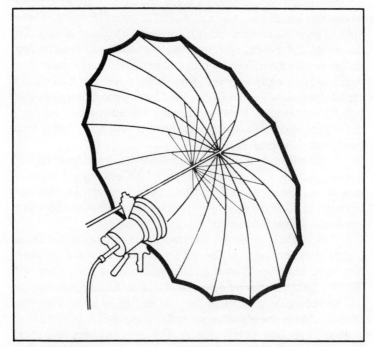

Fig. 4-13. A reflective umbrella (courtesy of Eastman Kodak Co.).

Fig. 4-14. A subject with a busy background.

width and come in lengths from 12 to 50 feet. At the present time, there are about 50 different colors including several shades of white.

Fig. 4-15. The same subject with a neutral background is much easier to see.

Fig. 4-16. In this shop, the subject is very close to the background.

One of the many desirable features of seamless backdrop paper is that it can be used behind most subjects without detracting from the overall appearance of the final photograph. The paper is there and yet appears not to be. Backdrop papers are also available in various light reflective or absorbing qualities as well. They are excellent for bust portraits in the studio.

In addition, there are two other things that the photographer can do in the studio to either make the background a part of the final photograph or not. These include placing the backdrop closer or further away from the subject and shooting the photograph at a lower F stop.

By moving the backdrop further away from the subject, it will tend to be less apparent in the final photograph. On the other hand, if the backdrop is placed close to the subject it will, in most cases, be very much part of the photograph (Figs. 4-16 and 4-17).

Shooting at a lower F stop setting will also decrease the depth of field. This simply means that only part of the final photograph will be in focus. The foreground and background will tend to be out of focus. This can often lead to a very interesting overall effect. If a higher F stop is used, more of the final photograph will be in focus (both the foreground as well as the background). See Figs. 4-18 and 4-19.

Fig. 4-17. In this shot, the subject has been moved away from the background. The result is that the photograph is not too busy.

Fig. 4-18. Shooting at a low F stop (in this case f/2) results in a narrow depth of field. Only part of the subject is in focus.

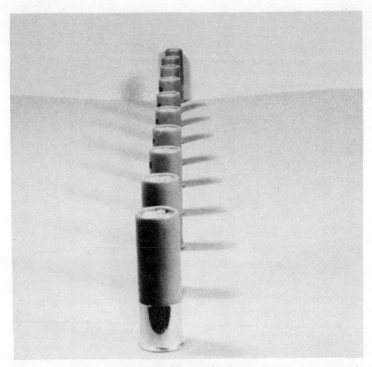

Fig. 4-19. Shooting the same subject at a high F stop (f/16) results in a much greater depth of field and much more is in focus.

In the lighting section of this chapter, I explained a bit about bounced light—as opposed to direct lighting—and the overall softness that can be achieved with this technique. In effect, what the photographer is doing with bounced lighting is using some type of surface to reflect the light onto the subject rather than directly pointing the light source at the subject. All types of surfaces can be used to reflect light.

When direct light from a spotlight strikes a surface, the texture of that particular surface will do certain things to the light. If the surface is flat white in color, for example, it will absorb some of the light but will reflect most of it. The same spot light shined on a flat black surface will have a much different effect. Most of the light will be absorbed by the surface and only a very small amount will be reflected. Reflected light in the photographic studio is commonly referred to as bounce light for obvious reasons.

As you can see, bounce light can come from any surface that is close to the subject and on which is shined a light. A certain amount

Fig. 4-20. Bounced light has a soft effect on the subject.

of experimenting is necessary to give you a good indication of what the different surfaces can do for you in the studio. Try bouncing light from a spotlight or floodlight off the ceiling wall, or seamless backdrop paper. While the sharper the angle of the bounce the more intense the light, the general overall effect of bounce lighting is always softer than if the same light were to shine directly on the subject (Figs. 4-20 and 4-21).

Professional studio photographers and cinematographers use minireflectors to help bounce light and highlight a specific part of the subject. A minireflector can be as simple as a piece of 2 x 3 foot white cardboard or as elaborate as a specially constructed aluminum foil covered reflector board 4 x 8 feet in size. Minireflectors are quite handy in the studio and outdoors because they are generally hand held and can be used quite effectively to throw a little extra, soft light exactly where you want it (to eliminate a shadow under the subjects chin for example).

Tenting is another technique used by professional photographers to help produce a soft light on the subject. Tenting, by way of definition, is the technique of surrounding the subject with reflecting surfaces. In many cases, tenting materials are simply white paper stretched over a lightweight frame. This diffuser is then placed between the subject and the light source. The end result is a very soft lighting effect.

Another possibility, and one used for small subjects, is to actually construct a tent around most of the subject. White linen, cotton and even translucent plastic sheeting are some of the more common materials used for this. Then spotlights or floodlights are directed onto the tent from the outside. Additionally, if colored acetate gels are placed over certain areas of this tent, or over the lighting source, special lighting effects can be achieved (Fig. 4-22).

With all of the lighting equipment and techniques available for studio photography today, it should be very apparent to you that there is no such thing as any one particular light or technique that can be used for every shooting session. There are instead, the proper lights and techniques for the particular shooting project at

Fig. 4-21. Direct lighting produces harsher tones and a whitish effect on the subject.

Fig. 4-22. Tenting results in very soft lighting tones on the subject.

hand. Artificial lighting is very much controllable in the studio, but it takes time and a certain amount of experimentation to know which to use for any given project. There are a few professional tricks of the trade that can make working with artificial lighting just a bit easier.

Proper exposure is crucial for predictable results when shooting photographs. When working with natural light, the F stop and shutter speed is relatively easy to determine. In each package of Kodak film, for example, will be a listing of F stops (usually at 1/250 or 1/500 of a second shutter speed) for the various and common natural lighting situations. F/22 should be used in a bright or hazy sun, on light sand or snow and F/8 should be used in open shade. These are rough guidelines to be sure, but more often than not—if they are followed—the film will be exposed correctly. In the studio, however, a different set of circumstances come into play and the studio photographer must take them into consideration for acceptable exposures.

The best way to determine shutter speeds and F stops when working under artificial lighting is to use a good light meter. There are many types currently available and even some of the better 35mm cameras have a built in (or attached as in the F series Nikons) light metering systems.

Unfortunately, more often than not, a light meter will tend to give higher light readings than actually exist. This is largely due to the fact that much of the light is reflected or being reflected off the surrounding backdrop or reflectors themselves. One way to determine correct exposures when working under these circumstances is to use a grey card to help you determine the correct exposure of the subject (Fig. 4-23).

A grey card, as the name suggests, is simply a piece of grey cardboard (usually dark grey on one side and light grey on the other). The card is held in front of the camera or light meter and the proper exposure for the card—rather than the subject—is determined. The grey card is removed and the picture is taken. In just about every instance, the grey card will call for an exposure that appears to be much more than is needed (overexposed) for the subject. This is in part because the grey card will absorb more light than it will reflect. The end result will usually be a photograph that is properly exposed.

You can make a very effective grey card from a piece of common grey cardboard such as the cardboard found on the back of a pad of paper or a shirt package. Your homemade grey card should be about 1 x 2 feet in size and you should use it to help you determine the proper exposure when you are working under artificial lighting in the studio. Keep the card handy by attaching a loop of string to one end and hanging the card on your tripod. Use the card to give you an indication of the proper exposure when there is a lot of reflected light.

You can make your own diffusion screen from lightweight lumber such as 1 x 2 or 2 x 2 inch stock. Make a frame approximately 3 feet wide and 6 feet long. Then stretch white cotton fabric over it much the same as if you were stretching a painting canvas. To help you achieve a soft lighting effect, place this screen between a flood light and your subject (Fig. 4-24).

Similar screens in various sizes can be built and covered with material that will reflect or absorb light. You will find many uses for these screens in your light studio. Some other materials that you might want to work with include fiberglass cloth and aluminum wire screening (fine mesh) which will reduce the intensity of light

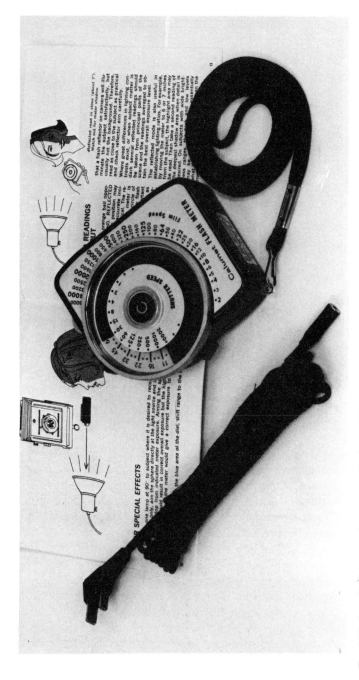

Fig. 4-23. A quality light meter is necessary for determining the proper exposure in the studio (courtesy of Calumet).

175

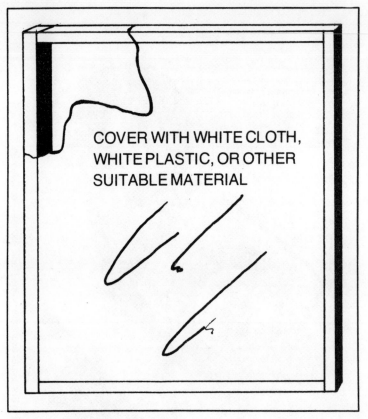

Fig. 4-24. Plans for a light diffusion screen.

without changing its character. Burlap, white opaque plastic, and yellow (or other colors) ripstop nylon also work well as diffusing or reflecting screen materials.

A simple but effective light reflecting screen can be made from a piece of cardboard that is 3 x 4 feet and covered with aluminum foil on one side. Cover one side of the cardboard with the foil as it comes from the box and cover the other side with crumpled foil for a very different type of reflective surface. Double stick tape is very handy for attaching the foil to the cardboard (Fig. 4-25).

Old movie screens also make good backdrops and light reflectors. You can usually pick one of these up for next to nothing by shopping garage sales and flea markets. Make sure the screen has no holes and that the stand works properly. Where possible, use the screen as a distant backdrop or light bouncing surface.

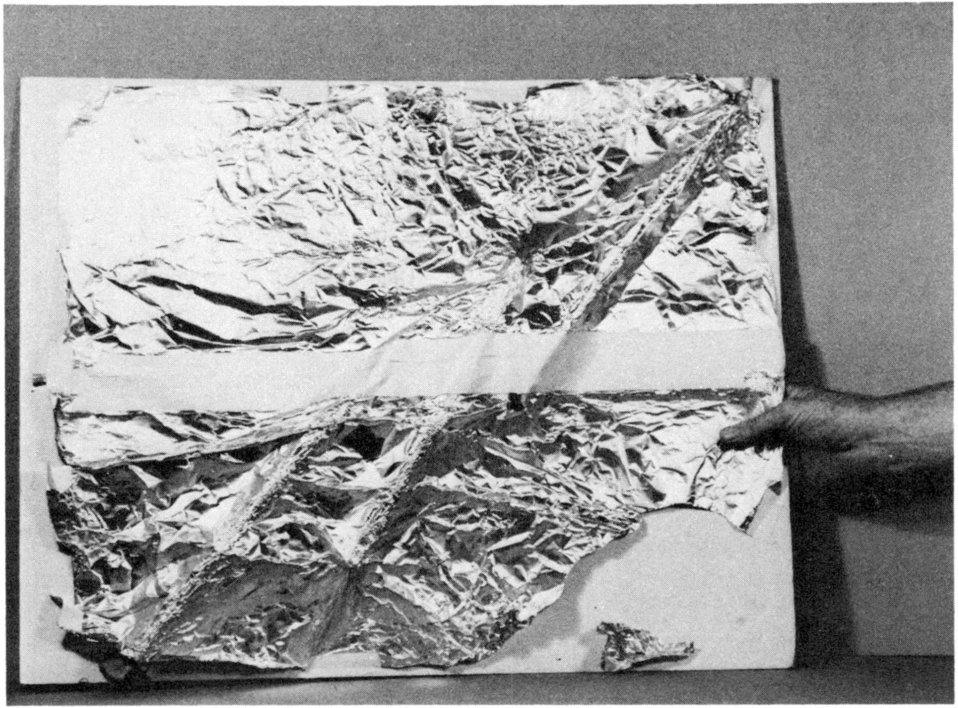

Fig. 4-25. Aluminum foil taped to a sheet of stiff cardboard makes a very effective light reflective surface.

To hold any type of lighting fixture, you will need some type of light stand. There are several different types for sale in photo shops. Stands range in price from a few dollars for a simple tripod affair, to great wheeled jobbies that cost over $100 (without the light fixture!).

If you have clamp attachments for your lighting equipment which will enable you to clamp the light wherever you want it, you can make your own light stands for practically nothing but a few hours of your time and several pieces of lumber (Fig. 4-26). Even simpler lamp holders can be made by filling a 3-pound coffee can (or similar container) with cement, then placing a piece of 2 x 2 inch lumber, about 6 feet long, into the wet cement before it hardens. It is fairly important that the light pole be vertical after the cement hardens. You might want to check the alignment of the pole with a carpenters level. Light stands such as either of those described above are simple to construct and have many uses around the light studio (Fig. 4-27).

Depending on the subject being photographed, you might find it handy to have several tables around the studio. One of the easiest ways of creating a table when you need it is to have several carpenter saw horses around. A few sheets of three-fourth inch thick plywood, in varying sizes, makes very suitable and quick table tops for photographing small objects. In addition, these

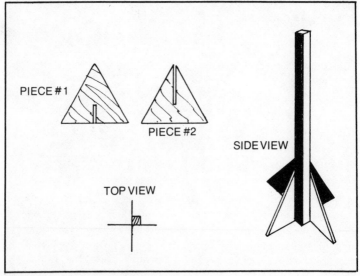

Fig. 4-26. Plans for plywood light stands.

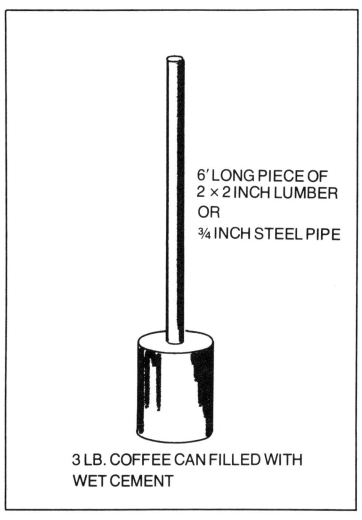

6' LONG PIECE OF
2 × 2 INCH LUMBER
OR
¾ INCH STEEL PIPE

3 LB. COFFEE CAN FILLED WITH
WET CEMENT

Fig. 4-27. Plans for a simple studio light stand.

make-shift tables can be assembled or disassembled in a few moments. Often seamless paper—either white or a color—will come in quite handy for covering the top of this quick table.

Speaking of all of that equipment, this is a good place to point out that no light studio is really complete or efficient without a certain amount of storage space. If your studio is small, you will probably be forced to store equipment and props in another room. The ideal situation is a photo studio with several large closets or small rooms off at one end and a photo processing lab in another nearby room as well (Fig. 4-28).

Because studio photography utilizes artificial lighting equipment, there is always a need for electrical power. Depending on the size of your studio, as well as your equipment, you might require more than the usual number of electrical outlets. If your lighting equipment draws a lot of power, you should install several electrical circuits in the studio to reduce the possibility of overloading any one circuit.

Additionally, some photographic lighting requires 220-volt current and you will have to install special circuits for this equipment. When you are first starting out—and often after you are established—a lot of your electrical current can come from long extension cords. Part of the attraction of extension cords is that they are quite portable and they can be moved whenever necessary.

Where you locate your photographic light studio will be determined, at least in part, by your avaliable space at the time. Obviously, if you make your living by shooting studio photographs you will require quite a bit more space than the amateur who occasionally takes photos of the family. But even the amateur can benefit considerably by having a home light studio.

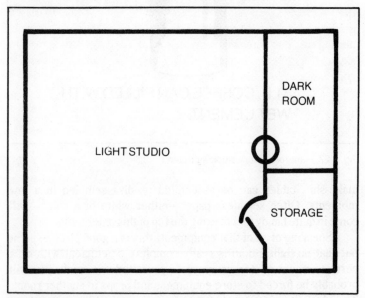

Fig. 4-28. Floor plan for studio.

Some of the basic requirements of a good photographic light studio—in addition to storage space and electrical service which is adequate—include ceilings that are higher than conventional. This will mean ceilings that are over 8 feet high. The reason for high ceilings is that you will have more freedom to place lights above, behind, or to one side of the subject without the lights themselves being too close. High ceilings also offer a greater feeling of freedom than lower ceilings and this tends to add a little to the creative processes of the photographer.

The room size of your studio really depends on the general type of shooting you plan on doing. If you are shooting small subjects you will obviously require less space than if you were photographing automobiles. A good photographic light studio should, generally, not be less than 15 x 15 feet. Of course, you can get by with less space, but more space would be even better. Artificial lighting tends to get hot to work around and the more space you have around the lights the cooler the overall room temperature will be.

One last point about a larger studio is that with a greater amount of space you are left free to set up and work on several projects simultaneously. In a small studio, you are more or less limited to one project at a time.

The home photographic light studio—whether in the corner of the basement or an entire floor of your home—offers the photographer a place to experiment with lighting. In the studio, it is not necessary to wait until the sun moves into a better location in the sky or for the clouds to move. The existing light is under the complete control of the photographer.

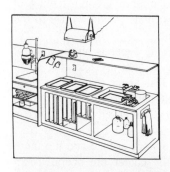

Chapter 5
Craft Workshops

Americans have more leisure time than ever before. Modern appliances make many household chores quite simple to accomplish. American industry and business has also experienced more advanced production methods and information storage systems. Consider for a moment the capabilities of electric typewriters and computers over manual typewriters and filing systems. As a result of all of our modern technology, we are all able to accomplish various tasks with greater speed and this leaves us with more leisure time. To help fill in spare hours, many people have turned to some type of craft orientated activity.

Home crafts can be defined as some type of hand operation that turns raw materials into a predefined style, shape or design. Some crafts such as fly tying originated around 600 B. C. Other crafts are quite modern and use materials such as plastics. Nevertheless, all crafts have one thing in common. Working at a craft can be a very rewarding form of self-expression. These is a craft for just about everyone.

At the present time, there are easily hunderds of different crafts pursued by thousands upon thousands of people across the United States. Stores specializing in materials have sprung up in every major city and many small cities and towns as well. American Handicrafts and Tandy Leather are just two of the largest types of suppliers of raw materials.

I will not argue whether or not turning clothespins into little toy soldiers, making beer can hats or making bead dolls can really be considered a craft on a par with making a stained glass window or weaving a tapestry. A craft is a rather personal thing that gives pleasure to the person making the item. In the majority of cases, homemade crafts are used by the maker or given as gifts to friends rather than sold on the open market.

In the past decade or so, many craftspeople have found that they can also sell the items that they make. Every shopping mall in the country has at least one craft show a year where local craftspersons offer their handmade items for sale. Some people have found that they can supplement their normal income by selling crafts. Still others make a reasonable living at this growing cottage industry.

In this chapter, I will discuss six rather different types of crafts. Each differs from the others in materials used, time necessary to accomplish the craft and ultimate use of the item. All are similar in that they can be done in the home and do not require any real specialized skills. The six workshops covered are macrame, fly tying, weaving, ceramics, stained glass and leather working. While it is not necessary to have a special place to do any one of the particular crafts, each can be done at the kitchen table, a craft workshop will enable you to pursue your chosen activity anytime the mood strikes you. Additionally, the hobby will be much easier to work at once you have a place to store materials, tools and works in progress.

PLANNING YOUR HOME CRAFT WORKSHOP

Part of the key to a successful home craft workshop is planning for your immediate and future needs. If you are a beginner, most experts agree that it is best to start off small. Don't overwhelm yourself with large outlays for materials and equipment. Grow with the hobby and acquire materials as you require them. Do not, for example, go out and buy 10 rolls of four-ply macrame cord in the beginning. You might find that you like working with two-ply cord much better.

Seek out as much information as you can about your craft before you actually set up your workshop. You might start out by reading some basic books on the subject. Here you should find solid information about material and equipment needs. In time, you will be able to determine which pieces of equipment you need to make the craft more enjoyable and easier to accomplish.

Magazines are also very good sources of information for the beginner. Every craft and hobby has at least one magazine or periodical that will contain articles written by people doing the same craft as you. Often you will also find technical articles and equipment evaluations. These specialized magazines are also billboards for manufacturers of the supplies, materials and equipment that you will need.

Take courses at adult continuing education, the "Y" and local colleges or universities to expand your knowledge of the craft. Very often a store that sells crafts will offer special courses in your craft as well. This information can be very helpful to you because it is generally a distillation of the many ways that can be used to accomplish a specific task or operation. Additionally, you will get a chance to work with different materials, learn new techniques and, if applicable, learn how to use specialized machines and tools. All of this information will help you to know more about your particular craft and in the long run make your craft more rewarding.

It is possible to lump all crafts into two rather broad categories. These categories are portable crafts and permanent crafts. A little information about these two groups of crafts will help in the planning stages to indicate whether or not a special place is really required for the work you will be doing.

Portable crafts include any type of hobby work that can be done just about anywhere. To be sure, every craft has certain operations that can be done anywhere—such as planning patterns for weaving—but this group mainly concerns itself with those crafts that can just as easily be accomplished at the kitchen table as in a special studio. Crocheting, bead work and macrame jewelry are three examples of portable crafts.

Portable crafts do not require a studio. They do, however, generally require a collection point or storage area for materials and supplies. Because portable crafts tend to utilize small materials and tools, you will not generally need a lot of storage space.

More often than not, a chest of drawers, a shelf or two in a closet or even a filing cabinet can handle your storage needs. About the only requirements are that the storage place for your materials be easily accessible and, ideally, close to where you normally do the work. For traveling, some type of carrying case will prove its worth rather quickly. Press an old and unused attache case into service as a portable storage system. With such a setup, you can take your materials and supplies wherever you go and, when time allows, do a little craft work.

Permanent crafts are those which require a specific place—a table or a room—in order to work at that particular craft. Often there will be a need for storing materials under special conditions such as fly tying materials and ceramic supplies. The craft itself will dictate the amount of space required. Some types of work can be done at a small table or bench while other crafts require lots of space. It is easy to see that permanent craft studios require a lot of consideration during the planning stages.

It is always best to draw a diagram of the studio during the planning stages. Determine your options and try several different arrangements of counters, workbenches and furnishings before you actually implement them. It is far easier to arrange your studio on paper than later after everything has been set into place.

If the work is commonly done while sitting in one place, a bench and comfortable chair or stool will be adequate for your needs. If you must work standing up, then a workbench of suitable height will be required. The height of the bench itself should be right for your height. Average heights for stand-up type work-benches are from 34 to 38 inches from the floor. If space permits, you should have a place for doing work while you are sitting or standing. This will make your craft studio all that more versatile.

Your studio should have storage space. This is also deter-mined in part by the type of craft that you are engaged in. If space is limited, try incorporating storage under workbenches or counters. Keep in mind that you might want to store other things besides raw materials such as finished projects and work in progress. One alternative for storing finished pieces, assuming that you are not really cramped for space, is to display the finished works in one area of the studio. One obvious way to store materials and supplies is on open shelves, on specially constructed racks, in closets, cabinets, or any combination of these. Some experts claim that you should plan for twice as much storage as you think you will need in your studio. When all things are considered, it is probably safe to say that you will never really have enough storage space. We all tend to fill empty spaces rather quickly (Fig. 5-1).

Lighting is important in any studio. Plan to have good overall lighting in addition to lights over specific work areas. Natural lighting from windows or skylights can be used on sunny days, but you should also have electrical lighting for night work or when the skies are overcast. Keep in mind that your eyes will become fatigued in poor light. You should also know that eyestrain will result if you only have light over your work area and darkness or semidarkness beyond.

Along with adequate lighting goes ample electrical outlets for electric tools. Some crafts require more than others, but the fact remains that you will probably have a need for some type of electrical service. If you are working with ceramics and have an electric kiln, know in advance that you will probably require a high voltage line (220 volts) to run the oven. Some kilns designed for the home ceramics hobbyist run on conventional (110 volts) current. If you are shopping for a kiln you should take this into consideration.

If water is present in the workshop—as it might very well be in a ceramics shop—you should make certain that the electrical outlets are suitably grounded to prevent electrical shock. A special grounding unit (Ground Fault Interrupter) installed in the circuit is your best insurance against potentially lethal electrical shock in the studio.

There are several other things that should be taken into consideration during the planning stages of your studio. Examples are plumbing, work surface material, floor covering, and specialized work areas. Because these considerations are really dependent on the type of craft you are engaged in, you will have to make the final determination as to need. In an effort to help you discover what your craft studio needs might be, what follows is a detailed discussion of six different types of craft studios. Your craft might be one of these or related in some ways. In any case, these six craft studios are offered as general guidelines to help you set up your own craft workshop in your home.

CERAMIC STUDIO

There are a number of desirable characteristics for any home ceramic workshop. In addition there are a few machines that not only make some ceramic operations possible, but make the work more enjoyable. Because working with clay cannot be considered a portable craft, one of the first requirements of a home ceramic workshop is a room where equipment can be set up and projects can be worked on as time permits.

Your ceramic studio will be most effective if it is large enough to work in comfortably. The floor should be easy to clean. Working with clay—both mallable and liquid forms—can be messy. Resilient floor coverings such as vinyl-asbestos tile or sheet vinyl are two good choices. These floor coverings resist stains and clay deposits can usually be wiped up with little effort. To remove globs of dried clay, you can use a scaper and a light touch. Keeping the floor waxed with any of the modern liquid waxes will also make cleaning the floor easier. If your workshop has a concrete floor such

Fig. 5-1. Many crafts lend themselves well to a display. These flies are tied to represent flies used around the year 1496.

as in a basement or garage, it should be covered with a glossy floor paint at the very least. A wooden floor is probably the poorest floor covering for a ceramic studio from the standpoint of keeping it clean.

Walls in the ceramic studio can be covered with almost any material that is easy to keep clean. Probably the most economical wallcovering is gypsum that is suitably taped and spackled and then painted with a semigloss (scrubbable type) paint. Certain areas will receive more abuse than others and you should take this into consideration during your planning stages. The area around the sink, for example, will be easier to keep clean if it is covered with a plastic laminate rather than simply painted. Give special attention to the wall or walls around your kiln. The wallcovering here must be fireproof. Thicker types such as five-eighths inch or double five-eighths inch thick gypsum panels should be used around the kiln area.

If you have the room, your ceramic studio will be much easier to work in if you have a large sink and running water (both hot and cold). If you do not have the space, you will have to rely on buckets of water. To avoid headaches with your plumbing system, you must have a special silt collecting trap in the sink drain. Even with such a device you should never dump clay residue into the sink. A pail of clear water near the sink will also help keep your drain lines clean and free running even if you have a special silt trap in the line. Stainless steel sinks are preferred over all other types in the ceramic studio. Enamel covered sinks tend to wear out quickly with the abrasive effects of bits of clay. A higher than normal faucet, sprayer, and foot operated or large lever type hot and cold water controls will make the sink easier to use as well.

You will need at least one large work table in your ceramic studio. The table should be sturdy enough so that it will not wobble or move as you work with the clay. The top of your work table should be covered with a material that is easy to clean. Plastic laminate—such as Formica—is one popular choice. However, many serious potters feel that this covering is too unnatural and it will scratch in time.

Wooden workbench tops are more pleasing to work on and can be made much stronger than plastic covered tables. You can make a wooden workbench top by laminating 2 x 4 inch lumber and sanding the top surface until it is relatively flat and smooth. Plans for such a top—often called a butcher block work surface—are shown in Fig. 5-2. If hardwoods such as maple or oak are used instead of common pine, the work surface will not only be more durable, but more pleasing to the eye as well. Additionally, if hardwoods are used, smaller size lumber such as 2 x 2 inch will be just as effective as 2 x 4 inch common pine.

Your home ceramic studio should also have a *wedging table*. If you don't know what a wedging table is, you're not really ready for a studio yet. There are two types of wedging tables: plaster and wood. You can make a wedging table quite simply from plywood as shown in Fig. 5-3. The two types are shown.

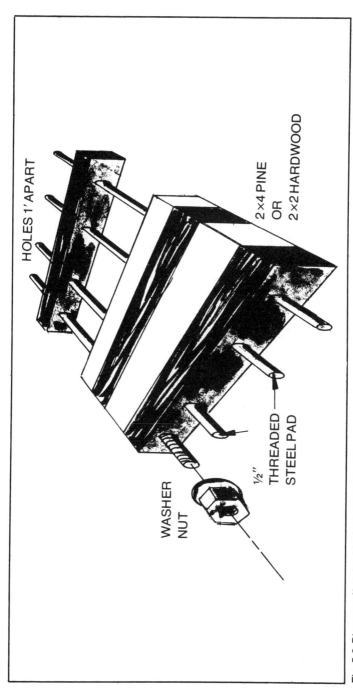

HOLES 1' APART

2×4 PINE
OR
2×2 HARDWOOD

THREADED STEEL PAD

½"

WASHER
NUT

Fig. 5-2. Diagram of butcher block type workbench top.

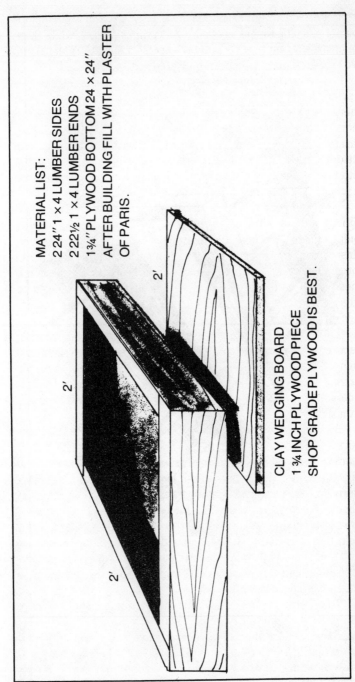

MATERIAL LIST:
2 24" 1 × 4 LUMBER SIDES
2 22½ 1 × 4 LUMBER ENDS
1¾" PLYWOOD BOTTOM 24 × 24"
AFTER BUILDING FILL WITH PLASTER
OF PARIS.

2'

2'

2'

2'

CLAY WEDGING BOARD
1 ¾ INCH PLYWOOD PIECE
SHOP GRADE PLYWOOD IS BEST.

Fig. 5-3. Plans for clay wedging box and board.

A potter's wheel is another necessary piece of equipment if you are planning to make pots in your ceramic studio. While there are many different types of potters wheels for sale, they all fall into two broad categories—electric powered and foot powered.

The electrical powered models are much preferred because they are faster and much easier to use than foot powered units. There are several models available that are designed for the small home studio and these tend to be lower priced than professional, classroom models. Also available are plans for building your own potters wheel. Check the current issues of magazines aimed at pottery craft for up to date information. A listing of magazines can be found in the appendix of this book.

No home ceramics studio can really be considered complete without a kiln. This is easily the most expensive piece of equipment that the home potter requires. As you might expect, kilns for firing pottery and ceramics come in many sizes and prices. For the hobbyist, a small electric kiln is probably the best bet. These small units—in sizes up to 11 x 11 x 11 inches—can be plugged into any electrical outlet and therefore do not require special wiring (as the larger kilns do).

Larger kilns, for the more serious potter, are fired by either electricity (most commonly 220 volts), natural gas or bottled gas. Each of these fuels will impart special characteristics to the ceramic piece being fired. Therefore, you must have a clear understanding of the results you are trying to achieve before you buy a kiln.

An alternative to the ready made kiln is one that you make yourself. Kiln building is not the type of thing for the casual potter. There is much to know about the theories of heat and its effects on clay. If you are interested in building your own kiln, seek out information from local or national pottery organizations and supply houses. There are also several good publications about building home kilns and a listing of these can be found in the appendix of this book. It is important to keep in mind that kiln building is an art in itself and should not really be attempted until you have investigated all aspects and made all information—both current and time proven—available to you.

Your home ceramic studio must have some special storage system for the different types of clays that you will be using. It is important to store different types of clays separately in a cool location and in a sealed container. Probably your best bet is a metal or plastic garbage container with a tight fitting lid or cover. If your studio gets hot—as it might when the kiln is running—you should give serious consideration to storing your clays in another room. Powdered and dry clay does not require the cool dark conditions that mixed clays do, but they still must be stored carefully. Develop some type of labeling system so that you know exactly what type of clays you have on hand and when they were purchased and mixed. Because clay is the basis for all pottery and ceramic work, give it the attention that it deserves.

As you work at the craft of pottery, you will undoubtedly accumulate a lot of tools, equipment and materials—not to mention finished pieces. By planning for this, before you actually set up the workshop, you will save yourself untold headaches as you develop your skills and work in the studio. As I mentioned earlier, you will almost never have enough storage space. But at the very least, you should try to keep your studio organized and orderly so that you will be able to work with a certain amount of freedom.

STAINED GLASS WORKSHOP

Stained glass—with its roots in Medieval times—gained popularity as a home craft about two decades ago (Fig. 5-4). Part of the attraction, I am sure, is that almost anyone can create light catchers, or window hangers, and even entire windows with only a few simple hand tools and a small investment in materials. There is a vast difference between a 6-inch square composed of matched pieces of stained glass and a stained glass window in a house of worship, but the mechanics are basically the same.

To make stained glass craftmanship easier to accomplish, as well as more rewarding, there are several specialized work areas that are commonly used by those craftspeople who take their work seriously. These include a workbench, cutting table and a light box. There are also a few specialized tools that help the hobbyist in cutting and joining the pieces of glass into design patterns. A discussion of these work areas will help you to set up your own stained glass studio and generally make the work that much easier to accomplish.

A special workbench is needed for stained glass work. The top should be flat, level and preferably made from wood. A section of the workbench top should be covered with a sheet of asbestos board that is about 2 x 3 feet and up to one-quarter inch thick. This section of the workbench is where you will solder the joints in the stained glass project. If you work on larger pieces, you should consider covering the entire workbench top with asbestos board.

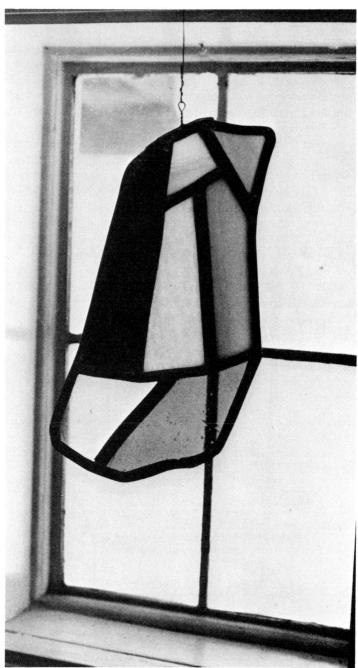

Fig. 5-4. A hanging stained glass window.

193

The height of the worktable should be comfortable to stand at, if you work in this manner, or at a suitable sitting height.

You will also need a special surface for cutting glass. This can be either at one end of your workbench or a separate table. The important thing to know is that the surface of the cutting table should be covered with a material that will prevent the glass from slipping while being cut and slightly cushion the glass as well.

Probably the best material for a cutting table surface is carpeting. Many craftpeople like indoor/outdoor carpeting with a short nap. You can buy a remnant at any carpeting store. Get one larger than the table top surface. Then simply cover the surface of the table by tacking the edges to the underside of the work surface. The cutting table should be sturdy enough to permit you to exert a bit of force during the actual glass cutting operation. The height of a cutting table should be sufficient enough to permit you to stand while you do the cutting (Fig. 5-5).

A light box is another necessity for the serious stained glass worker. The purpose of this unit is for viewing projects as they are assembled. A light box can utilize either natural or artificial light. Purists claim that stained glass should only be viewed in natural light, but this practice has a few limitations such as ruling out night work. A very suitable light box can be made from common lumber and illuminated with a small fluorescent light fixture. With such a unit, you will be able to view stained glass projects anytime of the day or night. Plans for an artificial light box are shown in Fig. 5-6.

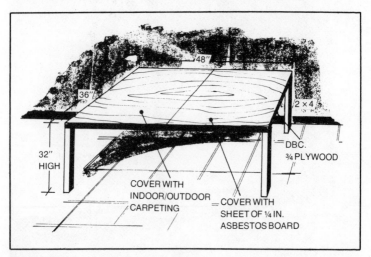

Fig. 5-5. Plans for a stained glass worktable.

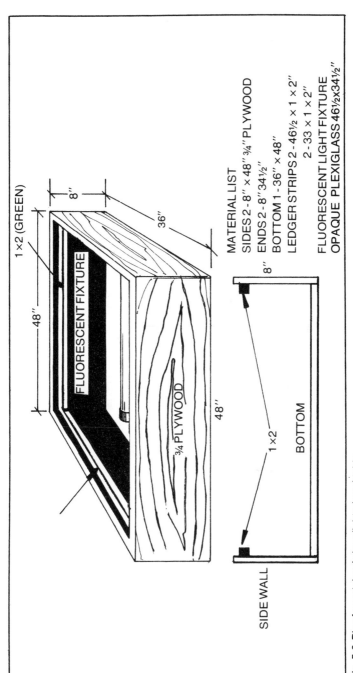

MATERIAL LIST
SIDES 2 - 8″ × 48″ ¾″ PLYWOOD
ENDS 2 - 8″ 34½″
BOTTOM 1 - 36″ × 48″
LEDGER STRIPS 2 - 46½ × 1 × 2″
2 - 33 × 1 × 2″

FLUORESCENT LIGHT FIXTURE
OPAQUE PLEXIGLASS 46½ x 34½″

1 × 2 (GREEN)

FLUORESCENT FIXTURE

¾ PLYWOOD

8″

36″

48″

48″

8″

1 × 2

BOTTOM

SIDE WALL

Fig. 5-6. Plan for a stained glass lighted worktable.

In addition to using your special light box for viewing stained glass projects, you can also use it for drawing designs of future projects. Because the surface is illuminated, you can easily draw designs on paper and view them much as if they were the actual stained glass pieces. You will find several uses for the light box in your stained glass studio.

There are really only a few simple tools that are necessary for most types of stained glass work. These include nipping pliers—most commonly with carbide tips—carborundum stone for smoothing the edges of cut glass and a quality soldering iron. Because the soldering iron is one of the most important tools used for stained glass work, you should not skimp on quality here. Buy one that is specifically designed for making the soldered joints between the pieces of glass and you will find the work much easier to accomplish.

One other tool that you might consider buying after you have mastered some of the basics of stained glass is a good bench grinder. With such a machine, you will be able to smooth the often raggedy edges of cut glass much quicker than if the same work was done by hand. A grinding wheel—fitted with a special Carborundum wheel—will practically pay for itself on the first large project you attempt. Remember that every edge on every piece of glass must be smooth for a snug fitting joint. A bench grinder will help you to do this type of work in a fraction of the time that it would take you to smooth the edges with a hand stone (Fig. 5-7).

The main materials you need for stained glass work are solder, lead channel or copper foil, flux and, of course, the glass itself. Because there are a number of different types of solders—combinations of tin and lead—fluxes, you should use only those materials that are compatible. If you buy your materials in a shop that specializes in stained glass supplies, there is very little chance that you can go wrong.

The glass used for stained glass work is available in a wide range of colors, thicknesses and different types. Just about every color in the spectrum, in types such as cathedral, opalescent, antique, handblown and even used glass, can usually be found in a store that specializes in this type of craft. Thicknesses range from about one-eighth of an inch to about one-fourth inch. You will generally find that you can get lower prices on your glass if you buy in quantity rather than by the piece. This makes a lot of sense. If you have an assortment of different types and colors of glass in your studio, you will find projects easier to get into and finish.

Fig. 5-7. A small bench grinder (courtesy of Black & Decker).

Your assortment of glass should be stored carefully. Large sheets are best stored in specially constructed vertical storage racks much the same as you would store LP record albums on. Small pieces of glass can best be stored in suitable size boxes and segregated according to thickness, color and basic type.

Stained glass work can be a rewarding and enjoyable pastime. For many people, it has also become a way to make a modest living as well. A stained glass studio in your home requires only a small investment for equipment and supplies. Having such a space will enable you to work with efficiency and develop those skills necessary to turn out long lived and beautiful stained glass pieces.

MACRAME WORKSHOP

The craft of macrame is more in the category of a portable hobby than one which must be done at any one particular place or location. To be sure, the larger projects such as plant hangers and wall hangings do require a certain amount of space to accomplish, but even these projects can be done wherever space permits. The smaller macrame projects such as jewelry and small wall decorations are most easily worked on while sitting and using a special board on which the work is pinned or anchored. An example of such a macrame work board is given in Fig. 5-8.

For larger projects such as plant hangers, your studio, if it can be called such, will consist of a ceiling hook from which the project hangs while the cords are being tied. It is generally agreed among serious macrame craftspeople that your ceiling hook should be of the type that can be adjusted in some manner. With such a hook, you will be able to work at one height—usually while standing— and raise the work up as it is completed.

One simple way to make a ceiling hook adjustable for height is to start by securely fastening a standard ceiling hook in the ceiling of your studio. If possible, make certain that the hook screws into a ceiling joist. Joists are usually spaced 16 inches apart. If this is not possible, use a toggle bolt type screw for the hook. Once the hook is securely in position, simply run a length of heavy cord through the eye of the hook and tie off one end somewhere in the room—the back of a chair for example. Tie the other end to the top of the plant hanger. As the plant hanger is tied, simply untie the other end, pull down and raise the plant hanger a bit higher and then resecure the cord.

In your macrame workshop, you might also want to attach several hooks around the perimeter of the room. These ceiling

Fig. 5-8. Macrame workboard for small projects.

hooks can be used for displaying finished plant hangers and wall hangings.

Good general lighting is required for working on macrame projects. In addition you might also want to have direct lighting over the area where you work.

About the only other requirement for your home macrame workshop is storage space for raw materials. Because many of the cords used for macrame are colorful, you might want to store the spools of cord on open shelves in the shop. Beads, which are often added to the straps of plant hangers and wall hangings, look attractive in clear glass jars and when similarly arranged on open shelves (Fig. 5-9).

WEAVING WORKSHOP

Weaving on a loom obviously falls into the permanent studio category. A loom can be a large machine that you would not want to throw in the back of the car to go over to a friend's house to use. In this day and age, it is not uncommon at all to find a full size loom set up in the living room and used by several members of the family. Weaving is an age old tradition and quite a rewarding craft. While it is not necessary to have a separate room for your loom, you will eventually want such a place when you become serious about the craft of weaving (Fig. 5-10).

Because your loom is the center of a weaving workshop, wherever the loom is located is where your workshop will be. There are two general types of looms currently available for the home weaver: table looms and floor models.

Table looms tend to be small and lower priced than floor type looms. While there are inherent limitations to a table loom, they are handy for working up new designs and for small projects. In addition, some table looms are actually small enough to be carried and can therefore be taken to classes given on the craft of weaving. A table loom is a good machine to learn the basics of weaving on and when not in use it can be stored in a closet (Fig. 5-11).

Floor model looms have been used by serious weavers for centuries. Although there are differences in capabilities, all floor model looms have one thing in common; they all take up some space. There are several types of floor model looms such as counterbalanced, counter-march and jack looms. Each has certain capabilities that the others do not. The width of the loom is important in that a wide loom will enable you to weave both wide and narrow pieces, but a narrow loom is rather limited. Experi-

Fig. 5-9. Macrame wall hanging.

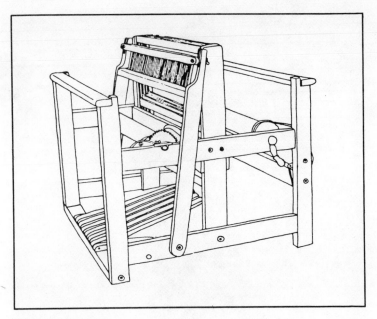

Fig. 5-10. A jack loom.

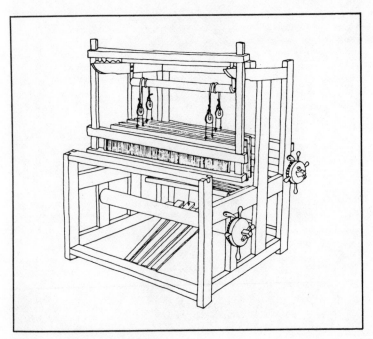

Fig. 5-11. A counterbalance loom.

202

enced weavers seem to agree that if you are serious about weaving you should sink as much money as you can into the widest loom possible so you can grow into larger projects as you develop the basic weaving skills (Fig. 5-12).

There are several sources of looms and materials and a listing of some of these can be found in the appendix. You should shop wisely for a loom and not make a purchase until you are certain the loom you are considering is at least adequate for your needs.

The materials used in weaving—largely cords and threads—are best stored on open shelves because they tend to add a certain charm to your weaving workshop. Many weavers do not have a separate place for their loom and supplies, but instead set up the equipment in one section of the living room. Many feel that the floor model loom is an attractive addition to the family room. This is, at least in part, the reasoning behind installing the loom in a conspicuous place in the home.

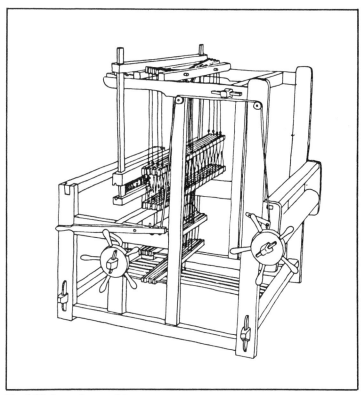

Fig. 5-12. A counter march loom.

FLY TYING WORKSHOP

The craft of tying artificial fishing flies is portable in that the fly tier requires only a handful of materials, a special vise and a few simple hand tools. There are several different types of fly tying vises. Some must be attached to a table top. Others have their own base which enables the user to set the vise almost anywhere. Also available is a tiny vise that is held in one hand while the other hand performs the necessary operations in making a fly. While fly tying can be accomplished almost anywhere, craftsmen who are serious about the work will have a fly tying bench where all their fly tying will be done (Fig. 5-13).

A fly tying bench makes a lot of sense on several levels. To begin with, your fly tying bench should be at a height that is comfortable to work at while sitting. From this position you should have free access to all of the materials that you require for the particular flies that you are tying. It is important to keep in mind that working at the craft of fly tying requires hours of sitting in front of the vise. To make this learning experience easier, as well as more enjoyable, you must work at a comfortable sitting height.

Adequate lighting should be available while you are tying flies. Many professionals have a special desk type lamp on the fly tying bench which provides specialized light. Because many types of flies are tiny—one centimeter—eye strain will be one of the results of inadequate lighting. Poor quality or sloppily tied flies are usually another result as well.

The typical fly tying bench should be large enough to hold all of the materials that you are using for the particular flies being tied. A bench measuring approximately 3 x 5 feet is just about right for most fly tiers. In addition, storage space for other fly tying materials—such as hooks, feathers, furs, thread, etc.—should also be close at hand.

Many professional fly tiers store materials in small cabinets either on top of the fly tying bench or next to it. One good storage system for the commonly small fly tying materials is a compartmentalized cabinet of the type commonly used for storing nuts, bolts and screws. With such a cabinet on the fly tying bench, the tier has access to hundreds of different materials. In addition, a small parts cabinet will help the fly tier to keep the materials organized and generally make the fly tying bench that much more efficient to work at.

The serious fly tier will accumulate some fly tying materials that are prone to damage by insects. Moths, for example, love

Fig. 5-13. A well organized fly tying bench with all necessary materials and tools close at hand.

feathers and furs and will seek them out unless they are stored carefully. The best way to store materials of this type is in a sealed container. Plastic containers with sealable covers—Tupperware is one brand—make excellent storage boxes and they are small enough to stack on one end of the fly tying bench without getting in the way of normal tying operations (Fig. 5-14).

In addition to the fly tying bench where the serious craftsperson can efficiently work, a traveling fly tying ktt is also quite useful. The kit should contain all of the materials necessary to construct a rather broad selection of flies. One popular way of carrying fly tying materials and equipment is a plastic sewing case. These boxes sell for a few dollars and have the ability of holding and protecting probably enough materials for making any imaginable fly. If you are just starting out, consider keeping all of your materials in a case such as this. Then you can easily carry your fly tying workshop wherever you go (Fig. 5-15).

The craft of fly tying is an enjoyable pastime that is older than most people realize. Knowledgeable estimates put the first artificial fly in the water around the year 1000 B. C. It is a craft that can be learned by anyone willing to invest the time necessary to learn the simple operations required. There are several good books on the subject. A listing of some of these can be found in the appendix.

LEATHER WORKSHOP

Leather working can be done almost anywhere there is a desk or tabletop. The materials required are easily obtainable and the tools are simple and few. A more serious leather worker, who creates wallets, pocketbooks, backpacks and other leather items, needs a more complete workshop. The leather working studio need not be large if it is well organized. Ideally, it should be away from normal household traffic so that the craftsperson can work undisturbed. If you are planning to set up a leather working studio, consider the following.

Light is especially important when you are working with leather. The grain of the leather must be carefully considered before it is cut and while you are working as well. In order for the craftsperson to see the grain, specialized lighting must be over the work area. In addition, direct lighting will also be necessary for decorating and finishing leather projects.

The real center of any leather working studio is the workbench. Because many operations can be done either while you are

Fig. 5-14. Plastic containers with tight fitting lids are ideal for storing fly tying materials.

standing or sitting, the workbench should be at a height that is comfortable to work at while you are standing. For sitting, a high stool is a good choice for the craftsperson. The drawers in the workbench are good places to store tools.

The workbench should be constructed of wood with a thick top. The butcher block workbench top described earlier in this chapter is especially good for leather working projects. If stamping designs is a common practice, a hardwood board—2 x 8 inches and about 2 to 3 feet long—should be available.

There are not many tools that are necessary for working with leather. Examples are cutters, punches, stamping dies, heavy shears, etc. All of these can be hung on the wall behind the workbench where they will always be within easy reach without being in the way. Metal stamping dies are most commonly stored in a special rack very much the same as the type of rack used to store twist drill bits.

Another requirement of your leather working shop is a safe place to store your raw materials. All leather should be protected from moisture because it has a tendency to mildew in the presence of dampness. Adequate fresh air circulation is the key here unless you live in one of the more arid parts of the country.

One last consideration for your leather workshop is a special place to finish leather projects. Because a number of finishing operations involve applying dyes to the leather, this work should be done in an area where accidental spills and splashes will not damage raw materials or other projects. You should also know that some types of dyes require good air circulation during use and drying. If your shop is small, you could simply cover your workbench with newspaper and do the finishing here. As you become more serious about your work, you will want a special area for finishing and drying leather projects.

GENERAL PURPOSE CRAFT OR HOBBY ROOM

If several members of your family have their own crafts or hobbies, it might be worthwhile to create a general purpose craft room in your home. This would be a place where any member of the family could work on a personal project. Ideally, the room should be large enough to permit more than one person to work at any given time. To make the craft room useful to everyone, consider the following points.

A sturdy table and several chairs should be either in the center of the room or against one wall in the craft room. The table should

Fig. 5-15. A sewing case will hold a vast assortment of fly tying materials.

be at a height that is comfortable to work at while you are sitting and large enough to accommodate at least two people.

A stand-up type workbench should also be installed along one wall in the room. It should be at a height that is useful to everyone using the room and it should be strudy and long enough so that more than one project can be worked on at any one time.

Storage space is essential for the craft room or the result will be chaotic clutter. Use as much space around the perimeter of the room for storage as possible. Potential storage areas are under the workbench, open shelving and cabinets.

Consider installing a sink with hot and cold running water. This will aid in keeping the rest of the house clean. Workers and projects can be cleaned here. And it will make some projects easier to accomplish.

Lighting should provide sufficient illumination for you to work anywhere in the room. A large fluorescent light fixture in the center of the room should provide enough light. If the room is very large—more than 10 x 12 feet—install more than one light fixture for good general lighting. If necessary, small lamps such as desk top high intensity types can be used for special projects where more than general lighting is needed.

The floor in the craftsroom should be easy to clean and it should be able to withstand accidental spills. Asbestos or vinyl floor tiles are probably the best choices because these materials are resistant to damage from spills. Keep the floor waxed for additional protection and have available a sponge mop for wiping up spills as they happen.

The walls in the craftsroom—where they are not covered with shelving—should be covered with a material that both adds charm and resists splashes and grime caused by dirty hands. Washable wallpaper or semigloss paint are two good choices.

One section of the craftsroom should be reserved for displaying finished projects. Open shelving is best for this and might serve as inspiration for younger family members to work at their particular craft or hobby.

If some members of the family require special tools, machines or working surfaces, seperate areas of the craftsroom should be available so that all types of work can be done in the room. If small children are visitors or members of the family, store chemicals, paints and tools in locked cabinets. Another possibility is to lock the craftsroom and not allow children to work without responsible supervision.

A general purpose craftsroom can provide years of enjoyment for any and all members of the family. The fact that you have such a place in your home will often be more than enough encouragement for family members to express themselves by working at a craft or hobby. By providing a special place for working on projects, you will also save some wear and tear on the other rooms in your home. Building or creating the room itself should be a family project with each member offering suggestions and helping with the construction.

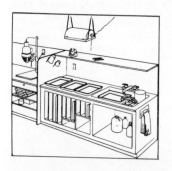

Chapter 6
Laundry &
Sewing Centers

In a typical American household, approximately two tons of dirty clothes will be washed every year and that does not include those clothing items that require dry cleaning. In the first half of this chapter, I will discuss some of the ways to make washing and drying clothing easier to accomplish. In the course of a year, you will probably be able to save about a week of time that would have been spent doing laundry. In addition, you can also save a few dollars by attacking your mountain of dirty clothes with a conscientious battle plan. The second half of this chapter is devoted to some suggestions for setting up a special place in your home for clothing repairs and making clothing—a home sewing center.

We have come a long way since grandmother's scrub board and wash tub. Some of the features that can be found on many automatic washers include the capability of washing small loads (in addition to full loads), variable agitation speeds (heavy duty for soiled work clothes to delicate for knits and delicate fabrics) and selective controls for water temperature. Modern laundry detergents have the capability of cleaning in cold water. This saves the expense of heating water for washing laundry. Some washing machines have compartments for loading detergent, bleach and fabric softener. These are added when the wash is loaded and dispensed at the correct time during the various cycles. There is no need to come back to add detergent, bleach or fabric softener. See Fig. 6-1.

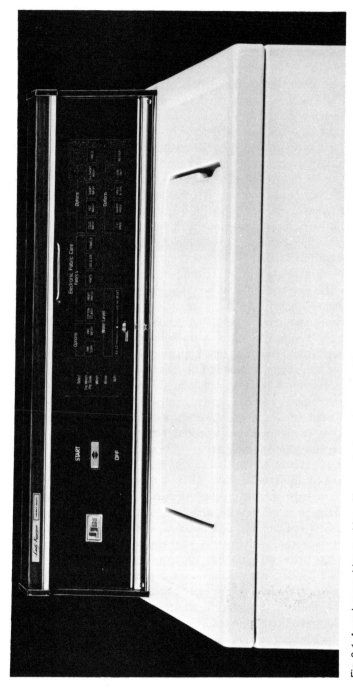

Fig. 6-1. A modern washing machine with many features (courtesy of Sears Roebuck & Co.).

213

In addition to these features, the modern washing machine comes in a variety of sizes. There are models that fit in perfectly with standard kitchen cabinets. They have decorator colors to match or contrast with kitchen appliances. There are also compact washer/dryer combinations that have been specifically designed to save space. Several makers offer combinations that measure about 24 inches wide and they are stored one on top of the other. Most have the washer below and dryer above.

In a setup such as this, the washer is rolled out for use while the dryer is supported on a rack or hung on the wall. One added feature for most combinations of this type is that no plumbing or special wiring is required. The washer is simply wheeled to the kitchen sink and hooked up to the faucet for use (Fig. 6-2).

Most automatic washing machines are top loaders, although front loading washers are available. Agitation is most commonly a back and forth action. The few models that are front loaders have a drum which rotates to create a tumbling washing action.

The modern, full-size washing machine will require special plumbing connections. These are hot and cold faucet hook-ups and a drain. In addition, a suitably grounded electrical outlet must be near the washer. Compact or so-called portable washers do not generally require any special plumbing or electrical connections. These are simply wheeled to the nearest sink and hooked up for use. After the wash has been done, this machine is wheeled back into storage.

Because the modern automatic washing machine is the virtual heart of the home laundry center, you must shop wisely. First determine your washing needs—a few loads a week for a small family or at least two loads a day for large families—and then shop around for the type of washer that will take care of your laundry requirements with the greatest efficiency. In some cases, you will not require more than a portable washer/dryer combination. If space is a problem, this type of setup might be your only choice. In other instances, such as when your family is growing in size, you might be better off in the long run to purchase a full size automatic washer. Consider the features and compare models. In the end, choose the washer or dryer combination that best fills your needs.

A modern temperature controlled tumble dryer is not a frivolous addition to the family laundry center. With a dryer, you can dry a load of wash much quicker than if the same load was hung outside to dry. A clothes dryer is a real time saver and does not limit you to doing laundry in the daylight hours. This is a real plus

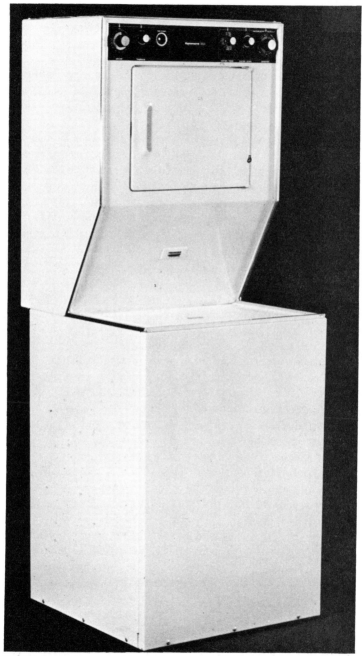

Fig. 6-2. A compact washer/dryer combination (courtesy Sears Roebuck Co.).

for working families or those families with several loads of wash to do a day. In addition, with so much of our clothing being permanent press, a clothes dryer is not a luxury. It is a necessity. When permanent press clothing is tumbled dried, usually at a cooler setting, it can be taken out of the dryer and put on hangers. It will be ready to wear with no ironing necessary. In the final analysis, a modern clothes dryer can save you a considerable amount of time and energy (Fig. 6-3).

While all clothes dryers have an electric motor to turn the drum, they can be heated by either electric or gas. A gas powered clothes dryer will usually cost more to buy, but it will be cheaper to run than the same size unit powered by electricity. Local utility rates come in to the picture here because some parts of the country have lower rates for natural gas than for electricity. With the present energy crisis in full swing, it is really impossible to predict what electricity or natural gas will cost in the future. A comparison of current utility rates is probably your best indication.

All dryers must have some type of venting system which carries the removed moisture away from the machine. The most common means for accomplishing this is with flexible exhaust air ducts which run to some point outside the home. There are a few models that do not require venting of moist air. These have special built-in condensers that do the job of removing the moisture.

It is foolish to under estimate the need for an exhaust system for your clothes dryer. A load of clothing will give off, on an average, about 8 to 10 pints of water. If this moist air is not vented to the outside of the home, the result will be high humidity and a steamy feeling in the room where the dryer is installed.

To compound the problem during the heating season, this excess humidity, if not suitably provided for, can cause blistering or peeling paint on exterior siding and other condensation related problems. If your clothes dryer requires an exhaust vent, you must install one.

Installing an exhaust vent for your clothes dryer is not difficult at all when you use modern materials. Special flexible duct work is available for just this purpose. The flexible duct material—standard variety is 4 inches in diameter—is run from the back of the dryer to and through an outside wall of the house. A special outside deflector fitting protects the duct work from the weather and pests. At the same time, it permits exhaust air an easy exit. Part of the beauty of flexible exhaust duct work is that it easily fits in floor, ceiling or wall cavities. Therefore, it is quite easy to work with.

Fig. 6-3. A clothes dryer (courtesy of Sears Roebuck & Co.).

When you are shopping for a clothes dryer, there are several things that you should take into consideration. The first is how the machine is powered. If it is electric, you must determine if it can be run on normal house current (100 volts) or if it requires a special (220 volts) line which will have to be installed for the unit. If the dryer is a gas powered model, it will require a gas connection as well as a conventional electrical outlet.

If a gas line is not present in the laundry center, you will have to have one installed. This will increase the price of the overall installation. Still another consideration for a gas powered clothing dryer is that most building codes require that any appliance powered by gas must have a venting stack to remove burned and unburned natural gas. Installing a venting stack, while not particularly difficult, will add to the cost of the dryer. The vent must run from the dryer straight up and through the roof.

If space is a problem, consider purchasing the stackable or portable washer/dryer combinations. Some manufacturers offer units that take up a small space. Typical dimensions are 24 to 27 inches wide, 25 to 27 inches deep and 60 inches high. Some other attractive points about the portable washer/dryer combinations are that they usually do not require special plumbing or electrical connections, and they often do not require special venting of exhausted moist air. While their general capacity will be less than a full size machine, they can easily handle lighter loads.

When shopping for a modern automatic washer and/or dryer, keep in mind that you can usually do better on the price if you buy both the washer and dryer. More often than not, both a washer and dryer can be had for a price that is considerably less than if both machines were purchased separately.

HOME LAUNDRY CENTER

Where you install your washer and dryer might not be totally under your control. This is especially true if you live in a home that is a bit on the small side. In the ideal situation, these machines should be placed in a room designated as the laundry room. Also in this room could be a sewing workshop for repairs and construction of clothing.

Unfortunately, most of us have rather limited space for washers and dryers. As a result, these machines are installed where they fit, rather than necessarily the best place. Some of the more useful and efficient installations are in the kitchen under existing counters. The front loading washers and dryers are generally ideal for this type of installation. Top loading washing machines obviously cannot be installed under kitchen counters. They must have nothing closer than about 18 to 24 inches from the top of the machine. Usually, installing a top loading washing machine at the end of a kitchen counter is the most workable arrangement. Because most clothes dryers are front loaders, they can be installed under counters (Fig. 6-4).

If both machines are installed next to one another, take the way that the dryer door opens into careful consideration. Some

Fig. 6-4. A washer/dryer combination (courtesy of Sears Roebuck & Co.).

dryers open down and form a shelf for loading and unloading. Other models have a door which swings from side to side. When you install side swinging dryers next to the washer, position the dryer so that the door swings towards the washer. This setup is more convenient and allows for quick transfer of wet clothing into the dryer. Some dryers have doors which are reversible so that the most convenient swing of the door can be made possible in a matter of minutes.

Storage space around the washing machine and dryer is not only a good idea, it is a necessity. When you consider some of the things that are necessary for cleaning clothes—such as detergent, bleach, fabric and water softeners, starches and stiffeners, stain removers and other laundry supplies—the need for adequate storage becomes apparent. A wide and sturdy shelf over the washer should be used for the more common supplies that are used on a regular basis. A cabinet off to one side is just the right place for storing extra supplies and infrequently used items.

A cabinet next to the washer is another useful addition to your home laundry center. A used or even new kitchen cabinet that is the same height as the washer is very handy. In addition, the top of the cabinet can be used as a work surface where operations such as spot removing and sorting can take place. From there it is a simple task to push the clothing into the top loading washer.

One other strong point in favor of a cabinet that can be kept closed or even locked is that dangerous laundry supplies such as bleach can be stored out of the reach of children. If small children frequent the area where the laundry is done, consider some type of special latch or lock that little hands cannot operate.

If you are creating a full-fledged laundry room, you will want a sink. Conventional, deep laundry sinks are reasonably priced at almost any home improvement center or plumbing supply house. In addition to helping with laundry related tasks such as presoaking, the laundry room sink is also a good place for cleaning paintbrushes and other commonly messy household tasks.

To make your home laundry center more efficient, you need some means of holding dirty clothes until they can be washed. Probably the most common way to do this is to place all dirty clothes in a special clothing hamper. A clothes hamper that is large enough for your family will not only help to keep all dirty clothes in one place, but it will actually encourage family members to pick up their clothing. The location of the clothing hamper is rather important. To be effective it must be in a place where clothing is normally discarded. The two obvious choices are the bathroom or bedroom.

One very good alternative to the conventional clothing hamper is a laundry chute. If you have the space to install a laundry chute, this could be a real solution to what to do with soiled clothing. One other requirement is that the laundry center must be located in the basement and the top of of the chute must be located on a floor above. Probably the best place for a laundry chute is in the bathroom. Another good location is in a hallway which services bedrooms and the bathroom.

The best laundry chutes are the simplest. All you really need is an opening that is large enough to permit passage of clothing. Some experts suggest a chute with dimensions of about 8 x 12 inches. The actual chute can be framed out during house construction or after the house is built along the lines of conventional forced air heating ductwork.

This material is commonly available from a plumbing and heating dealer or home improvement center. Some type of door is necessary at the top end of the chute and special swinging types are available. At the bottom end of the chute, a basket or a wheeled laundry cart will help to keep things organized in the laundry and aid in getting the dirty clothing to the washer.

The laundry center should have space for hanging clothing. This is especially important when a lot of the family clothing is permanent press. As clothing comes from the dryer it is placed on hangers. Portable hanging clothing racks are available or you can attach some type of hanging bracket in a convenient location. This small addition to the laundry room will make cleaning operations much easier to accomplish and the result will be less time spent doing laundry.

Another good addition to any laundry center is an area where clean clothing can be ironed. This addition, while not necessary, will make the laundry center that much more efficient. In all probability, however, you will not have the extra space to spare for an ironing center. The next best thing is to have some type of wall mounted holder for both the ironing board and iron. These wall hangers are quite handy and especially when space is limited. The real value is in providing a space for storing ironing gear, while at the same time making the gear easily accessible.

An alternative to a conventional ironing board is one that folds into the back of a specially constructed cabinet (Fig. 6-5). With such an arrangement, the entire cabinet is reserved for those items and supplies normally used in the ironing task. These items include starch and an atomizer for dampening clothing prior to ironing.

I think it is apparent that a laundry center in your home will take a lot of the drudgery out of this necessary task. When you think in terms of doing tons of wash every year, the reasons for having a space that is set up for efficiency makes an incredible amount of sense.

SEWING WORKSHOP

Earlier in this chapter I briefly mentioned the ideal clothing workshop which would contain an area for doing laundry and

Fig. 6-5. This small ironing board folds into the door of a closet. It is very handy and right there when you need it.

222

Fig. 6-6. There have been many developments in sewing machines since Singer introduced this model in 1851 (courtesy of Singer Mfg. Co.).

223

another area that would be used for repairs and construction of clothing. One alternative to the ever escalating prices for new clothing is to keep existing clothing in good condition by repairing it as soon as the need arises. Still another possibility is to make your own clothing at home (Fig. 6-6).

Most clothing repairs—if a garment can be repaired—are relatively simple. Probably the hardest part is digging out the needle and thread or pulling the sewing machine out of the closet and setting it up. You can make sewing projects—from mending a sock to making a dress—much easier to start if you have a sewing workshop.

The sewing area need not be more than a small table on top of which sits the sewing machine. Next to it would be the commonly used sewing materials such as thread, scissors, needles for both hand sewing and for your machine (Fig. 6-7).

On the other hand, if you sew quite a bit you will require a true sewing workshop. This will include a space for your machine, storage space for fabrics and other related sewing materials, a specially constructed worktable for cutting and laying out projects, an area for ironing and possibly a closet or suitable rack for hanging work in progress as well as finished projects. This could also be the room where you do the laundry. In short it would be a total clothing workshop.

Whether your aim is to build the ultimate sewing workshop or simply establish a special place to sew, the heart of your workshop will be your sewing machine. The sewing machines of today are in a word, amazing. Even low priced sewing machines have capabilities that were unheard of just a decade ago (Fig. 6-8).

Just about any modern machine is easy to use for normally difficult tasks such as threading and loading bobbins. Most new machines come with an instruction manual that will explain all of the features of the machine and probably tell you more than you want to know.

In addition, there is usually a control panel that is used for controlling the machine during different functions. Some of the more up-to-date capabilities include a wide variety of stitches such as regular, stretch, blind, basting, zigzag, mending and generally a broad assortment of decorative stitches. The choice of stitch as well as length is most commonly controlled by the simple twist of a dial or the push of a button.

Attachments increase the capabilities of most machines until they can really be considered professional in performance. Some of

Fig. 6-7. Your home sewing center need not be large if it is well organized (courtesy of Masonite Corporation).

the more common attachments include pleating, buttonholing, quilting and special zipper concealers.

Some sewing machines are called open arm models and they differ from conventional sewing machines in that they have the capability of sewing in small areas. Sewing cuffs, sleeves and pant legs are just three of the more common tasks that these machines can easily accomplish.

When you are shopping for a sewing machine, there are a few things that you should be aware of. The first is that it is not uncommon for one particular type of sewing machine head to be offered as a portable, in a cabinet and on a specially designed worktable. The portable is easy to move around and would be a good choice if you have a limited space problem. The cabinet models—many of which are practically sewing workshops in themselves—are pieces of furniture (often in different styles). This type would be a good choice if you plan to put your sewing machine in the living room.

The sewing machines that come on specially designed worktables are more or less professional models. The worktable itself is designed for function rather than for fashion. This last choice is probably the best for the serious seamstress. Because the selling price is a result of the cabinetry involved, the portable and worktable models will usually be less expensive than the cabinet sewing machines.

Before you buy a sewing machine, you should work with the machine for a few hours. There are quite a number of features that you might not really need and the only way to find out is to use the machine. Most sewing machine stores have some type of lending or renting policy so you can take the machine home and give it a real test.

You might also ask friends about their particular sewing machine preferences. Find out as much as you possibly can about all of the machines in your price range and base your final purchase decision on how well any one machine does a particular sewing task. You will want a machine that will take care of all of your present and future sewing needs. A sewing machine can be a big investment, but money well spent if the machine will help you mend and repair clothing for many years. Probably the best advice anyone can give you is to shop wisely.

If you decide on a portable sewing machine—a good choice if cost is a factor—you will need a suitable height table to set the machine on for sewing. Some of the requirements of a sewing

226

Fig. 6-8. The Singer Sewing Machine Company has always come up with advances just as they did in 1902 when this photograph was taken (courtesy of Singer Mfg. Co.).

machine table are that it must be sturdy, large enough to support the machine and materials being worked on and have a drawer or other arrangement for holding often used tools such as scissors.

The height of the table is an important consideration. Twenty-eight to 30 inches is about right for most people. If it is higher than this, you will find working at the machine very tiring—even over short periods of work. If the only table you have to sew on is high, a higher than normal chair might be the answer to the problem. Sewing, like typing, requires that the machine be at a comfortable position for best overall results.

As a side note, the same shops that sell sewing machines will usually also sell special sewing tables. This might be a good choice if you are in the market for the best table to sew on.

Worktable

The efficient sewing workshop will have, in addition to a quality machine, a special worktable on which patterns are laid out and fabrics are cut. This cutting table should be large enough to spread out material comfortably. A good size for a cutting table for the serious sewing workshop is 3½ to 4 feet wide and 5 to 6 feet long.

You can make a suitable table out of three-fourth inch thick plywood, but make certain that you pay particular attention to the edges all around the table. For best results, you should fill the edges of the plywood top with a suitable wood filler material. This small act will prevent the fabric from becoming snagged or torn by the tables edges.

If you do not have the space for a full-size cutting table, consider using a drop-leaf table with extra leaves installed. For large projects, it is a simple matter to open the table and add the extra leaves.

One very good alternative to the standard cutting table is a special cutting board that can be folded up and stored when not in use. Cutting boards have a lot of appeal for someone without much working space. They can be unfolded—most are made from thick cardboard—into a surface which is ideal for cutting. Most cutting boards have lines or other marks that are a real aid during the cutting process.

Along with the cutting table or cutting board, the sewing workshop requires cutting and measuring tools. An assortment of large and small scissors with both straight and bent blades should take care of most of your cutting needs. In addition, you might also want a pair of pinking shears and one of the new cordless electric scissors.

A seamstress needs measuring tools just as much as a carpenter does. Included in the workshop should be the following: a measuring tape (most commonly made from cloth and with numbers printed on both sides), a yardstick, a 6- to 12-inch ruler (handy for marking cuffs and hems) and a hem marker that can be used by itself.

If you are serious about making your own clothing, you will surely want to have a dress form—female and/or male models. With such a mannequin, you will be able to custom make clothing easily for yourself because you will have a life size form on which to measure and fit. All of the newer dress forms are fully adjustable so the mannequin should last a lifetime.

Another handy item around the sewing workshop is an ironing board and steam iron to go with it. When you are making clothing, a steam iron is often very handy for pressing a seam before stitching. You can either use a small ironing board—ideal for quick pressing sleeves or pant legs prior to stitching—or use a full-size ironing board and make this part of your sewing workshop the ironing center for your home. Refer to the first part of this chapter for some suggestions about storing ironing boards when they are not in use.

Storage Space

Your sewing workshop should have ample storage space. Some of the things that are commonly needed in the workshop include fabric (both new and uncut as well as scraps), thread, patterns, various tools, findings and other small items, and hanging projects (both work in progress as well as finished).

The key to an effective sewing workshop storage system is planning. A project will be less likely to get started and it will be a real headache to finish if materials are spread throughout the household. You should have a drawer or peg rack for storing thread. Take advantage of the fact that spools of thread are attractive when displayed with some thought to organization. A spool of red thread will be much easier to find if it is in a special thread holding rack than if it is in a drawer full of other spools of thread (Fig. 6-9).

Fabric for projects not yet started should be stored carefully in an area that is protected from damage by moisture, accidental spills and insects. A special cabinet or part of a closet should be used for storing such precious goods. Scraps, left over material or extra

Fig. 6-9. An effective home sewing workshop has areas for storage and for working on projects (courtesy of Masonite Corporation).

material is always of use so it should be stored with a little care as well. Consider using clear plastic boxes with tight fitting lids. Another good storage idea is to use clear plastic bags such as those used for freezing, with zip-lock type closures.

Findings and other small items can most easily be stored in small clear glass jars such as baby food jars. Jars of buttons and bangles set on an open shelf not only look good in the sewing shop, but you will be able to locate these items much easier when they are in plain sight. If you don't have the space, consider using plastic bags, ice cube trays or even empty pill containers.

Projects that are being worked on as well as those which have been completed should be hung up to be stored. After you have spent hours working on a piece of clothing, it seems like a real waste to simply drape the garment over the back of a chair. Make sure your sewing workshop has space for hanging projects to keep them unwrinkled and nice looking. A special closet can be used for hanging storage or you can use a free standing clothes rack. At the very least, you should have some type of wall-mounted hooks for hanging projects.

A sewing workshop in your home—even if it is just a table in one corner of the living room—is not just a quaint idea. It is a sensible way to cut down on the rising costs of new clothing. Basic sewing techniques are relatively simple to learn. With modern sewing machines it is easier than ever to master sewing.

If you have never learned to sew or if your skills are a bit rusty, consider taking a course to bring you up to date. Stores that sell sewing machines, fabric shops and continuing education programs are all good places to start the learning process. Once you have mastered some of the basic techniques, you can then start making and repairing clothing in your own home sewing workshop. Hours of rewarding projects as well as real savings on the clothing bill can all be yours for just a small investment in time and energy.

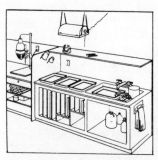

Chapter 7
Food Preservation
and Storage Workshop

A survey conducted by the Department of Agriculture several years ago determined that approximately one family in four raised and preserved part of their total annual food supply. You might ask why, in this age of supermarkets—with vast arrays of canned fruits and vegetables—would anyone want to bother with canning jars, boiling water baths, home dehydrators and freezers. The truth of the matter is that Americans are concerned about quality and the costs of feeding a family and have decided to do some things about them.

It is possible to chop your annual food costs in half by freezing, canning and drying fruits, vegetables, and meats. There are several prerequisites, however, that include a source of inexpensive materials to preserve. You must have a place where you can efficiently and quickly prepare these foods for preservation and you must be willing to invest the time necessary to accomplish the various tasks.

The best way to acquire inexpensive fruits, vegetables and meats for preserving is, of course, to grow or raise them yourself. During the Great Depression and the World War II years, most households had a garden where a good portion of the food necessary to feed the family was grown. After the war, many people slowed down or even stopped food production and a lot of very productive home gardens were turned into lawns. These were the prosperous years and the 1950s and 1960s witnessed gigantic

Fig. 7-1. With a little work, the home garden can produce much of a familie's annual food needs.

supermarkets that offered everything from canned tomatoes to "garden fresh" vegetables.

Part of the attraction, no doubt, was that it was much easier to shop for food than it was to grow the same items. This was true at least until the last few years. In the late 1960s, Americans experienced what was called the "back to the land" or "back to the basics" movement. Many people felt rather far removed from the basic can of tomatoes and decided to do something about it.

Fig. 7-2. A modern freezer.

Food cooperatives sprang up all over the country and many families began digging up their back lawns and planting gardens. Modern seeds, fertilizers and equipment made home gardening easier than ever and the production from a small backyard garden could be amazing.

It became entirely possible to raise enough tomatoes in the backyard to last a family for a year. It is estimated that the average American consumes 54 pounds of tomatoes and tomato related food stuffs per year (Fig. 7-1).

A number of books and magazines sprang up about producing food for the family. There is also a current weekly television program aimed at helping produce the family victory garden.

The reasons for the popularity of the home garden vary among individuals. Some people garden to save money, to have better quality food, for recreation or any combination of reasons. Whatever the reason, the fact remains that a small garden plot can produce a large portion of a family's food needs. The obvious extension of the family food garden is preserving home grown food for enjoyment throughout the year.

Gardening with an eye on producing part or all of a family's food needs requires a certain amount of conscientious work. Preserving the fruits of your labor requires additional time and energy as well. You can, however, take a lot of the drudgery out of food preservation by setting up an efficient raw food preparation center in your home.

I will concentrate in this chapter on how you can create a special space for just such tasks. I will not deal with specific freezing, canning or drying techniques. But I will discuss how to make your food preservation area efficient. I will also discuss the major equipment necessary for food preservation. Information about techniques and how to can specific fruits and vegetables can easily be found in other sources. A listing is included in the appendix of this book.

FREEZING

Many people feel that freezing is the quickest, safest and best method of preserving food. The truth of the matter is that some foods freeze better than others. Meats, for example, lend themselves better to freezing than any other modern preservation method. Some fruits and some vegetables such as squash do not freeze well at all. Nevertheless, freezing is probably the simplest and least time consuming of all food preservation methods (Fig. 7-2).

Of course, before you can freeze meats, fruits and vegetables, you must have a freezer and the cost of a new or used unit could offset any saving you hope to realize by preserving your own food. Most experts agree, however, that over a period of several years a home freezer will pay for itself in time saved when compared with other food preservation methods.

In addition to the basic cost of a home freezer, you must also take into consideration that the unit needs electricity to run. It is no secret that utility rates rise every year and this fact could have a bearing on whether or not a home freezer can really help to cut your food costs. While it might be true that the food you are preserving costs little or nothing, the cost of storing the food in your freezer can be substantial. This is especially true in parts of the country where electrical rates are high.

One other point about the power necessary to run any freezer is that there is always the possibility that the power will go off and leave you with 18 cubic feet of spoiling food. In certain parts of the country, where brown-outs and black-outs are common, this could be a problem and should be taken into consideration when you decide on the best means of preserving food. It is generally accepted that a full freezer will remain frozen for two days, even during the warm months, if the unit is kept closed. A freezer with less than a half load will not remain frozen for more than a day however.

In addition to a freezer, you will also need containers for freezing foodstuffs. It is important to keep in mind that the purpose of packaging is to keep food from drying out and to preserve food value, flavor, color and texture. Any container used for freezing should be easy to seal and waterproof so that it will not leak. The packing material should also be able to withstand low temperatures without becoming too brittle or cracking.

To retain the highest quality in frozen food, packaging materials should be moisture-vapor-proof to prevent evaporation. Many of the packaging materials on the market for freezing food are not moisture-vapor-proof, but they are sufficiently moisture-vapor-resistant to retain satisfactory quality of fruits and vegetables during storage.

Glass, metal and rigid plastic are examples of moisture-vapor-proof packaging materials. Most plastic bags, wrapping materials and waxed cartons made specifically for freezing are moisture-vapor-resistant. Poor choices for freezer packaging are ordinary waxed papers and paper cartons such as those which

Fig. 7-3. Some of the choices for freezer containers. The best choices are on the right.

various dairy products come in—milk, ice cream, yogurt, etc. (Fig. 7-3).

The shape of your freezer storage containers is also a consideration. Rigid containers that are flat on both top and bottom stack well in a freezer. Round containers and those with flared sides or raised bottoms waste freezer space. Non-rigid containers that bulge waste freezer space as well.

Frozen food can be removed easily, before it is thawed, from containers with sides that are straight from top to bottom or that flare out from the bottom. Food must be thawed before it can be removed from containers with openings that are narrower than the body of the container.

Care in sealing is as important as using the right container. Rigid containers usually are sealed either by pressing or by screwing on the lid. Some rigid cardboard cartons need to have freezer tape or special wax applied after sealing to make them airtight and leakproof. Glass jars must be sealed with a lid containing composition rubber or with a lid and a rubber ring.

Most bags used for freezer packaging can be heat-sealed or sealed by twisting and folding back the top of the bag and securing with a string, a good quality rubber or plastic band or other sealing device available on the market. Some duplex bags are sealed by folding over a metal strip attached to the top of the bag. There are also zip-lock type closings that work quite well providing the plastic bag itself is made from thick (at least 5 mils thick) plastic sheeting.

All foods to be frozen should be labeled clearly. Include the name of the food, the date it was packed and type of pack if the food is packed in more than one form. Gummed labels, colored tape, crayons, pens and stamps are made especially for labeling frozen food packages (Fig. 7-4).

After the fruits, vegetables and meats have been prepared for packaging, they should be frozen as quickly as possible. Put these foods in the freezer a few packages at a time as you complete the packaging or keep packages in the refrigerator until you have packed all of the foods you are planning to freeze at this point. Then transfer them to the home freezer and freeze at 0 degrees Fahrenheit or below.

Put no more food into the home freezer than will freeze within 24 hours. Usually this will be about 2 or 3 pounds of food to each cubic foot of the freezer's capacity. Overloading slows down the rate of freezing. Foods that freeze too slowly might lose quality or

Fig. 7-4. It is important to label all packages that go into the freezer. Note the contents and the date.

even spoil. For quick freezing, place packages against freezing plates or coils and leave a little space between the packages so that the cold air can circulate freely.

After freezing, packages can be stored close together. Store them at zero degrees Fahrenheit or below. At higher temperatures foods lose quality much faster.

Most fruits and vegetables maintain high quality for 8 to 12 months at zero degrees Fahrenheit or below. Citrus fruits and citrus juices maintain high quality for four to six months. Unsweetened fruits lose quality faster than those packed in sugar or syrup. Longer storage will not make foods unfit for use, but it might impair quality.

It is a good idea to post a list of frozen foods near the freezer and keep it up to date. List foods as you put them into the freezer, with date, and check foods off the list as you remove them.

CANNING

Home canning of fruits, vegetables and even meats is probably second only to freezing as the most popular form of preserving foods. Canning has a lot of appeal in that the process is relatively simple to accomplish, inexpensive—only a few pieces of equipment, jars and lids are required—and the results are pleasing to look at as well as use the year round. When all is said and done, canning is probably the most economical and practical method of preserving food at home. Among other things, it is a way to save food that might otherwise be wasted.

The wise homemaker will can only the amount of food that can be consumed within one year—until the next harvest. Food held longer will be safe to eat if it has a good seal and no signs of spoilage, but there might be nutrient or quality loss. This is especially true if the foods are stored at temperatures above 70 degrees Fahrenheit.

The home canner needs to know some things about microorganisms such as yeasts, molds, and bacteria, on the food, in water, in the air and the soil as causes of spoilage in foods. Knowing about these minute forms of life, which are so abundant everywhere, will help to make the work safer as well as more interesting.

In addition to the action of these organisms, the spoiling of fruits and vegetables is hastened by natural changes in color, flavor and texture of the food being canned. These changes result from the action of enzymes or microorganisms found in nature which break down and decompose foodstuffs.

Volumes of procedures for safe canning are abundant. The would-be home canner must familiarize him or herself with this information to insure that the food being preserved is safe for consumption. A listing of the more significant and informative publications about home canning can be found in the appendix.

Most canning equipment and supplies can be purchased at hardware stores, housewares departments, supermarkets and through mail-order companies. Jars and lids are available in many retail stores and especially during the canning season. The wise shopper can often find sales on equipment that will reduce the cost of home canning.

Canning jars are the backbone of the home canning operation. Standard canning jars are made from specially tempered glass that can withstand high temperatures. The manufacturers name or symbol in glass will identify the product. With careful handling, jars should last for an average of about 10 years. You should avoid using antique canning jars because there can be hairline cracks not visible to the eye which will cause the jars to break.

It is important to use canning jars in sizes suitable for the food being canned and your family's needs. Canning jars generally are

240

sold in half-pint, pint, and quart sizes. They will have wide or narrow mouths. Large mouth jars are convenient for packing such foods as whole tomatoes and peach halves. Quart jars are convenient for vegetables and fruits if your family has four or more members (Fig. 7-5).

Examine the sealing edge of jars for nicks, cracks or sharp edges that would prevent a good seal. Discard any jars with such imperfections.

Containers such as used mayonnaise jars should not be used because they might break when subjected to the high heat required for home canning. The tops of these jars will not fit standard canning lids and this prevents a good seal.

Closures are jar lids and rings that come with new canning jars. The sealing compound of lids recommended for one use will not hold a seal effectively after the first use.

Select lids appropriate for the jars being used. You might find the two piece units (flat lid with sealing composition and ring), one piece lids or flats with separate gaskets made of metal or plastic. Always follow the instructions for pretreatment as indicated on the box or container by the manufacturer. If no name is indicated on the lid, use black wax marking pencil or crayon and mark the identity of each lid. If there are problems, contact the manufacturer whose name and address is on the box or container (Fig. 7-6).

Screw ring bands can be reused if they are kept clean and dry in a protective container with a tight-fitting lid. Never use bands with rust or pried up or bent edges.

Fig. 7-5. Canning jars come in many different sizes and shapes.

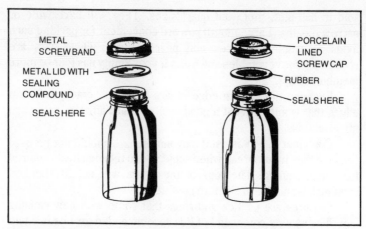

METAL
SCREW BAND

METAL LID WITH
SEALING
COMPOUND

SEALS HERE

PORCELAIN
LINED
SCREW CAP

RUBBER

SEALS HERE

Fig. 7-6. The right type of lid is crucial to the success of home canning.

A boiling water bath canner is needed for processing high acid foods, such as some fruits, tomatoes, tomato and fruit juices and pickles. Water bath canners in several sizes are generally available. The container must be deep enough for a rack to hold the jars off the bottom of the canner. The depth allows water to be over the jars of food by at least 1 to 2 inches. Keep 1 to 2 inches of space above the water to allow for boiling. This prevents water from boiling over the side of the canning pot (Fig. 7-7).

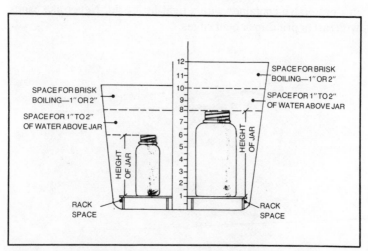

SPACE FOR BRISK
BOILING—1" OR 2"

SPACE FOR 1" TO 2"
OF WATER ABOVE JAR

HEIGHT
OF JAR

RACK
SPACE

SPACE FOR BRISK
BOILING—1" OR 2"

SPACE FOR 1" TO 2"
OF WATER ABOVE JAR

HEIGHT
OF JAR

RACK
SPACE

Fig. 7-7. When canning, it is important that boiling water completely surround the canning jars. Place the jars on a rack and make sure that the top of each jar is covered with at least 2 inches of boiling water.

Fig. 7-8. A special wire rack must be used when canning.

243

The canner must have a tight fitting lid. Or you can use a large kettle with a tight fitting lid and a wooden or wire rack to hold the jars off the bottom. There should be free circulation of water to every part of the surface of the jar and lid for best results.

If you are going to buy a water bath canner, check the height and the lid to be sure it is tight fitting. Preferably the rack should have dividers so that jars will not touch each other or fall against the sides of the canner during the canning process (Fig. 7-8).

A steam pressure canner is absolutely essential for canning low acid foods such as some vegetables and insures the destruction of spoilage causing microorganisms. Ten pounds of pressure is used for processing food in standard canning jars at sea level. This pressure corresponds to 240 degrees Fahrenheit.

The standard steam pressure canner is made of heavy metal that withstands high pressure developed by steam. It consists of a kettle with a tight fitting lid equipped with an accurate weight or dial gauge to register the pounds per square inch inside the canner. The lid must lock or seal to prevent the escape of steam and in fact make pressurized canning possible.

The canner must have some type of safety valve, pet cock or steam vent that can be opened or closed to permit venting of the steam. In addition to the pressure gauge, the steam canner must also have a rack to hold the jars at least one-half inch up from the bottom of the canner.

A dial gauge indicates pressure on a numbered instrument face. A weighted gauge has no dial, but automatically limits pressure with weights preset for 5, 10 or 15 pounds of pressure (Fig. 7-9).

To insure the pressure canner's proper working condition, check the dial gauge for accuracy each year before the canning season gets into full swing. You should also check the gauge if the dial glass is broken, dented or if any parts are rusty. The manufacturer or your county extension office can give you information on the availability of testing equipment in your area. Study and follow the manufacturers directions for using your pressure canner and you will greatly reduce the chances of mishap.

It makes a lot of sense to run through the process of operating your pressure canner on your range in a trial before you get into the canning season. Make certain that the canner operates properly. You should also make a note of the dial setting of the range, if you use an electric range, for holding pressure steady. If the canner does not operate as it should you must get it checked or repaired by a qualified person.

Trying to use a pressure canner obtained from garage, rummage or auction sales or handed down to you from someone's attic could prove dangerous. You will not have any idea as to the care, handling or storage of the canner. A manufacturer's manual on care, directions for use and replaceable parts might be difficult or impossible to find.

General kitchen equipment is quite helpful for washing, peeling, coring and slicing in the preparation of fruits and vegetables. Some of the more handy and common kitchen tools include a vegetable brush for cleaning foods, a blancher or wire basket for scalding fruits and vegetables such as tomatoes and peaches that will loosen skins prior to peeling and a colander for washing delicate fruits such as berries (Fig. 7-10).

A food mill is handy for making purees and straining fruits for making juices and as strainer for straining juice. A long handled fork or plastic spatula aids in fitting and packing food and removing air bubbles. A wide mouth funnel is very convenient for filling jars and a jar lifter helps to avoid burns in handling hot jars. An automatic timer is handy for processing foods accurately (Fig. 7-11).

The number of pints of preserved food you will get from a given quantity of fresh food depends on the quality, variety and maturity of the fruit or vegetable, on the size of the pieces and on the packing method used. After jars of food have been processed—

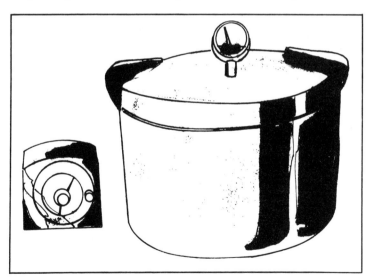

Fig. 7-9. A pressure canner is necessary for canning low acid foods such as green beans.

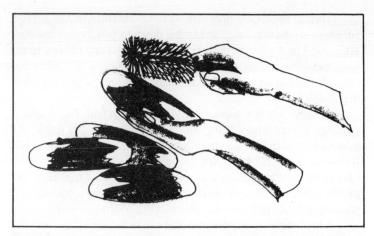

Fig. 7-10. A small scrub brush should be used to clean rough skinned vegetables before canning or pickling.

Fig. 7-11. This food sieve is very handy when working with tomatoes.

in either the hot water bath or pressure canner—they should be allowed to cool. After the jars have cooled to the point where they can be picked up without burning your hand, but before 24 hours have passed, check each jar to be sure the seal is good.

To test a jar that has a flat metal lid, press the center of the lid. If the lid stays down and will not move, the seal is good. Most modern canning lids have a special section on the top that will appear indented when the seal is correct. Turn jars with porcelain-lined zinc caps partly over in your hands. If they do not leak, they are sealed properly (Fig. 7-12).

After the jars have thoroughly cooled, the metal screw bands should be carefully removed. Wipe the outside of each jar with a damp cloth and label the jars to show the date and the contents.

Fig. 7-12. After canning, the jar lid should remain indented when pressed down with your thumb.

Store the sealed jars in a cool dry place. If you find a jar that did not seal properly, use the food right away or can the food again immediately. Empty the contents, pack and process the food as if fresh.

When you are selecting canned foods for use at the table, check the dates on the jar labels to be sure that you are using the food that has the earliest processing date. Before opening any jar for use, look at it carefully for any signs of spoilage. If it leaks, if it has a bulging lid, if it spurts liquid when it is opened or it it has an off odor or mold, do *not* use the food. Do *not* even taste it. Destroy it out of the reach of children and pets.

Canned vegetables might contain the toxin that causes botulism without showing any visible signs of spoilage. Therefore, boil all home canned vegetables in a covered pot before tasting or serving. Heating generally makes any odor of spoilage more evident. If you are ever in doubt about any home canned food or if an off odor is present, do *not* use it.

DRYING FOODS

Drying as a method of preserving fruits, vegetables and meats is the oldest method of preserving foodstuffs. In many parts of the world, this method is still widely used today. Even though you might never have thought about drying some of your garden harvest, you probably use some dried food products every day; consider herbs as the prime example.

Drying is appealing because the procedure is relatively simple and requires little equipment. Only minimal storage space is needed. Food can be dried in the sun, in the oven or in a food dehydrator. Drying requires a method of heating the food to evaporate the moisture present and some means of removing the resulting moisture.

Trays of wood slats, plastic mesh or aluminum screen may be placed in the sun on support blocks or strips to allow air movement around and through the trays. Galvanized wire is not recommended as a tray material because high acid foods will react with the zinc coating on the wire.

If insects or birds are a problem—as they might be when drying is done out of doors—a wooden frame can be constructed over the trays to support a plastic mesh or cheesecloth cover. Further protection can be provided by using a totally enclosed frame and a transparent panel to form a solar drying oven (Fig. 7-13).

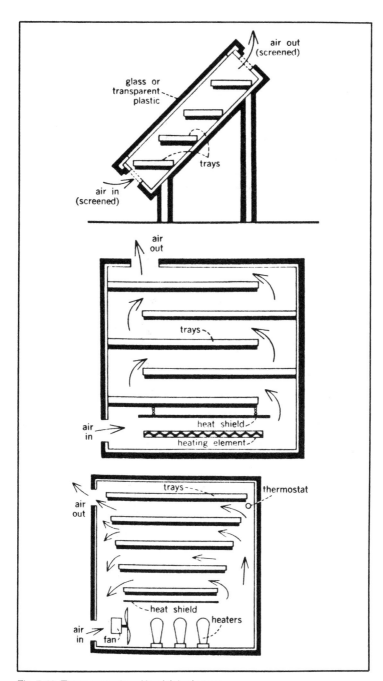

Fig. 7-13. Three examples of food dehydrators.

To dry fruits, vegetables and meats in the kitchen oven, the thermostat should be set at its lowest temperature setting— generally about 140 to 150 degrees. Because oven vents for removing moisture from roasting and baking are adequate for drying only small quantities of food at one time, the oven door should be left partially opened during the drying process. For larger loads, the air circulation can be increased by placing a household fan outside the oven and directed at one edge of the partially opened oven door (Fig. 7-14).

Dehydrator cabinets can be purchased in many sizes and types. They can be built in the home workshop using plans available from state universities or the U.S. Department of Agriculture. Ask your county extension office about plans for a homemade food dehydrator. All dehydrator cabinets are provided with a heat source and vents for carrying off the moist air during the drying process.

Simpler units rely on natural convection to carry moist air away and the heating unit is limited in output so that the cabinet never exceeds safe drying temperatures near the end of the drying period. This type will be slow in achieving drying temperatures if sizable amounts of food are processed at one time.

Trays of food must be rotated during the processing period to insure an even drying of all of the pieces. Trays nearest the bottom are exposed to the hottest, driest air and will dry most rapidly.

If the natural convection type cabinet is equipped with a thermostat, it can be fitted with a larger heating unit. This will provide higher drying temperatures during the early stages, but will not give even drying across all trays.

By using a fan to force air across the trays more rapidly, even drying can be obtained across each tray as well as between the trays. The forced air system can be used with or without a thermostat.

Most food products release moisture rapidly during the early stages of drying. This means that they can absorb large amounts of heat and give off large quantities of water vapor while remaining at a temperature well below that of the drying air. Maximum drying rates can be achieved by providing a larger, thermostatically controlled heat source and a fan for circulating air.

To conserve energy and still obtain rapid, even drying across all trays of food, much of the drying air can be reheated and recirculated. This is particularly effective during the last 70 to 90 percent of the drying period when relatively small amounts of

Fig. 7-14. Oven drying is done at the lowest setting possible—145 to 150 degrees F.

water are absorbed by the air as it passes over the partially dried food.

The recirculating system requires either a thermostat or separate switch controls on part of the heating unit to adjust heat output to match the drying load. The amount of air recirculated is determined by the size of the permanent inlet and outlet openings in the drying box. It can be further controlled by adjusting the door to a partially opened position.

Detailed plans for constructing the recirculation type dryer can be obtained by sending 25 cents to the Western Regional Agricultural Engineering Service (WRAES), Oregon State University, Corvallis, Oregon, 97331 and requesting WRAES Fact Sheet number 18.

Drying fruits and vegetables is a relatively simple process, but there are a number of recommended techniques. See the appendix for books on the subject. You might need to use a "trial and error" approach to find the drying process that works best for the particular food you are drying and for the part of the country you live in.

Fruits and vegetables can be dried in pieces or pureed and dried in a thin sheet that is commonly known as fruit "leather". Fruits and vegetables selected for drying should be of the highest quality obtainable—fresh and fully ripened. Wilted or inferior produce will not make a satisfactory dried product. Immature produce lacks flavor and color. Overmature produce will be tough and fibrous or soft and mushy.

Prepare produce immediately after gathering and begin drying as quickly as possible. Wash or clean all fresh food thoroughly to remove any dirt or spray. Sort and discard defective food because of decay, bruises or mold. Any piece could affect the entire batch.

For greater convenience when you finally use the food and to speed drying, it is advisable to peel, pit, or core most fruits and vegetables. Small pieces dry more quickly and uniformly.

A temperature of 135 to 140 degrees Fahrenheit is most desirable for dehydrator or oven drying. Moisture must be removed from the food as quickly as possible at a temperature that does not seriously affect the foods flavor, texture color and nutritive value.

If the initial temperature is too low or if air circulation is insufficient, the food might undergo undesirable microbiological changes before it dries adequately. If the temperature is too high and the humidity too low, as when drying small loads in the oven, the food surface might harden. This makes it difficult for moisture to escape during the drying process.

It is important that oven or dehydrator drying continue without interruption to prevent microbial growth. To promote

Fig. 7-15. Dried fruits and vegetables should be stored in a sealed container.

even drying, you should rotate trays occasionally and stir food if necessary. Drying time varies according to fruit or vegetable type, size of the pieces and tray load. Dehydrator drying generally takes less time than oven drying. Sun drying takes considerably more time, but ironically it is probably the most widely used method of food preservation in the world today.

Before testing foods for dryness, remove a handful and cool for a few minutes. Foods that are warm or hot seem softer, more moist and more pliable than they will actually be after cooling.

Foods should be dry enough to prevent microbial growth and subsequent spoilage. Dried vegetables should be hard and brittle. Dried fruits should be leathery and pliable. For long term storage, home-dried fruits will need to be drier than commercially dried fruits sold in grocery stores.

Fruits cut into a wide range of sizes should be allowed to "sweat" or condition for a week after drying to equalize the moisture among the pieces before placing in long term storage. To condition, place fruit in a non-aluminum, non-plastic container and put in a dry, well ventilated and protected area. Stir the food gently each day.

Dehydrated foods are free of insect infestation when removed from the dehydrator or oven. However, sun dried foods can be contaminated and should be treated before storage. Insects or their eggs can be killed by heating the dried food at 150 degrees Fahrenheit for 30 minutes in the oven. An alternative is to package the food and place it in the home freezer for 48 hours.

Dried foods should be thoroughly cooled before packaging. Package in small amounts so that the food can be used soon after the container has been opened. Pack food as tightly as possible, without crushing, into clean, dry insect-proof containers. Glass jars or moisture-vapor proof freezer cartons or bags—the heavy gauge plastic type—all make good containers. Metal cans with fitted lids can also be used if the dried food is first placed in a plastic bag (Fig. 7-15).

Label packaged foods with the packaging date and the type of food. Containers of dried food should be stored in a cool, dry, dark place. You should check food occasionally to insure that it has not reabsorbed moisture. If there is any sign of spoilage—off color or mold growth—discard the food. Food affected by moisture, but not moldy, should be used immediately or reheated and then re-packaged.

FOOD PRESERVATION WORK CENTER

Whatever method you choose to use—keeping in mind that a combination of all methods is often the most workable arrangement—you will need a place to prepare the fruits and vegetables before "putting them up". In just about every instance, the steps include gathering the fruits and vegetables, washing them, carefully sorting through the material and discarding undesirable pieces, and then putting the food into containers. Additionally, some fruits and vegetables require cutting up and blanching or cooling before they can be canned or frozen.

Because home preservation of fruits and vegetables takes place only during about a two month period during the summer, it would really be impractical to create a home center that was used just for the purpose of handling food. The obvious place where you will do this work is in your existing kitchen. There are a number of modifications that you can make during the canning season that will help you to accomplish the task of preserving food quicker and much more efficiently (Fig. 7-16).

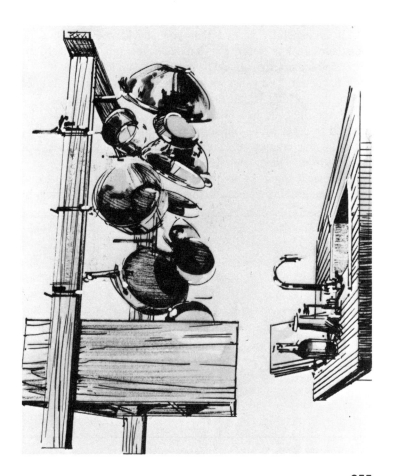

Fig. 7-16. A home center for handling food (courtesy of Georgia-Pacific).

The first step in the food preservation process is to wash the fruit or vegetable. Washing is necessary for all foods whether or not they will be cut up before packaging. The obvious reason for a thorough washing is to remove dirt, insects, sprays and surface bacteria or yeasts. Dirt contains some of the hardest bacteria to kill so washing is necessary.

To help the work go faster, remember that the point of home processing is to get the food from the vine, tree or plant into storage as quickly as possible; wash small loads at a time. A double kitchen sink is very handy for this washing. You will do a more effective job of cleaning the food if it is dipped in and out of the water. One handy tool for this is a metal wire basket or other suitable container that will allow the food to be washed and drained at almost the same time. This way the dirt that has been washed off will not have a chance to go back on the food (Fig. 7-17).

It is generally agreed that you should not let fruits or vegetables soak in water. Fresh foods have a tendency to absorb water and the practice should be avoided. Also, foods tend to lose their flavor and food value when soaked for long periods of time. During the washing, handle the food gently to avoid bruising.

After the food has been washed thoroughly, it should be allowed to drain while you sort through it. A large wire rack is handy for this draining and sorting. A drain board under the rack will help to keep the wash water off the floor.

The next step is to prepare the fruit or vegetable for packing into containers. In some cases, this will mean cutting or paring. In

Fig. 7-17. A wire basket for washing fruits and vegetables.

other cases, it will simply mean packing the whole pieces into jars or freezer containers.

All of the above operations require space and you will almost never have enough during the canning season. In most cases, you will be using all available space in your existing kitchen. To make this space more useful, you should clear the counter top around the sink area so fruits and vegetables can be washed, sorted and prepared in one area.

Another area or work surface should be used for packing the food into containers. Your kitchen table should be pressed into service for this operation. If cooking, hot water bath or pressure canning will be the next step, you should set your kitchen table between the sink and counter area and your range so there can be a free flow of work from the sink, to the jars and to the stove. Another table or counter can be very useful for the hot jars of food as they come out of the canner on the range.

In a number of cases, you will not have much freedom because it would be difficult or impossible to rearrange fixtures and the range just to accommodate your canning tasks. But you can make your kitchen easier to work in by rearranging those pieces of furniture—such as the kitchen table—that can be moved so there will be a free flow of work from the sink to packages, to the canner and to storage. By setting up your kitchen in this manner, you will be able to quickly get the fresh food into a container and seal it.

STORING HOME PRESERVED FOODS

Proper storage of home preserved foods, especially of home canned products, and close scrutiny before serving are essential. If proper storage requirements are not met, home preserved foods will lose their quality or spoil. Proper storage will protect canned foods from loss of quality and in some cases spoilage. Canned foods should be stored in a clean, cool, dry area away from bright light—particularly sunlight—and in an area where the foods will not freeze or be exposed to high temperatures. Under these conditions, the canned food will remain at high quality for at least one year.

Excessive dampness will rust cans and metal lids. If this condition becomes severe, leakage will occur and the food will obviously spoil. Freezing will cause expansion of the food and the lid might loosen, the jar might crack or can seams might be stressed.

As a rule of thumb, home canned foods will remain high in quality for one year if they are stored properly. It is generally agreed among experts that after one year of storage, home canned foods begin to lose a bit of their quality.

Containers for home preserved foods are designed to resist any chemical reactions between the product and the container. However, some foods—particularly high acid foods such as tomatoes—will slowly react with the metal in the can or the jar lid. Corrosion and container failure will follow during subsequent storage. This action occurs from the inside out and can take place even under good storage conditions (Fig. 7-18).

Jars should be dated when stored and used within one year from the processing date. Always rotate stock on the shelves so as to use the oldest container first. Can no more units of any single product than your family can consume in the course of one year.

The last and perhaps the most important quality control steps are the final inspection and serving procedures. If ever a home canned food is suspect—for any reason—destroy the jar and contents.

Foods stored in your home freezer can generally be considered safer than canned foods stored in a pantry or closet. This is because the bacterium that causes botulism cannot grow in the freezer. Proper freezing of food stuffs prevents the growth of microorganisms that cause spoilage and those that can cause illness.

After home packaged foods have been frozen, they should be stored close together at a temperature of zero degrees or less. At this temperature, they will retain the highest quality for the longest time. You should keep in mind, however, that some foods deteriorate faster than others, even in the freezer, and for this reason it is important to label all packages and use the oldest foods first. If foods are stored at or below zero degrees Fahrenheit for prolonged periods, taste might be affected but there will not be any question as to the safety of the food. Nevertheless, if frozen foods—after thawing—appear or smell odd, they should be destroyed rather than consumed.

STORING FRESH FRUITS AND VEGETABLES

Many fruits and vegetables lend themselves well to being stored fresh. But the home gardener must gather them at proper maturity and observe correct temperature, humidity, ventilation and cleanliness rules.

Fig. 7-18. Canned foods should be stored in a cabinet out of direct sunlight and at moderate temperatures —55 to 65 degrees F.

Basements or outdoor cellars can serve as temporary storage for some produce. A cellar, mostly below ground level, is best for root type vegetables. It can be designed to run into a bank and be covered with at least 2½ feet of soil. Sometimes outdoor root cellars are made with a door at each end.

Modern basements are generally too dry and warm for cool, moist storage. However, a suitable storage room can be built by insulating walls and ceiling and ventilating through a basement window. You can ventilate by extending a ventilating flue from half of the window down almost to the floor. Cover the other half of the window with wood and the outside openings of the ventilator with a wire screen for protection against animals and insects.

Keep your basement food storage room cool by opening the ventilators on cool nights and closing them on warm days. If properly cooled, the room temperature can be controlled between 32 and 40 degrees Fahrenheit during the winter months. To maintain the humidity, sprinkle water on the floor when produce

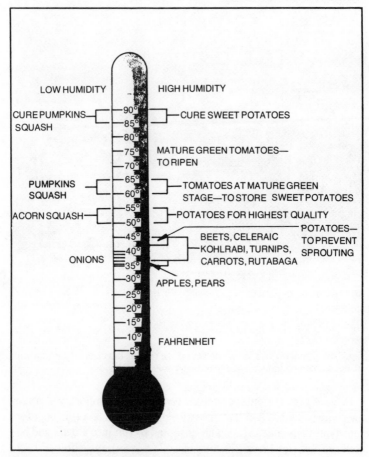

Fig. 7-19. A vegetable/fruit temperature storage guide.

Table 7-1. Home Storage Chart.

	Where to store	Storage conditions Temperature (F) Humidity		Storage period
Vegetables:				
Beans and peas, dried	Any cool, dry place	32-40		
Beets	Storage cellar or pit	32-40		**Fall-winter**
Cabbage	Storage cellar or pit	32-35		**Fall-winter**
Carrots	Storage cellar or pit	32-40		**Fall-winter**
Celery	Roots in soil in storage cellar	32-40		**Fall-winter**
Onions	Any cool, dry place	As near 32 as possible		
Parsnips	Leave in ground or put in storage cellar	32-40	Moist	Fall-winter
Potatoes	Storage cellar or pit	45-48	Moist	Fall-winter
Pumpkin, winter squash	Unheated room or basement	55-60	Dry	Fall-winter
Rutabagas	Storage cellar or pit	32-40	Moist	Fall-winter
Sweet Potatoes	Unheated room or basement	55-60	Dry	Fall-winter
Tomatoes (green or white)	Unheated room or basement	55-60	Dry	1-6 weeks
Turnips	Storage cellar or pit	32-40	Moist	Fall-winter
Fruits:				
Most apples	Fruit storage cellar	30-32	Moist	Fall-winter
McIntosh, Yellow Newton & Rhode Island Greening	Fruit storage cellar	35-38	Moist	Fall-winter
Grapes	Fruit storage cellar	31-32	Moist	4-6 weeks
Pears	Fruit storage cellar	30-31	Moist	Fall-winter
Peaches	Fruit storage cellar	32	Moist	2 weeks
Apricots	Fruit storage cellar	32	Moist	2 weeks

begins to wilt. A slatted floor and slatted shelves will provide floor drainage and good air circulation. A reliable thermometer is needed for operation of any home storage room (Fig. 7-19).

It is important to keep in mind that requirements for fruits and vegetable storage differ. Controlled cold storage or refrigerated storage is best. But you should also know that people have been storing fresh produce in root cellars for centuries. With a little thought and thorough planning you should be able to achieve good results (Table 7-1).

There are a number of good books on the subject of natural food storage and a listing of some of these can be found in the appendix. A root cellar or food storage room in your home makes a lot of sense. When you think about all of the time necessary for growing and canning your own food, it seems reasonable that you should also create a special room in your home where you can store your yield. Once you have a larder, you can be reasonably certain that the fruits of your labor will survive storage and supply you with food throughout the year.

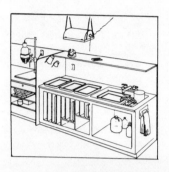

Chapter 8
Automobile
Workshop

The costs of maintaining an automobile have been steadily rising for the past decade and many motorists are now at the point of doing some of the work themselves in an effort to ease some of the costs. This makes a lot of sense when you consider that a set of spark plugs costs about $8 (for eight) and that a general auto mechanic will usually charge about $5 to put them into your car. By installing your own spark plugs you could, theroetically, save yourself $5. Similar savings can be realized by performing many of the other necessary and routine maintenance tasks such as changing your oil and filter, replacing other filters, points, condenser, cap, rotor and spark plug wires.

Automobile maintenance is not for everyone. You must be willing to invest time for repairs and maintenance. You must also be willing to learn —through any of the many publications—how to go about keeping your automobile in first-class running order.

Probably the greatest motivating force behind the current do-it-yourself auto repair trend is the very real savings that are possible. While you probably will not be able to do all of your maintenance and repairs—such as rebuilding your engine after it turns 150,000 miles—you can do a lot of this work and in the long run you will save a pile of money. You will also have a more efficient running automobile and this will help to save a little energy as well.

The bulk of this chapter is devoted to suggestions for setting up an automobile workshop in your home and tools that are handy

262

for this type of work. It is far easier to take care of your automobile if you have a specific place where you can accomplish repairs and maintenance tasks quickly and as efficiently as possible. In this chapter I will also discuss many of the tools that can make maintaining your automobile easier than ever before.

LOCATION

The obvious location for an automobile workshop is, of course, a garage or other suitable outbuilding. With a garage, you can work on your automobile anytime the need arises. You can work during other than daylight hours, during inclement weather and during the cooler months. There are several requirements for a suitable garage. Keep in mind that I am discussing the ideal automobile workshop for the do-it-yourselfer and chances are very good that your home garage will fall short of the mark. You must work with what you have, but you should be able to pick and choose some of the more useful points of the ideal garage and incorporate them into your existing facilities. If you are planning to build a garage, all the better.

A garage for automobile maintenance must be more than simply a place to park the car out of the weather. The basic space requirements will depend, at least in part, on the size of your automobile. A multicar garage is best for the home mechanic. With a two or more car garage you have the freedom to work on a project—such as rebuilding an antique automobile—at your leisure. Projects such as this are best done indoors to protect the parts from the elements. Additionally you will be able to work on several projects simultaneously.

FLOORS

The floor of your garage should be concrete. Any other material is unsuitable. Because many maintenance tasks require that the automobile be jacked up and supported by jack stands, a hard durable surface is necessary for safety. Experts agree that a concrete garage floor should be painted with a special coating that resists the actions of petroleum products—gasoline and oil. Probably the best floor covering is a good concrete paint or porch and deck enamel.

A very good reason for painting your garage floor is that it will be much easier to keep clean. Puddles of oil can be quickly removed from a painted floor, but they will stain an unpainted floor. A second reason is that a painted floor tends to keep dust to a minimum and dust can be an enemy of an efficient running automobile.

Painting a concrete floor is a bit different from other painting tasks. First of all, a special paint is required. You should not even think about painting a concrete floor (or any masonry surface for that matter) until it is at least eight weeks old. If possible, the concrete should age for at least six months for best results. The main reason for this waiting period is that when concrete is poured it contains certain oils and other additives which will prevent paint coatings from adhering to the surface of the concrete.

In time, these additives rise to the surface of the concrete—as it cures and hardens—and they can be swept away. This curing period will also give the concrete a chance to shed small particles of surface sand and mortar which are really not part of the masonry.

After the concrete has cured or on concrete floors that are several years old, there are a few surface preparation tasks which must be done to further increase the chances of a sound paint coating. Begin by scrubbing the surface of the garage floor with a stiff wire brush to dislodge loose particles. Some areas such as oil stains or heavily soiled areas will require special treatment.

These areas must be scrubbed with a solution of trisodium phosphate and water or with paint thinner. Both items are commonly available at any paint store. Use a stiff brush. After scrubbing, the area should be washed with a strong stream of water from a garden hose. A good rinsing of these problem areas, as well as the entire floor, will further ensure that the paint coating will adhear well. After washing, the concrete floor should be allowed to dry for about 24 hours (Fig. 8-1).

Previously painted concrete floors usually require less in the way of surface preparation. The main task is to sweep the floor, remove any oil or heavily soiled spots and wash the floor with a strong detergent. Additionally, any peeling paint should be removed with a scraper. After the floor has been rinsed and it has dried sufficiently, it can be painted.

It is a fallacy to think that you can paint a garage floor with just any paint you have lying around. While it may be true that any good exterior latex paint can be used—providing, of course, that the can label indicates that the coating is suitable for use on concrete—you will get better long-term results if you use a special concrete paint.

Grey high gloss or semigloss floor paints are most commonly used for concrete garage floors. These formulations contain certain additives which are resistant to the various types of alkali

264

Fig. 8-1. Before painting a concrete floor you must remove oil stains. Paint thinner works well for this.

commonly found in concrete floors. By using such a paint over a properly prepared concrete surface, you can be reasonably certain that the paint coating will perform well over a period of several years.

Painting a concrete floor is really quite simple. Begin in the back corner of the garage and pour about 1 quart of the paint onto the floor. With a long napped roller, on an extension handle, begin rolling the paint out evenly over the floor. The extension handle on the roller will enable you to reach a good distance, but you must keep a sharp eye so that the coating is spread uniformly over the entire surface.

After you have spread the initial puddle of paint, move on to another area and pour more paint onto the floor. Spread it evenly over an area of several square feet. Continue in this fashion until the entire floor has been adequately covered (Fig. 8-2).

You should be able to paint almost all of the garage floor with the roller, but you will encounter some areas that require a little brush work. These areas include the edge of the floor where it meets the walls, around doorways and around workbenches, etc.

After the floor has been coated, it is best to partially close the garage door and stay out of the garage for 24 hours. The garage door is left open slightly to provide ventilation and to insure that the paint dries thoroughly.

Once the garage floor has been painted, it should be allowed to dry 24 hours before you can walk on it. A further drying period will be necessary before you can park a car on the floor. After about two days, the floor should be dry and hard enough for normal traffic.

WORKBENCHES

The workbench for your automobile workshop has several requirements that are not common to other types of work. Generally, a woodworking workbench is unsuitable for the garage. The two most important requirements for an automobile workbench are that it must be strong and solidly constructed. You cannot expect just any old worktable to serve your needs. Another requirement is that the surface of the workbench must be made from a material that is impervious to gasoline and oil.

These requirements rule out a lot of choices for a suitable automobile workbench. Probably the best type of workbench is one that is constructed totally or partially of metal. While metal workbenches are available, their cost might be prohibitive. One alternative is to build a workbench from three-fourth inch thick plywood and cover the top with a single sheet of galvanized sheet metal (Fig. 8-3).

Your automobile workbench must be large enough to allow you to work on several projects at any one time. Additionally, the bench should be located in an area that is convenient to working on your automobile. Generally, the back of the garage is the best place. Located here, the bench will be handy to the front of the automobile when the car is pulled into the garage.

You might also want to construct another workbench on the side wall of the garage. This bench—if your garage space permits—need not be as large as the main workbench, but it should provide adequate workspace. If your garage is a little on the small side, consider building a hinged workbench on a sidewall of the

Fig. 8-2. A sweeping with a stiff broom will remove most of the surface scale and dirt.

building. When not in use, the bench top can be folded down flush with the wall.

In addition to the standard and auxiliary workbenches in your home garage, a wheeled card cart will come in very handy. With a cart, such as that described in Fig. 8-4, you can have a portable

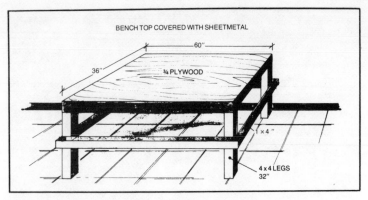

Fig. 8-3. Plans for a heavy-duty automobile workbench.

workbench that can be moved quite close to the automobile you are working on at the moment. Additionally, such a cart is very handy for holding tools that are frequently used and spare parts.

Your auto workshop will also require electrical wiring. At the very least, you will need electrical power for lighting and running small tools. In the more advanced shop, you might also need 220-volt service for arc welding equipment.

Adequate lighting is essential to doing professional type work. Fluorescent fixtures should be located over the main

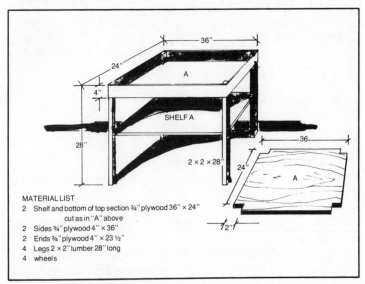

MATERIAL LIST

2 Shelf and bottom of top section ¾" plywood 36" × 24"
        cut as in "A" above
2 Sides ¾" plywood 4" × 36"
2 Ends ¾" plywood 4" × 23 ½"
4 Legs 2 × 2" lumber 28" long
4 wheels

Fig. 8-4. Plans for a wheeled cart.

workbench and over the area where the front end of an automobile will be located.

For specialized lighting problems—when you are working on the exhaust system for example—you should also have at your disposal a trouble light on a long cord. Trouble lights are generally available in auto parts stores and other hardware type stores. You can also make such a light quite simply and for probably half the cost. Figure 8-5 shows a trouble light which should be more than adequate for most purposes.

Your auto workshop will also require a certain amount of storage space. If all you do is change oil and do tuneups, your storage space requirements will not be as great as the do-it-yourselfer that rebuilds transmissions and engines. A general purpose storage system that should fill most needs is shown in Fig. 8-6. Notice that the top of these shelves is reserved for tire storage and the rest of the unit can be used for storing other automobile parts. If your storage requirements are not as great, this shelving system can be pressed into service for storing other tools and equipment commonly found in the average garage.

Other storage ideas include using old kitchen cabinets, other types of shelving and using the space under the auto workbench as a convenient place to store automotive related parts, tools and equipment. All related material should be stored close to the area where automobiles are worked on. It is much easier to start and finish automobive projects when all necessary tools, equipment and supplies are handy to the work area.

TOOLS

In order to perform maintenance and repair tasks, the do-it-yourselfer requires a collection of mechanics tools. The first

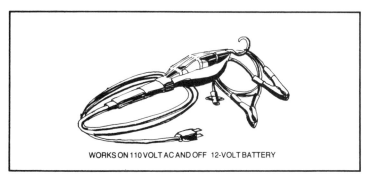

WORKS ON 110 VOLT AC AND OFF 12-VOLT BATTERY

Fig. 8-5. An automobile trouble light.

basic consideration is the general type of work you will be doing. If your maintenance tasks are simple—such as changing oil and filter, tuneups and replacement of minor parts, you will not generally require very much in the way of tools. A listing of the basic mechanic's tool requirements would include the following.

Adjustable wrench: 6- or 10-inch.

Socket set: three-eighth inch drive, including spark plug socket.

Open-end wrenches: assortment from three-eighth to three-sixteenth inch.

Screwdrivers: 4-inch, 6-inch and 10-inch in both standard and Phillips.

Pliers: including needle-nose, wire cutters, locking jaw and slip-joint.

Torque wrench: for socket set.

Thickness gauges: from 0.0015 to 0.035.

Hacksaw: with spare blades.

Allenhead Wrenches.

Lug wrench to fit the car.

Tire pressure gauge.

Trouble or drop light.

Wire brush.

Point file.

Spark plug gapping tool.

Small ball pein hammer.

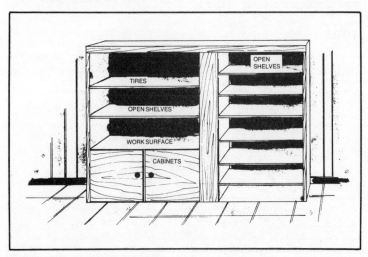

Fig. 8-6. A storage rack for a garage.

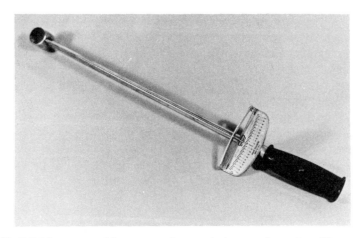

Fig. 8-7. A torque wrench is necessary for many tasks on modern automobiles.

This basic list of mechanic's tools will enable you to perform a wide range of routine maintenance and repair tasks. You should have tools in either SAE or metric. It depends on the type of car you will be working on. This assortment of tools will fit easily into a standard size tool box and that is where they should be kept when they are not in use. As you become more proficient at working on automobiles, you will undoubtedly acquire more tools and equipment and then the need for adequate storage space for tools will become apparent.

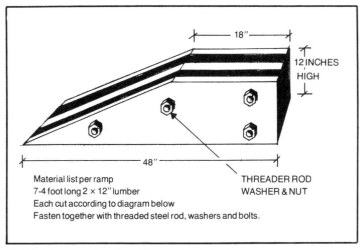

Fig. 8-8. A homemade automobile ramp (make two).

There are many ways to store tools, but really only a few good ways for these types of tools. Probably the best way is in a mechanics tool chest. These units—Sears Roebuck sells one popular model—consists of a drawered cabinet on top of a wheeled cabinet. You have undoubtedly seen tool storage chests such as these at your local garage. They are unbelievably handy because of all the drawers. Unless you have a lot of automotive tools and a need to keep them organized, a chest of this type might cost more than you are really willing to invest. One good alternative is to hang your frequently used automotive tools on a pegboard over the main workbench in the shop. Then all of the tools will be easy to spot and reach.

In addition to the basic tools previously mentioned, there are any number of other tools that are handy or even necessary around the home auto workshop. Some of the more necessary tools include the following.

Floor jack.
Jack stands.
Creeper.
Ramps - used instead of jack and jack stands (Fig. 8-8).
Battery charger, jumper cables and tester.
One-half inch drive socket set.
Brake tools.
Grease gun.
Oil drain pan.
Long spout (flexible) funnel (Fig. 8-9).

A listing of nice-to-have automotive tools is given below. Most of these tools and pieces of specialized equipment can be rented rather than purchased.

Engine hoist.
Engine stand.
Clutch pilot tool.
Wheel puller.
Hydraulic press.
Paint sprayer.
Body and fender tools.
Air compressor.
Gas or Arc welding equipment.
Fender covers.
Valve spring compressor tool.
Ring compressor tool.

272

Fig. 8-9. A floor jack and jack stands will make working on your automobile very easy.

The home auto workshop that has the tools listed above should be able to tackle almost any auto repair. It is probably fair to say that the tools represent several thousands of dollars worth of investment and chances are that you will never have need for all of these tools. Nevertheless, as you develop certain automotive repair skills you will probably come in contact with all of these tools.

There are also a number of useful electronic testing tools (Fig. 8-10) that are quite common in the automobile repair shop. A well rounded list would include the following.

Timing light.
Tachometer.
Dwell meter.
Compression tester.
Volt/ohm meter.
Remove starter switch.

Still another very handy piece of equipment to have in the home auto workshop is a parts' cleaner. Success in do-it-yourself automobile maintenance very often depends on cleaning parts before disassembly and then making certain that all components shine before reassembling. For this reason, it makes a lot of sense for the do-it-yourselfer to build a parts washing station for the shop. Plans and instructions for such a piece of equipment are given in Fig. 8-11.

RECORD KEEPING

In order to maintain your automobile in first-class running condition, you must perform various tasks on a regular basis. For example, engine oil should be changed every 6000 miles or according to the manufacturers recommendations. Other useable parts such as filters, plugs, points, etc., must also be changed or at least cleaned on a regular basis.

This will insure that you get the best gas mileage from your automobile. In these days of ever increasing gasoline prices, that is what automobile maintenance is all about. The only problem, unless you make routine automobile maintenance your life, is keeping track of the various tasks so that you will know when they are required again. One very effective method used by many serious do-it-yourself auto mechanics is to keep a log book listing the necessary and routine tasks.

Table 8-1 is a sample page from an automobile maintenance log book. You can copy it or make another one up that is more in

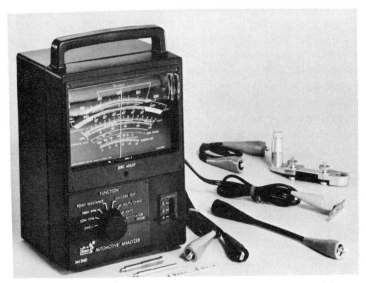

Fig. 8-10. Electronic testing gear for tuning automobiles (courtesy of Sears Roebuck & Co.).

tune to your personal needs. Basically, you want to know when you last performed a specific maintenance task such as changing the engine oil and oil filter. It only takes a few minutes to jot down the date and mileage of your vehicle when you perform this maintenance. Whenever you have an idea that certain parts or fluids need to be changed, you can check the log book to be certain of the time and mileage interval.

A log book is also a handy place to keep track of the type or make of parts you are using. For example, if you use Champion Spark Plugs on one particular tuneup, you can check them somewhere down the line and see if they are holding up. You are very likely to learn that Bosch Spark Plugs out-perform Champion Spark Plugs.

Table 8-1. Page From an Automobile Maintenance Log Book.

DATE	SPEEDOMETER READING	OIL	TYPE	OIL FILTER	PLUGS	POINTS	FILTER AIR	PCV	CAP	ROTOR	TRANS FLUID	TIRES TYPE
2/7	63,000	X	QS	X	X	X				,X		
4/2	70,000	X	QS	X			X				X	

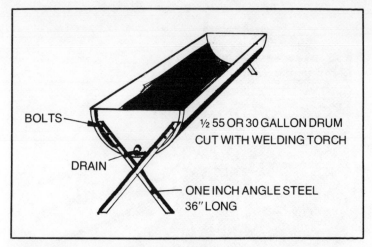

BOLTS

DRAIN

½ 55 OR 30 GALLON DRUM
CUT WITH WELDING TORCH

ONE INCH ANGLE STEEL
36" LONG

Fig. 8-11. Plans for a parts cleaning unit.

By keeping track of both interval and type of parts you are using, you can do your own comparison study and eventually learn which parts work best for your particular automobile. Routine automobile maintenance and repairs (as required) is the key to an energy efficient vehicle. By keeping track of when you are performing these tasks, you will find yourself well on the road to doing all that you can to save money and costly repairs.

For more information on do-it-yourself car maintenance, see TAB book No. 1029, *The Complete Handbook Of Practical Car Repair.*

Chapter 9
Plywood
Project Plans

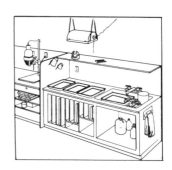

Throughout this book I have discussed specific types of home studios and workshops. Each chapter has a particular hobby, craft or function as its center. In each of these chapters I covered some of the better ways of setting up an entire room as a work center. In this chapter, I would like to offer additional suggestions for storage and small workshops in an effort to help you create the space you need.

In days gone by, it was relatively easy to sell a home and invest in a larger one as general space requirements increased. At the present time, however, it has become painfully clear to most homeowners that the price of a larger home is beyond the realm of possibilities. As a result of this, many homeowners now add on to their present homes to create the additional space they require.

Still another alternative is to better utilize existing space by making it more efficient. For example, two of the projects in this chapter explain how to build a room divider. By seperating a large room into two or more sections—with the partitions themselves being useable storage or work space—you have made one large room into at least two more efficient spaces. And you have done this for the very low cost of the plywood, glue, nails and some paint.

All of the projects in this chapter employ plywood as a basic building material. Therefore, I will discuss some of the grades and types of plywood that are best suited for these projects. Plywood is a very useful building material that has allowed carpenters and builders to accomplish tasks with seemingly lightning speed. Laying subflooring is one example.

Softwood plywood is a flat panel made from a number of thin sheets of wood veneer. It is glued under pressure with the grain of each sheet perpendicular to the grain of adjacent sheets. This cross bonding produces great strength in both directions and the glueline forms a bond that is actually stronger than the wood itself.

Plywood is truly one of the most amazing of all modern building materials. It is split-proof and it will not easily puncture. Pound for pound, a plywood panel is one of the strongest building materials made. It is rigid, stable and weighs far less than most metals, lumber or hardboard of equivalent strength. It is easily worked, nailed, glued, and finished. Plywood is also easily obtained at any lumber yard in the country.

The most common size for a sheet of plywood is 4 feet wide by 8 feet long. Many home improvement centers and lumber yards will also sell a half-sheet (4' x 4') especially in the shop grades of plywood. Thicknesses range from one-fourth inch to three-fourth inch. Generally, plywood is available in two basic types: interior and exterior grades. The basic differences are that the glue used for exterior grades of plywood is waterproof and not effected by moisture. Interior grades of plywood often use lower veneer grades and a glue that is less than totally waterproof. The general rule is that exterior grades of plywood can be used anywhere, while interior grades are limited to those areas and projects that do not have waterproofing of materials as a prerequisite.

Based on the above information, it is easy to see why many do-it-yourselfers tend to overbuy plywood. They commonly substitute exterior grades for interior grades on the theory that if exterior grades will stand up to the weather, they will do even better indoors. Unfortunately, this can be a costly presumption. Except where moisture or humidity is a problem—such as in the bathroom or kitchen—interior grades of plywood will perform just as well in the relatively controlled environment of the home. Possibly of greater importance, interior grades of plywood are generally lower priced than exterior grades. Practically all of the plywood produced in the United States is inspected by the American Plywood Association or some other certifying agency and it bears a special agency grade stamp. You can therefore assume that plywood is one product that you can buy with confidence and that it will perform as specified.

All of the plywood projects in this chapter can be made from interior grade plywood except where noted in the materials list for specific projects. Some of the projects call for plywood that is of a grade with one finished side. In those cases, only one part of the project is visible. For those projects, grade designations such as A-B or A-D are suitable. For those projects where both sides of the project will be seen, the grade designation of the plywood should be A-A. This means that both the face and the back of the plywood panel is finished with a high quality veneer.

Because all of the projects in this chapter are assembled with nails and glue, I will discuss some of the different types of adhesives currently available to the do-it-yourselfer. Currently, there are three types of glue which are suitable for various woodworking projects. These include: solvent glue, water based glue and hide glue.

Solvent glues consist of an adhesive base (vinyl resin or acrylic resin) and a solvent which makes the glue spreadable. As the solvent in these glues evaporates, the adhesive sets. One easy way to identify solvent glues is to check the container label. There will always be a reference to at least one of the following ingredients: toluene, methyl ethyl ketone, or acetone. Of the two basic types of solvent glues, acrylic resin base is a bit stronger than vinyl base. Solvent base glues—such as many types of contact cement—are highly flammable and others are toxic. When using these fast acting glues, it always makes sense to heed all cautions on the container label.

Water base glues are similar to solvent base glues as far as strength is concerned, but they take much longer to setup and harden. This is actually a real aid for the woodworker in that the pieces of a project can be positioned with greater freedom.

Most water base glues take about 12 to 24 hours to harden and for this reason the project must be clamped securely to prevent movement of the pieces as the glue sets up. Water base glues are probably the least expensive of all adhesives to buy and use. Additionally, all water base adhesives are non-toxic and non-flammable. They are very safe to use.

Undoubtedly, the most popular brand of water base adhesive is Elmer's Glue-All, the famous white glue. This is a good general purpose glue with many uses around the home. For woodworking projects, Elmer's Professional Carpenters Wood Glue is a slightly better choice. I recommend it for all of the projects in this chapter.

Hide glue, or animal glue as it is often called, is actually made from the hooves, bones and hides of various animals. Hide glue is one of the oldest types of adhesive and there are several ways in which it is sold: liquid, powder and flake.

The most practical form of hide glue for the do-it-yourselfer is the liquid form. It can be used straight from the container providing the ambient temperature is between 65 and 75 degrees Fahrenheit. This is an excellent glue for woodworking projects but, surprisingly not many do-it-yourselfers use it. This is probably because hide glue adhesive has an odor which many people find objectionable.

Hide glue is similar to water base adhesive in that it does not set up quickly and clamping of the project is necessary. One of the features of hide glue is that it is one of the best gap filling adhesives available. If joints are not exactly perfect and tight, the hide glue will take up the difference and still result in a strong joint.

All of the plywood projects in this chapter give materials needed and dimensions of the project parts. While it is entirely possible to modify these specifications to fit special needs—the first room divider project for example—it will be best to build these projects according to the plans given.

The actual cuts required for any given project should ideally be made on a good table saw. The second best way to cut up the pieces is with a hand-held circular saw. However, some type of guidance system should be used to insure straight cuts. If you do not own a table saw or hand-held circular saw, your best bet will be to have the lumber yard custom cut the pieces for you.

Simply bring a copy of the plans along with you when you go to buy the plywood and have the cutting shop at the lumber yard do the work for you. While there will be a charge for cutting, it will usually only be a few dollars and you can be certain that the pieces will be cut properly.

All of the projects—which were provided by the Georgia-Pacific Corporation—are simple to assemble provided you have a clear understanding of what you are trying to achieve. Keep this book handy during assembly so you can consult the diagram as you work.

After your plywood project has been assembled, you will want to finish it off with some type of coating. For all practical purposes, you can either paint it a solid color or stain it and then apply a clear coating of varnish or polyurethane. Your main intention should be to finish off the project so that it will blend in with the surrounding furniture and fixtures. While the type of finish you choose will have a bearing on the amount of surface preparation necessary—clear finishes generally require a more thorough sanding—there are a number of things that must be done to all plywood projects before any finish coating is applied.

Surface preparation includes all of the operations that are necessary to prepare the plywood project for a coating of finish material. In many cases, this will mean filling the ends of the project—where the edge of the plywood panel is visible—sanding, applying a first coat of finish (primer if the project is to be painted a solid color or stain if the finish coating will be clear), sanding lightly and then applying a finish coating (often at least two coats).

To fill the edges of exposed plywood in a project, you will need a special edge filler material. There are several types on the market at this time. One brand is Zar Wood Patch. Begin spreading the filler material along and into the edge of the plywood with a putty knife or spatula. It is important to force the filler into the end grain of the plywood so that it will penetrate for a good bond. You should exercise a certain amount of care as you apply the filler. The intention is simply to fill the exposed edge rather than build up the edge. After the filler has dried, the edge should be sanded with 220-grit sandpaper—in a sanding block—to create a smooth, flat, square edge.

The plywood edge filling method should be performed for all exposed edges on the plywood project. Most edge filling materials designed for this work will take a stain well. If the project is to be painted a solid color, you will not be able to see any edge grain or joints if the filler material has been applied properly and then sanded smooth with the surrounding areas of the project.

The next step in surface preparation is to sand, sand, sand. In addition to the edges and joints, you will have to sand the body of the project itself. Your goal is to achieve as flat and smooth a surface as possible. You will be able to do this by sanding with the grain and working with finer grades of sandpaper. You can use a hand sanding block for small areas, but you will find the work will go much quicker if you use an electric sander for larger work. In any event, the final sanding should be done with a paper of about 220-grit. When all of the sanding has been completed and just prior to applying the stain or primer, the project should be vacuumed to remove all traces of sanding dust.

If the project will be stained and later coated with a clear finish, you will have to seal the pores of the plywood before staining. It is entirely possible to use a stain that both seals and stains in one operation. You should investigate such a stain at your local paint store. If the project will be painted a solid color, the first coating will be with a good quality, oil base primer.

After the first coating has dried—either sealer/stain or primer—the next step is to lightly sand the surface so that the finish coating will be able to adhere well. This can easily be done with either 300-grit sandpaper or with fine steel wool. The intention here is simply to rough up the surface slightly and, as the experts say, "give it some tooth." After light sanding, the surface must be either vacuumed or wiped with a tack cloth. This step is necessary to remove all traces of sanding dust. Omit this step and the finish coating will have a rough texture.

A tack cloth is a very handy item for removing dust just prior to applying a varnish (as well as sanding between coats). You can buy a tack cloth at any paint store or you can make one in a few minutes as explained below.

A tack cloth is simply a piece of cotton cloth about 1 x 2 feet in size. Half of an old pillow case is ideal for a tack cloth, providing it is clean. Begin making a tack cloth by washing the material in soap and water. Rinse the cloth and make sure that no soap residue remains. Then wring it out until it is almost dry. Next, pour about 2 ounces of turpentine into the cloth and work it until it is evenly distributed. Then wring it dry once again. The next step is to pour about the same amount of varnish into the cloth. Work the varnish thoroughly into the cloth until it is uniformly spread into the material. The cloth will have an even yellow cast when it is about right.

As the name implies, a *tack cloth* must remain tacky during use. If it should become dry as you use it to pick up dust, you can rejuvenate it by adding small amounts of turpentine and water to keep it damp. If the cloth is too damp, hang it up to dry slightly. When not in use, you can store your tack cloth in a glass container that is tightly closed.

Because of its stickiness, you can use a tack cloth to pick up dust and other small particles that would impair the finish coating. A tack cloth actually does a better job of vacuuming and should be used after sanding between coats of paint or varnish.

Apply the finish coating—either clear or solid color paint—to the project and let it dry undisturbed for about one day. Inspect the work and, if necessary, give it another coat. After the paint or varnish has dried for at least one day, the project is ready to be pressed into service.

MATERIALS LIST

Makes one full set of (modules)

Qty.

2 Panels ½" x 4' 8' Interior Grade Plywood (good two sides) A-A

1 Panel ½" x 4' x 4' Interior Grade Plywood (good two sides) A-A

Glue

Wood Filler

Fine Sandpaper

4d Finishing Nails

Clear Sealer or Interior Semi-gloss Enamel Paint

Fig. 9-1. Boxes and cubes example and material list (courtesy of Georgia- Pacific).

The following plywood projects can be applied to any type of workshop or studio in your home. Some of these projects—such as the storage cubes—might even be suitable for your living room. While some of these are rather limited in application, you might be able to find just the solution to some of your space limitation problems and have a special area for working on smaller projects. At the very least, many of these projects are inexpensive ways of helping you to better utilize your existing space.

PROJECT #1: BOXES AND CUBES

Plywood boxes and cubes are very simple to build and all of the cubes shown in Fig. 9-1 can be made from two and one-half sheets of one-half inch thick plywood (A-A grade). Once you have made a few of these cubes, you will discover their versatility. A few cubes can serve as storage units when they are stacked in a corner. Or stack in two columns and span the space between with a shelf or desk. You can use a bank of cubes as a room divider and storage wall. The storage combinations you can achieve with these easy-to-build cubes are infinite.

Simply follow the diagram (Fig. 9-2) and you can cut all of the parts needed for a full set of cubes. Spend enough time to make sure all cuts are exact and then the boxes will go together smoothly. The end result will be a storage system that is quite functional.

To help you build the cubes, all joints should be glued and nailed with 4d finishing nails. Countersink all nail heads with a punch. Then fill the holes to conceal.

When you finish off each cube, it is important that all exposed edges of the plywood be filled with special filler—as described earlier in this chapter. After the filler has dried, each edge should be sanded smooth. The cubes lend themselves well to being finished off with a semigloss paint. White is the most popular color.

PROJECT #2: A SIMPLE FOLD DOWN TABLE

Here is a handy little fold down table or desk that you can build very easily. It is a useful addition to any workshop or studio. Because the table folds up and out of the way, you will not have to sacrifice valuable floor space. This entire project (Fig. 9-3) can be made from one half sheet (4 x 4 feet) of one-half inch thick plywood that is sanded on one side (A-B or A-C grade).

The few special instructions required for this fold down table are as follows. Start off by carefully measuring and cutting all of the

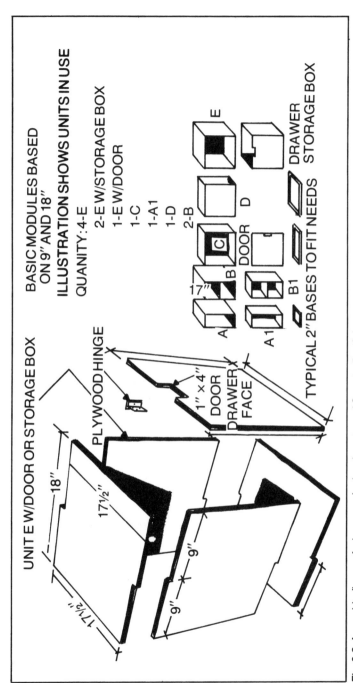

Fig. 9-2. Assembly diagram for boxes and cubes (courtesy of Georgia-Pacific).

MATERIALS LIST

Qty.
1 Panel ½" × 4' × 4' Plywood
  A-B or A-C Grade
1 21" Piano Hinge
1 27" Piano Hinge
4 1" Metal Angle Brackets
  Molly Bolts (if required)
  Fine Sandpaper
  White Glue
  6d Finishing Nails
  Interior Semi-gloss Enamel
  Paint

Fig. 9-3. Simple fold down table with a materials list (courtesy of Georgia-Pacific).

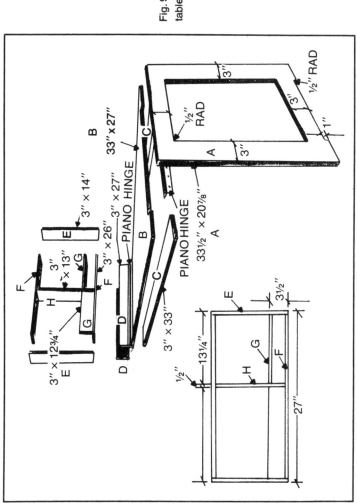

Fig. 9-4. Assembly diagram for fold down table (courtesy of Georgia-Pacific).

287

pieces required and indicated in the diagram (Fig. 9-4). Then assemble the cabinet pieces using both glue and 6d finishing nails. Notch the table top (section B) so that the upright base (A) fits snugly into place. Then glue and nail the braces (C) into their indicated position.

Next, attach the table top to the support brace and the wall brace (D) using the piano hinges. To complete the project, the remaining wall brace (D) is attached directly to the wall using either molly bolts or by screwing the brace directly into the wall studs.

Attach the wall brace (D) on the table top to the now secure wall piece (D) and the table is ready to be pressed into service after it has been primed and painted. You will have to fill all exposed edges of the plywood table and cabinet before finishing. A good quality semigloss enamel makes a nice, durable finish.

PROJECT #3: A VERTICAL STORAGE CABINET

This is a good basic storage cabinet for any workshop or studio. The project can be completed in just a few hours. Because this cabinet is made from exterior grade plywood, it can be used in any room or even outside the home in a carport. While Fig. 9-5 shows the cabinet being used to store sporting equipment, it can easily be pressed into service for storing long pieces of equipment in the photographic light studio. Tripods, light stands and rolls of seamless backdrop paper will easily fit. A simple to make "drop bar" on one side of the cabinet will help to hold vertically stored items in place.

It is a simple cabinet to build and one that will hold an enormous amount of hard to store items. Exercise care in cutting the pieces and assembling and then finish off to blend in with surroundings (Fig. 9-6).

PROJECT #4: A FUNCTIONAL POTTING TABLE

This is a very useful, illuminated, potting table that is simple to build. Note in the materials list that this potting table uses 2 x 4s and pegboard as well as exterior grade plywood. A little more work is required for building this table, but once completed it can serve as a work center for many gardening needs from starting seeds to repotting established plants. Consider using a special fluorescent light fixture and you will be able to grow plants on the table as well.

Special instructions for building this table include the following points. Use only water proof glue for assembling the pieces.

Materials List

2 panels ¾″ × 4′ × 8′ G-P
  Exterior Good Two Sides
  plywood
1 piece ¼″ × 3′ × 8′ G-P
  Exterior Good One Side
  plywood
2½′, ½″ quarter round nailing
strip
1 lb, 1½″ finishing nails
1 lb, 2″ finishing nails
Glue   Wood filler
1 door bolt
4 pin hinges
1, ¾″ hinge for drop bar
Clothes pins as required
Paint as required

Fig. 9-5. Vertical storage cabinet with a materials list (courtesy of Georgia- Pacific).

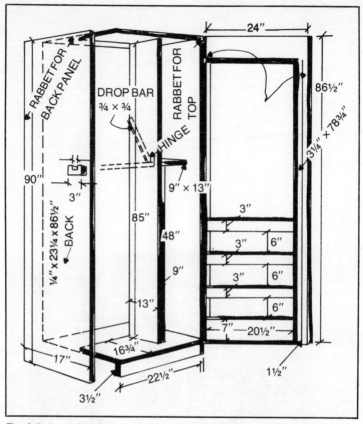

Fig. 9-6. Assembly diagram for vertical storage cabinet (courtesy of Georgia-Pacific).

Resorcinol glue is recommended. The soil box on the left-hand side of the potting table should be either lined with plastic sheeting or painted (inside) with creosote or similar waterproofing substance. Consider covering the top of this work table with plastic laminate material (such as Formica Brand) so that the surface will be easy to wipe clean. Add heavy-duty swivel type casters to the bottom of the table so that it can be wheeled anywhere.

The basic construction tasks can be done as follows. Use 2 x 4 dimensional lumber (fir or pine) to make three rectangular frames—each measuring 2 x 5 feet. Cut the sides of the table from three-fourth inch thick exterior plywood according to Fig. 9-8.

Assemble the frames to the sides using both waterproof glue and galvanized finishing nails. Cover the shelves (frames) with

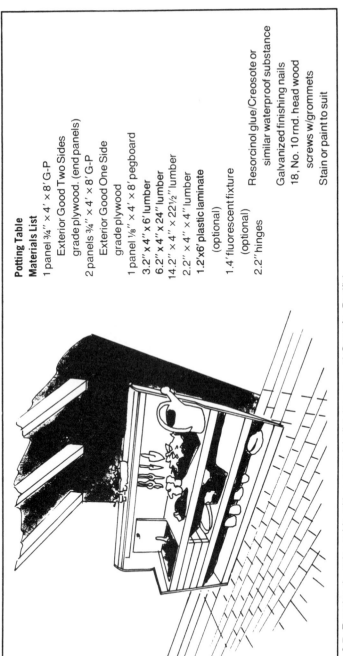

Potting Table
Materials List

1 panel ¾" × 4' × 8' G-P
   Exterior Good Two Sides
   grade plywood. (end panels)
2 panels ¾" × 4' × 8' G-P
   Exterior Good One Side
   grade plywood
1 panel ⅛" × 4' × 8' pegboard
3.2" × 4" × 6' lumber
6.2" × 4" × 24" lumber
14.2" × 4" × 22½" lumber
2.2" × 4" × 4" lumber
1.2'x6' plastic laminate
   (optional)
1.4' fluorescent fixture
   (optional)
2.2" hinges

Resorcinol glue/Creosote or
   similar waterproof substance
Galvanized finishing nails
18, No. 10 rnd. head wood
   screws w/grommets
Stain or paint to suit

Fig. 9-7. Functional potting table with a materials list (courtesy of Georgia- Pacific).

291

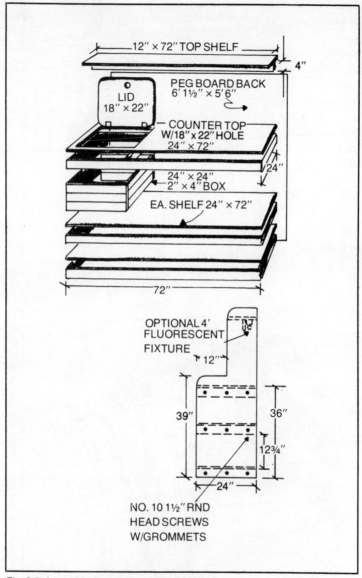

Fig. 9-8. Assembly diagram for potting table (courtesy of Georgia-Pacific).

three-fourth inch thick plywood. The next step is to cover the back of this workbench with a sheet of pegboard. The project is then complete except for filling edges, sanding and coating with a primer and quality semigloss paint.

Additions to the basic potting table include a fluorescent light fixture that is 4 feet long. This will be a real aid in helping you to clearly see what you are doing on the table. You can also add a plastic pan to the soil storage area instead of simply filling with potting soil. This will allow you to easily remove and dump the soil if the need should ever arise.

The entire project should take only a few hours. Make sure that you follow the plans so that the potting table will come out as in the illustrations. One alternative for the sides of the table is shown in Fig. 9-9.

PROJECT #5: A SIMPLE ROOM DIVIDER

This is a decorative wooden screen that can be used to direct traffic to create a small private area for working on projects (while you are still basically in the room) or as a shield inside an entry door

Fig. 9-9. Alternate sides for potting table (courtesy of Georgia-Pacific).

(Fig. 9-10). One of the features of all room dividers is that they help to define space.

Figure 9-11 shows one of the two ways of building and installing this particular room divider. The basic frame is constructed from 1 x 2 inch lumber and the special grooved faced exterior paneling (Texture 1-11 or T 1-11 for short) is attached to this frame. Next, the entire frame is hung from the ceiling using eye bolts and strong wire.

Another way to build this basic room divider is to begin by building a wall out of 2 x 4s and then covering these studs with the T 1-11. This second way of building a room divider results in a much sturdier partition, but also one that is permanent. The T 1-11 exterior siding plywood used for this room divider will finish quite nicely with a wood stain that is followed by several coats of a clear flat finish such as polyurethane.

There are a number of variations to this basic room divider design. A less expensive alternative, for example, would be to cover the frame with gypsum panels rather than plywood. Still another possibility is to build this room divider 4 feet high rather than from floor to ceiling. This half wall will serve almost the same purpose while at the same time not defining the room quite as much. Use your imagination and the basic room divider design and come up with a partition that is tailored to your needs.

PROJECT #6: A ROOM DIVIDER WITH PLENTY OF STORAGE

This project (Fig. 9-12) is a little more advanced than the previous room divider. You also get a great deal of storage space. At the same time you will be partially dividing a room into more functional units.

As you can tell from Fig. 9-13, there are quite a few cuts required for this project. Therefore it is important that you make certain of your measurements and that you cut with precision. If you do not have a table saw at your disposal, I would recommend that you have all of the pieces cut at your local lumber yard. This will add a few additional dollars to the total cost of the project, but at least you can be reasonably certain that the pieces will be cut according to plan.

Just as much care, and then some, is required during the assembly of this room divider. Work very carefully and with the diagram close at hand. White glue (water base) and 6d finishing nails are the materials you will require for assembly.

After the room divider is all put together and the glue joints have dried—at least overnight—you can begin the finishing. The

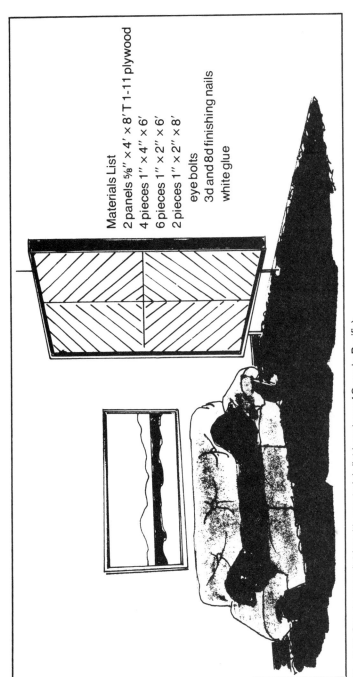

Materials List
2 panels ⅝" × 4' × 8' T 1-11 plywood
4 pieces 1" × 4" × 6'
6 pieces 1" × 2" × 6'
2 pieces 1" × 2" × 8'
eye bolts
3d and 8d finishing nails
white glue

Fig. 9-10. Simple room divider with a materials list (courtesy of Georgia-Pacific).

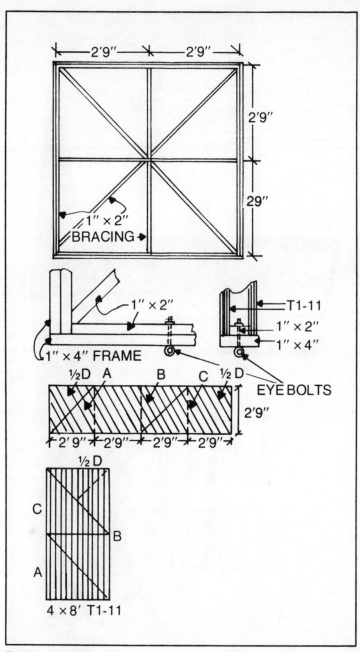

Fig. 9-11. Assembly diagram for a simple room divider (courtesy of Georgia-Pacific).

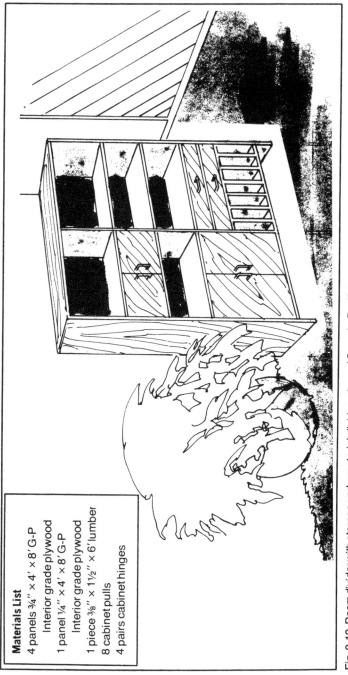

Materials List

4 panels ¾" × 4' × 8' G-P
   Interior grade plywood
1 panel ¼" × 4' × 8' G-P
   Interior grade plywood
1 piece ⅜" × 1½" × 6' lumber
8 cabinet pulls
4 pairs cabinet hinges

Fig. 9-12. Room divider with storage and a materials list (courtesy of Georgia-Pacific).

bulk of this work will be filling the exposed edges of the plywood. It is very important to work carefully. Keep in mind that your intention is to simply fill the end grain of the plywood and not build it up.

Sand all parts of the divider and either stain and cover with a clear coating or prime and paint a suitable color. White is a good basic color that will blend in well with most types of decor. On the other hand, if you prefer a stain, go with a lighter tone so that the natural beauty of the veneer can show through well.

If you decide to build this room divider with storage space, allow yourself plenty of time for the project. Accomplish all cutting

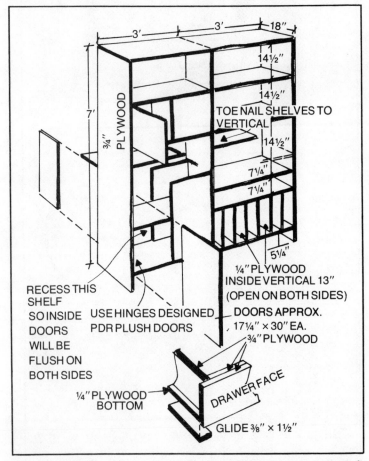

Fig. 9-13. Assembly diagram for a room divider with storage (courtesy of Georgia-Pacific).

Fig. 9-14. A suggestion for a below-the-stairs storage cabinet (courtesy of Georgia-Pacific).

and assembly tasks in an unhurried manner. Then finish off the project with several coats of finish material. If you take the care necessary to build this room divider according to the diagram, you will end up with a functional piece of furniture that will easily give a lifetime of silent service.

PROJECT #7: BELOW STAIRS STORAGE CABINETS

One area of the home that is often overlooked as a good storage area is the space found under existing stairways. In most cases this area—most commonly in the basement—does not provide any usable floor space, but it is an ideal spot for a built-in closet or storage shelves and cabinets. It is important to do thorough planning with a ruler and paper before you begin such a project.

Because your stairway might be different than that shown in Fig. 9-14, it might be helpful to talk rather generally about some of the things necessary for transforming any stairway into useful storage.

Use 2 x 4 inch dimensional lumber to frame out under the stairs. Attach the studs to the top of the stair stringer and to a plate along the bottom. Space studs 16 or 24 inches apart. Internal shelving can be made from three-fourth inch thick plywood (any grade) or from chip board. Cover the inside of the cabinet with either one-fourth inch thick decorative paneling or gypsum board. The outside face of the cabinet—that which is visible—can be covered with any number of finish materials including gypsum (later painted or covered with wallpaper), paneling or even rough sawn boards for a rustic look.

Doors for the cabinet can be easily made by first constructing a frame from 1 x 3 inch lumber. Then cover these with one-fourth inch thick unfinished plywood or paneling.

To really customize the cabinet, consider what will be stored in the space. Then build the type of shelves or racks to hold the material. Plan the project carefully so that you end up with a cabinet that is both functional as well as one that will blend in with the surroundings.

Chapter 10
Building Materials

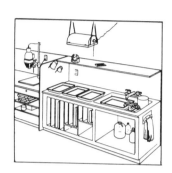

Anyone who plans to attempt any project around the home should not only have a knowledge of construction techniques and the use of tools, but also know how to choose the proper material for a particular project. Therefore, this chapter will deal with building materials, masonry materials, choosing grades and types of lumber, joints, fasteners, wood preservatives, etc.

LUMBER

Wood is used for such basic building materials as solid lumber, plywood, particle board and hardboard. All of these materials will find use for projects around the home, but the handyman must know how to select and order these basic materials.

Most woods for furniture must have good appearance, be comparatively free from warp, excessive shrinking and swelling, and have sufficient hardness to resist swelling. Therefore, most furniture woods are hardwoods; that is, the wood of any broadleaf (deciduous) tree. Softwoods are generally used for paneling, built-ins, trim, framing, etc. They are the wood from cone-bearing (evergreen) trees. Following is a list of some of the more common woods in use today.

SOFTWOODS

Douglas Fir. Douglas fir is somewhat more difficult to work with hand tools than soft pine, but it holds fastenings well and can be glued satisfactorily. It is used for lumber, timbers, piling and plywood. The heartwood is orange-red to red.

Ponderosa Pine. This wood is not easily split and has a good resistance to nail withdrawal; it also glues easily. Its principal use is for lumber and veneer. Knotty ponderosa pine has come into wide use as paneling for interiors. The heartwood is yellowish to orange-brown.

Shortleaf Pine. Shortleaf pine has the widest distribution of the southern pines and ranks with the lightest of the important southern pines. Its principal uses include lumber for interior finishes, ceilings, frames, sashes, sheathings, subflooring, and joists as well as for boxes and crates. Many telephone poles are shortleaf pine. The heartwood ranges from yellow to light brown.

Sugar Pine. This is a West Coast tree that is very lightweight—averaging about 25 pounds per cubic foot. The wood is used almost entirely for lumber in buildings, boxes and crates, sashes, doors, frames, general millwork and foundry patterns. It is suitable for all phases of house construction. The heartwood is light brown to pale reddish brown.

Western White Pine. As the name implies, this tree grows in the Western part of the continent. It is moderately light in weight. Practically all these trees are sawed into lumber. The lower grades are used for subflooring as well as wall and roof sheathing. The highgrade wood is used for siding, trim and paneling. The heartwood is cream colored to reddish brown.

Redwood. Redwood grows along the California coast. This is one in a group of woods that has an outstanding decay resistance and a high resistance to termites. It's one of the best lumbers to use on outdoor projects such as outdoor furniture, house siding, etc.

Sitka Spruce. Here's another West Coast tree which is used for lumber, barrel making and paper pulp. A lot of this wood also goes into boxes and crates. The heartwood is light pinkish yellow to pale brown.

Other softwoods include cedar, cypress, hemlock, and several species of white and "yellow" pine. Cedar—especially red cedar— has the same decay and termite resistance as California redwood although the logs are much smaller. Therefore, wide boards are rare.

HARDWOODS

White Ash. This deciduous tree grows throughout the Eastern United States and is a heavy wood with an average weight of 42 pounds per cubic foot. The wood is noted for its excellent bending qualities, its ability to hold fastenings, and its resistance to splitting. It is standard wood for canoe paddles, handles for shovels, hoes, racks, baseball bats, etc. It is good for bent parts on outdoor furniture.

Basswood. Basswood is a lightweight hardwood, but weak and moderately stiff. Most basswood is used for boxes and crates, but some goes into doors and general millwork. Heartwood is creamy white to creamy brown.

American Beech. This is one of the heavier woods in the United States, rated high in strength and shock resistance. It is used for lumber, distilled products, veneer, railroad ties, pulpwood, barrel making and furniture. It is especially suitable for food containers because it does not import taste or odor. The heartwood is white with a reddish tinge.

Yellow Birch. Yellow birch is heavy and hard and is therefore difficult to work with hand tools. It is used principally for lumber, veneer and crossties. Because of its pleasing grain pattern and ability to take a high polish, it is widely used for cabinets and furniture. The heartwood is light reddish-brown.

Black Cherry. The wood is stiff and strong, making it difficult to work with hand tools. The majority of black cherry is sawed into lumber to make furniture, woodenware, and interior finishes. The heartwood is light to dark reddish brown.

Cottonwood. Eastern, swamp, and black cottonwood are moderately light in weight. Most trees are cut into lumber and veneer and then remanufactured into containers and furniture. The heartwood is white to light grayish brown.

American Elm. This tree, with moderately heavy wood, grows in most of the United States. It is used principally in the manufacture of furniture and containers. Due to its excellent bending qualities, the wood has been used for barrels and kegs. The heartwood is brown to dark brown.

Hickory. The hickories grow throughout the Eastern United States with 40 percent grown in the lower Mississippi Valley region. The wood is very heavy, hard, strong and exceedingly high in shock resistance. The majority of the true hickory goes into the making of tool handles. Other uses include farm implements, athletic goods and lawn furniture . Heartwood is brown to reddish brown.

Mahogany. African mahogany comes from the Gold, Ivory, and Nigerian coasts of West Africa. West Indies mahogany comes primarily from British Honduras, Bermuda, and the keys of Southern Florida. Tropical American mahogany comes from Mexico, Central America and parts of Peru. It is of moderate density and hardness and has excellent working and finishing characteristics. A high resistance to decay is one of its most important properties. It is used in quality furniture of all styles, and is one of the best woods for boat construction. The heartwood varies from a pale to a deep reddish brown.

Mahogany, Philippine. This wood is grown primarily in the Philippine Islands and is very similar to genuine mahogany in general properties, although it is somewhat coarser in texture. It is a little more difficult to finish, but it is inexpensive, easy to work with and simple to glue. The heartwood varies in color from pale to dark reddish-brown for some varieties while others are light-red to straw-colored.

Sugar Maple. The sugar maple grows in a large portion of the U.S. with its highest concentration in the Northeast and the lake states. It is heavy and hard and has a high resistance to shock. Sugar maple ranks high in nail withdrawal resistance and glues easily. It takes stain readily and is capable of high polish. It is used principally for lumber, distilled products, veneer and crossties. Most of the lumber is made into furniture, flooring, woodenware and novelties. It is especially suitable for bowling alleys and dance floors. The heartwood is light reddish brown.

White Oak. The white oak family grows mainly in the Eastern half of the United States, although some species are found in some of the Northwestern states. The wood is heavy, very hard and must be seasoned carefully to avoid warping. Most white oak is made into lumber for flooring, furniture and general millwork. It is the leading wood for the construction of boats and ships. White oak is grayish brown.

Red Oak. Red oaks are generally found east of the Great Plains and are similar in properties to the white oak family. Most of the red oak cut in this country is converted into flooring, furniture, millwork, caskets and coffins, boats and woodenware. Preservative-treated red oak is used extensively for crossties and fence posts. The heartwood is grayish brown with a reddish tint.

Pecan. Pecan is primarily a southern wood, but it can be found in most of the Eastern United States. It is a heavy wood with an average weight of 48 pounds per cubic foot. It is one of the toughest and strongest American woods in common use. Pecan is used for furniture and can be stained and finished to resemble walnut. The heartwood is reddish-brown in color, often with darker streaks.

Sweetgum. Sweetgum grows in the eastern, southern and central states. It is a moderately heavy wood and has a low decay resistance. It is high in ability to resist splitting by nails and screws. Lumber, veneer and plywood are its principal uses. It is reddish brown and variegated with streaks of darker color.

Black Walnut. Black walnut grows in the eastern, central and southern states. It is classified as a heavy wood and is hard, stiff and strong with great durability. It finishes beautifully with a handsome grain pattern. The outstanding use of black walnut is for furniture, but large amounts are used for gunstocks and interior finish. The heartwood is chocolate brown and occasionally has darker, sometimes purplish-streaks.

Yellow-Poplar. Yellow-poplar grows in many eastern and southern states. It is moderately light in weight and has an excellent reputation for taking and holding paint. It stains and glues quite satisfactorily. It does not impart taste or odor to foods and therefore is used for food containers. Other uses are lumber, veneer and pulpwood. It is brownish yellow with a greenish tinge.

Lumber-grading methods vary, but usually follow the following method:

Select Lumber

☐ 1 and 2 Clear: Highest quality lumber—generally clear and free from defects. Suitable for natural finishes and fine cabinetwork.

☐ C select: May have minor imperfections. One side may be without blemish.

☐ D select: Lowest finishing grade. Has minor defects and blemishes, but ideally suited for painted finishing.

Common Lumber

☐ No 1: May have small, sound knots. Takes paint well. Usable with minimum waste.

☐ No. 2: Utility grade. Has larger and more numerous knots. Often used for knotted paneling.

☐ No. 3: Numerous defects. Some waste in use.

☐ No. 4: Lowest grade usable in building.

☐ Bottom quality. Suitable only for crating, rough concrete forms, etc.

PLYWOOD

Plywood is probably the most versatile wood that the homeowner can buy. As mentioned previously, Douglas fir is used extensively for plywood; it is the least expensive type manufactured. Other kinds include hard-wood-faced plywood, which are available in many beautiful hardwoods.

All plywoods have their own grading system and it is important to know these when ordering material. Interior plywood, for example, should be used only in dry locations, while exterior plywood is for use in damp (or wet) locations. The laminated layers will not come apart on exterior plywood even when placed in boiling water. Tables 10-1 and 10-2 give the various grades of fir plywood—for both interior and exterior use.

HARDBOARD

Hardboard is a dense wood sheet material which can be used for wall paneling, counter tops, doors, drawer bottoms, floors and many other workshop projects. It can be cut with hand or power saws and can be nailed, screwed, drilled, routed, planed, sanded, etc. —just like any other wood product.

Because hardboard is entirely free from grain, it won't split or crack. Furthermore, it will bend around framework or take self-supporting bends. However, it requires that nails or screws be secured to some other material because the hardboard, itself, will not hold nails or screws.

When cutting hardboard, use a colored pencil to mark the cutting line. The dark surface will hide conventional lead pencil marks. Use a fine-tooth crosscut or combination blade (8 to 12 points to the inch); hold the hand saw at a flat angle and bend the hardboard slightly to overcome saw "buckle."

The rough edges from a cut can be smoothed with a file or rasp or rounded with a small plane. Always use a shallow set on the plane and then sandpaper it. You might also want to apply a wash-coat of shellac before final dressing. Then, practically any finish normally applied to wood surfaces may be used to finish the hardboard.

FASTENINGS

The basic types of nails are wire nails, box nails, finishing nails, and casing nails as shown in Fig. 10-1. Common wire nails are used for rough, heavy work. Box nails are thinner and therefore

Table 10-1. Grades and Uses of Exterior Plywood.

Grade	Uses
A-A	Outdoor, where appearance of both sides is important.
A-B	Alternate for A-A, where appearance of one side is less important.
A-C	Siding, soffits, fences. One "good" side grade.
B-C	For utility uses such as farm buildings, some kinds of fences, etc.
C-C	Excellent base for tile and linoleum, backing for wall covering.
C-C	Unsanded, for backing and rough construction exposed to weather.
B-B	Concrete forms. Re-use until wood literally wears out.

will not split the wood as easy as common nails, but are used for the same purpose. The small head on finishing nails may be set below the surface. Casing nails are used for trim.

Common screw types include the flathead, which is set flush with the surface; oval head, which is more decorative; and the roundhead, which does not require countersinking. All of these types are shown in Fig. 10-2.

Some nails—like gypsum-board fasteners—have tapered threads and broad flat heads for better holding (see Fig. 10-3). Masonry nails are threaded and made of high-carbon steel for driving into masonry; they are good for anchoring items to foundations, walls, and so forth. See Fig. 10-4.

Machine bolts have heads while a carriage bolt has a square collar that locks it against turning in wood as shown in Fig. 10-5. The machine bolt is normally used in metal and the carriage bolt in wood.

Lag screws (Fig. 10-6) have square heads for turning with a wrench or pliers and coarse threads for pre-bored holes in wood. These screws are excellent for securing wood members when a hole can't be bored clear through to accept a carriage bolt.

Hooks and eyes have a variety of uses for outdoor projects. A U-bolt, for example, is a very strong "eye" that can be used to

Table 10-2. Grades and Uses of Interior Plywood.

Grade	Uses
A-A	Cabinet doors, built-ins, furniture where both sides will show.
A-B	Alternate of A-A—one side high standard, the other, solid and smooth.
A-D	Good one side for paneling, built-ins, backing, underlay, etc.
B-D	Utility grade. Has one good side. Backing, cabinet sides, etc.
C-D	Underlay for tile, linoleum, and carpet and similar uses.
C-D	Sheathing and structural uses such as temporary enclosures, subfloor.
B-B	Concrete forms, re-use until wood wears out.

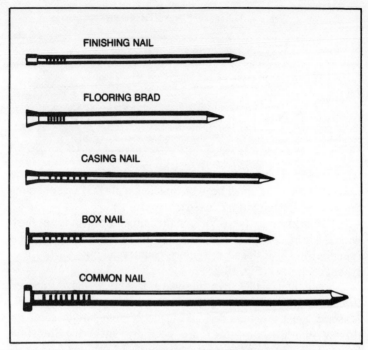

Fig. 10-1. Common types of nails used in outdoor building projects.

secure a hammock, clothesline, etc. A hook and eye is also very handy for securing wood members in place that will frequently have to be removed. For example, the roof of a dog house may have to be removed periodically to clean the interior. Four hooks and eyes placed at the corners of the roof where it attaches to the lower structure will hold the roof in place and also make it easy to remove when necessary.

Fig. 10-2. Common screw types.

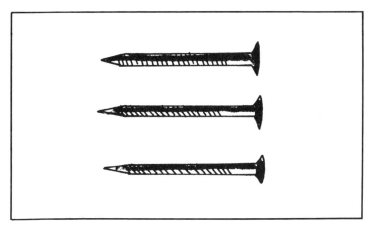

Fig. 10-3. Gypsum-board fasteners have tapered threads and broad flat heads for better holding.

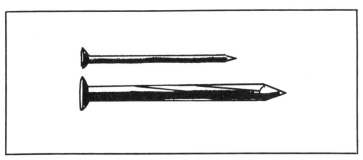

Fig. 10-4. Masonry nails are threaded and made of high-carbon steel for driving into masonry.

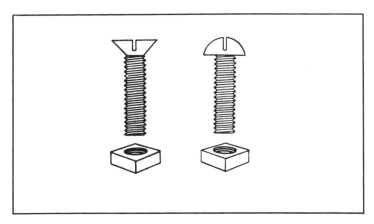

Fig. 10-5. A machine bolt.

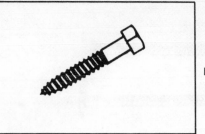

Fig. 10-6. A typical lag screw.

CONCRETE

Ready-mixed concrete is easy for the handyman to use as all that is necessary is to add water according to directions. Basically, there are three types available: mortar mix, sand mix, and gravel mix.

For large jobs, the homeowner will save money by mixing his own concrete. In general, use one part cement to two parts sand and three parts gravel. However, the job will determine the best mix to use. The following mixes are recommended for the homeowner:

☐ Footings and Foundations: The mix should consist of 1 bag of cement to 3 cubic feet sand and 5 cubic feet of gravel with the maximum aggregate size 1½″. You will need from 5 to 7 gallons of water per bag of cement, depending upon the dampness of the sand.

☐ Columns, chimneys, retaining walls, etc.: Mix proportions of cement to sand and gravel at 1:3:4; that is, one bag of cement, 3 cubic feet sand, and 4 cubic feet of gravel with 1½″ being the largest aggregate size. The amount of water will range between 4¾ gallons to 6¼ gallons— depending upon the dampness of the sand.

☐ Watertight wall, swimming pools, etc.: Mix proportions of cement to sand and gravel at 1:2:3 respectively. The amount of water will range between 4¼ to 5½ gallons.

Table 10-3. Materials Needed for Concrete.

Mix Formula	Cement (bags)	Sand (cu. ft.)	Gravel (cu. ft.)
1:3:5	4½	15	22
1:3:4	5	15	20
1:2½:3½	6	15	21
1:2:3	7¼	14¼	21
1:2:2	8	16	16

☐ Driveways, terraces, tennis courts, steps, etc.: You will need 1 bag of cement to 2½ cubic feet sand and 3½ cubic feet of gravel with the aggregate size no larger than 1 inch.

☐ Topping for pavement, steps, tennis courts, etc.: Mix 1 bag of cement to 1 cubic feet sand and 1¼ cubic feet of gravel—¾″ maximum aggregate size—and about 4½ gallons of water.

☐ Posts, garden furniture, tanks, bird baths, etc.: You will want to use a 1:2:2 mix with about 3¾ gallons of water. The largest gravel size should be ½″.

You can see that concrete ingredients consist of cement, sand, gravel and water. You can mix the ingredients on any flat, hard surface or platform. Unless you have or rent a concrete mixer, a standard wheelbarrow is hard to beat for mixing small batches of concrete around the home. Mix all the dry ingredients first and then sprinkle water over the concrete. Let it soak a minute or two before thoroughly mixing with a concrete hoe.

Once you have worked with concrete for a while you will be able to accurately judge the water needed by the way the material handles. However, never use more than indicated in the formulas. A little less won't hurt anything, but never use more water.

When planning your concrete project, calculate the amount of concrete needed in cubic yards. Then determine the amount of materials needed to obtain the required amount of ready-to-pour concrete.

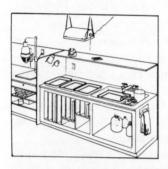

Glossary

abrasive. Any of the coated papers (sandpaper), coarse fabrics and other materials (pumice and rottenstone) or steel wool used for transforming a coarse surface into a smooth one.

air-dried lumber. Lumber that has been piled in yards or sheds for any length of time. In the United States, the minimum moisture content of thoroughly air-dried lumber is 12 to 15 percent and the average is somewhat higher. In the South, air-dried lumber might be no lower than about 19 percent.

airway. A space between roof insulation and roof sheating for the free movement of air.

alligatoring. Coarse checking pattern characterized by a slipping of the new paint coating over the old coating to the extent that the old coating can be seen through the fissures.

anchor bolts. Bolts to secure a wooden sill plate to concrete or a masonry floor or wall.

apron. The flat member of the inside trim of a window placed against the wall immediately beneath the stool.

areaway. An open subsurface space adjacent to a building used to admit light or air or as a means of access to a basement.

asphalt. A residue from evaporated petroleum. It is insoluble in water, but soluble in gasoline and it melts when heated. Used widely in building for waterproofing roof coverings of many types, exterior wall coverings, floor tile, and protecting other surfaces from moisture.

astragal. A molding that is attached to one of a pair of swinging doors, against which the other door strikes.

attic ventilators. In houses, screened openings provided to ventilate an attic space. They are located in the soffit area as inlet ventilators and in the gable end or along the ridge as outlet ventilators. They can also consist of power driven fans used as an exhaust system. (See louver).

backband. A simple molding sometimes used around the outer edge of plain rectangular casing as a decorative feature.

backfill. The replacement of excavated earth into a trench around and against a basement foundation.

balusters. Usually, small vertical members in a railing used between a top rail and the stair treads or a bottom rail.

balustrade. A railing made up of balusters, top rail, and sometimes bottom rail, often used on the edge of stairs, balconies and porches.

base (baseboard). A board placed against the wall around a room next to the floor to finish properly between floor and plaster.

base molding. Molding used to trim the upper edge of interior baseboard.

base shoe. Molding used next to the floor on interior baseboard. Sometimes called a carpet strip.

beam. A structural member transversely supporting a load.

bearing partition. A partition that supports any vertical load in addition to its own weight.

bearing wall. A wall that supports any vertical load in addition to its own weight.

bed molding. A molding in an angle such as between the overhanging cornice, or eaves, of a building and the sidewalls.

blind nailing. Naling in such a way that the nailheads are not visible on the face of the work. This is usually done at the tongue of matched boards.

brace. An inclined piece of framing lumber applied to a wall or floor to stiffen the structure. Often used on walls as temporary bracing until framing has been completed.

butt joint. The junction where the ends of two timbers or other members meet in a square-cut joint.

cap. The upper member of a column, pilaster, door cornice, molding and the like.

casement frames and sash. Frames of wood or metal enclosing part or all of the sash that can be opened by means of hinges affixed to the vertical edges.

casing. Molding of various widths and thicknesses used to trim door and window openings at the jambs.

checking. Fissures that appear with age in many exterior paint coatings. At first they are superficial, but in time they can penetrate entirely through the coating.

checkrails. Meeting rails sufficiently thicker than a window to fill the opening between the top and bottom sash made by the parting stop in the frame of double-hung windows. They are usually beveled.

column. In architecture: a perpendicular supporting member, circular or rectangular in section, usually consisting of a base, shaft and capital. In engineering: a vertical structural compression member which supports loads acting in the direction of its longitudinal axis.

combination doors or windows. These are used over regular openings. They provide winter insulation and summer protection and often have self-storing glass or screen inserts. This eliminates the need for handling a different unit each season.

concrete. A mixture of cement, gravel, sand and water. It can be reinforced for shrinkage or temperature changes.

condensation. In a building: beads or drops of water (and frequently frost in extremely cold weather) that accumulate on the inside of the exterior covering of a building when warm, moisture laden air from the interior reaches a point where the temperature no longer permits the air to sustain the moisture it holds. Use of louvers or attic ventilators will reduce moisture condensation in attics. A vapor barrier under gypsum lath or dry wall on exposed walls will reduce condensation in them.

conduit (electrical). A pipe, usually metal, in which wire is installed.

construction, drywall. A type of construction in which the interior wall finish is applied in a dry condition. Generally it is in the form of sheet materials or wood paneling, as contrasted to plaster.

construction, frame. A type of construction in which the structural parts are wood or depend upon a wooden frame for support. In codes, if masonry veneer is applied to the exterior walls, the classification of this type of construction is usually unchanged.

corner bead. A strip or formed sheet metal, sometimes combined with a strip of metal lath, placed on corners before plastering to reinforce them. Also, a strip of wood finish three-quarters round or angular placed over a plaster corner for protection.

corner braces. Diagonal braces at the corners of frame structures to stiffen and strengthen the wall.

cut-in brace. Nominal 2-inch thick boards, usually 2 x 4s cut in between each stud diagonally.

cornerite. Metal-mesh lath cut into strips and bent to a right angle. Used in interior corners of walls and ceilings on lath to prevent cracks in the plaster.

cove molding. A molding with a concave face used as a trim or to finish interior corners.

crawl space. A shallow space below the living quarters of a house. It is normally enclosed by the foundation wall.

cross-bridging. Diagonal bracing between adjacent floor joists placed near the center of the joist span to prevent joists from twisting.

crown molding. A molding used on cornice or wherever an interior angle is to be covered.

d. See *penny.*

dado. A rectangular groove across the width of a board or plank. In interior decoration, a special type of wall treatment.

decay. Disintegration of wood or other substance through the action of fungi.

deck paint. An enamel with a high degree of resistance to mechanical wear. It is designed for use on such surfaces as porch floors.

density. The mass of substance in a unit volume. When expressed in the metric system, it is numerically equal to the specific gravity of the same substance.

dewpoint. Temperature at which a vapor begins to deposit as a liquid. Applies especially to water in the atmosphere

dimension. See *lumber dimension.*

direct nailing. To nail perpendicular to the initial surface or to the junction of pieces joined. Also termed *face nailing.*

doorjamb, interior. The surrounding case into which and out of which a door closes and opens. It consists of two upright pieces, called jambs, and a horizontal head jamb.

315

dressed and matched (tongued and grooved). Boards or planks machined in such a manner that there is a groove on one edge and a corresponding tongue on the other.

drier paint. Usually oil-soluble soaps of such metals as lead, manganese or cobalt. In small proportions, they hasten the oxidation and hardening (drying) of the drying oils in paints.

drywall. Interior covering material such as gypsum board or plasterboard which is applied in large sheets or panels.

ducts. In a house, usually round or rectangular metal pipes for distributing warm air from the heating plant to rooms or air from a conditioning device or as cold air returns. Ducts can also be made from other materials.

efflorescence. A white residue left on the surface of masonry after water has evaporated.

emulsion. A liquid preparation in which minute particles remain in suspension. Most commonly used to describe latex coatings.

enamel. The term used to describe color finishes that contain a high varnish content. The most important characteristic is that enamels dry to a hard finish. They can be flat, semigloss or high gloss.

epoxy. Extremely tough coating made from synthetic resins. They are often two part mixtures.

expansion joint. A bituminous fiber strip used to separate blocks, bricks or units of concrete to prevent cracking due to expansion as a result of temperature changes. Also used on concrete slabs.

extender (painting). An inexpensive, inert pigment that is often added to coatings to increase the mass and lower the cost. It can be used to control certain properties in a coating such as gloss, viscosity and sheen.

fading. Loss of color due to exposure to the sun.

feathering. The blending of the edges of a finished area. Also, in sanding, when an edge and flat surface are leveled so that the result cannot be seen or felt.

filler. Powder, paste or liquid used to fill the pores in certain open-grained woods such as oak; also patching plywood edges; sheetrock.

film. The dry coating on a surface.

fireresistant. Applies to materials for construction not combustible in the temperatures of ordinary fires and that will withstand such fires without serious impairment of their usefulness for at least one hour.

fire-retardant chemical. A chemical or preparation of chemicals used to reduce flammability or to retard spread of flame.

flame spread rate. The results obtained from a carefully controlled test to determine the rate at which a dry coating will burn on various substrates such as plywood, shingles, dry wall, etc.

flat paint. An interior or exterior paint which contains a high proportion of pigment and dries to a flat lusterless finish.

flue. The space or passage in a chimney through which smoke, gas or fumes ascend. Each passage is called a flue. Together with others and the surrounding masonry they make up a chimney.

footing. A masonry section, usually concrete, in a rectangular form wider than the bottom of the foundation wall or pier it supports.

foundation. The supporting portion of a structure below the first floor construction or below grade, including the footings.

framing, balloon. A system of framing a building in which all vertical structural elements of the bearing walls and partitions consist of single pieces extending from the top of the foundation sill plate to the roofplate and to which all floor joists are fastened.

framing, platform. A system of framing a building in which floor joists of each story rest on the top plates of the story below or on the foundation sill for the first story. The bearing walls and partitions rest on the subfloor of each story.

fungi, wood. Microscopic plants that live in damp wood and cause mold, stain and decay.

fungicide. A chemical that is poisonous to fungi.

furring. Strips of wood or metal applied to a wall or other surface to even it and normally to serve as a fastening base for finish material.

gable. The triangular part of a wall under the inverted "V" of the roof line.

glazing. Any work that involves fitting glass into windows or doors.

gloss. The luster of a paint or clear coating.

grain. The natural pattern in wood or other natural materials such as slate or stone.

green lumber. Lumber that has been freshly cut or inadequately dried and which tends to warp or bleed resin. In contrast, see *air dried lumber*.

grounds. Guides used around openings and at the floorline to strike off plaster. They can consist of narrow strips of wood or of wide subjambs at interior doorways. They provide a level plater line for installing of casing and other trim.

grout. Mortar made of such consistency (by adding a liquid) that it will just flow into the joints and cavities of the masonry work and fill them solid. It is also in tile setting.

gypsum plaster. Gypsum formulated to be used with the addition of sand and water for base coat plaster.

header. A beam placed perpendicular to joists and to which joists are nailed in framing for a chimney, stairway or other opening. Also, a wood lintel.

heartwood. The wood extending from the pith to the sapwood. The cells of which no longer participate in the life process of the tree.

hiding power. The ability of a coating to completely cover a surface and hide the color beneath.

holidays. A term used to describe areas where a paint coating has not completely covered the surface. Also, areas that the paint brush missed.

humidifier. A device designed to increase the humidity within a room or hours by means of the discharge of water vapor. They can consist of individual room size units or larger units attached to the heating plant to condition the entire atmosphere of the house.

INR (Impact Noise Rating). A single figure rating which provides an estimate of the impact wound insulating performance of a floor ceiling assembly.

Insulation board, rigid. A structural building board made of coarse wood or can fiber in one-half and 25/32 inch thicknesses. It can be obtained in various densities and with several treatments.

Insulation, thermal. Any material high in resistance to heat transmission that, when placed in the walls, ceiling or floors of a structure, will reduce the rate of heat flow.

Interior finish. Material used to cover the interior framed areas or materials of walls, floors and ceilings.

jamb. The side and head lining of a doorway, window or other opening.

joint. The space between the adjacent surfaces of two members or components joined and held together by nails, glue, cement, mortar or other materials.

joint cement. A powder that is usually mixed with water and used for joint treatment in gypsum or wall board finish. Often called "spackle", this material is also available in a premixed version.

joist. One of a series of parallel beams, usually two inches thick, used for the support of floor and ceiling loads and supported in turn by larger beams, girders or bearing walls.

kiln-dried lumber. Lumber that has been kiln dried often to a moisture content of 6 to 12 percent. Common varieties of softwood lumber, such as framing lumber, are dried to a somewhat higher moisture content.

knot. In lumber, the portion of a branch or limb of a tree that appears on the edge or face of the piece as the tree trunk is sliced lengthwise.

landing. A platform between flights of stairs or at the termination of a flight of stairs.

lath. A building material of wood, metal, gypsum or insulating board that is fastened to the frame of a building to act as a plaster base.

latex paint. A water thinned finish.

lattice. A framework of crossed wood or metal strips.

let-in brace. Nominal 1-inch thick boards applied into notched studs diagonally.

leveling. The ability of a coating to dry flat and free from ripples, brush marks, etc.

light. Space in a window sash for a single pane of glass. Also, a pane of glass.

lintel. A horizontal structural member that supports the load over an opening such as a door or window.

louver. An opening with a series of horizontal slats so arranged as to permit ventilation, but to exclude rain, sunlight or vision.

lumber. The product of a sawmill and planing mill not further manufactured other than by sawing, resawing and passing lengthwise through a standard planing machine, crosscutting to length and matching.

lumber, dimension. Yard lumber from 2 inches to, but not including, 5 inches thick and 2 or more inches wide. Including all framing members such as studs, rafters, joists, plank and small timbers.

lumber, dressed size. The dimension of lumber after shrinking from green dimension and after matching to size or pattern.

lumber, matched. Lumber that is dressed and shaped on one edge in a grooved pattern and on the other in a tongued pattern.

lumber, timbers. Yard lumber 5 or more inches in least dimension. Includes beams, stringers, posts, caps, sills, girders and purlins.

lumber, yard. Lumber of those grades, sizes and patterns that are generally intended for ordinary construction such as framework and rough coverage of houses.

masking. Temporary covering of an area to prevent paint from falling on that area.

mastic. A pasty material used as a cement (as for setting tile) or a protective coating (as for thermal insulation or waterproofing).

metal lath. Sheets of metal that are slit and drawn out to form openings. Used as a plaster base for walls and ceilings and as reinforcing over other forms of plaster base.

mil. One-thousandth of an inch. A coating thickness measurement.

mildew. A fungus that thrives in warm, damp environments.

millwork. Generally, all building materials made of finished wood and manufactured in millwork plants and planing mills are included under this term. It includes such items as inside and outside doors, window frames and doorframes, blinds, porchwork, mantels, panelwork, stairways, moldings, and interior trim. It normally does not include flooring, ceiling or siding.

miter joint. The joint of two pieces at an angle that bisects the joining angle. For example, the miter joint at the side and head casing at a door opening is made at a 45-degree angle.

moisture content of wood. Weight of the water contained in the wood. This usually expressed as a percentage of the weight of oven-dried wood.

molding. A wood strip having a curved or projecting surface used for decorative purposes.

mortise. A slot cut into a board, plank or timber, usually edgewise, to receive tenon or another board, plank or timber to form a strong joint.

mullion. A vertical bar or divider in the frame between windows, doors or other openings.

muntin. A small member which divides the glass or openings of sash or doors.

nap. The length of the fibers of a paint roller cover or sleeve.

natural finish. A transparent finish which does not seriously alter the original color or grain of the natural wood. Natural finishes are usually provided by sealers, oils, varnishes, water repellent preservatives and other similar materials.

newel. A post to which the end of a stair railing or balustrade is fastened.

NGR (non-grain raising). A term used to describe stains which do not contain water and therefore will not swell the fibers in wood.

non-bearing wall. A wall supporting no load other than its own weight.

nosing. The projecting edge of a molding or drip. It is usually applied to the projecting molding on the edge of a stair tread.

notch. A crosswise rabbet at the end of a board.

OC (on center). The measurement of spacing for studs, rafters, joist, and the like in a building from the center of one member to the center of the next.

oil stains. Wood stains that are formed by mixing oil-soluble dyes in an oil. The term is often applied to pigmented wiping stains.

opaque. The opposite of transparent. Any coating that has unusual hiding power is said to be opaque.

open-grained wood. Woods with large pores such as oak and walnut.

orange peel. The irregular surface of a film that resembles the dimpled skin of an orange. A paint failure resulting when a covering fails to level.

orange shellac. The natural color of shellac: deep amber.

paint. A combination of pigments with suitable thinners or oils to provide decorative and protective coatings.

panel. In house construction, a thin flat piece of wood plywood, or similar material, framed by stiles and rails as in a door or fitted into grooves of thicker material with molded edges for decorative wall treatment.

paper, building. A general term for papers felt and similar materials used in buildings without reference to their properties or uses.

paper, felt. A building material, generally paper or asphalt saturated felt, used in wall and roof construction as a protection against the passage of air and sometimes moisture.

parting stop or strip. A small wood piece used in the side and head jambs of double-hung windows to separate upper and lower sash.

partition. A wall that subdivides spaces within any story of a building.

paste filler. Wood filler in paste form which must be thinned before it can be used.

peeling. Paint failure usually caused by moisture or grease under the topcoat.

penetrating finish. Any coating which, when applied, sinks into the surface leaving almost nothing on the surface.

penny. As applied to nails, it originally indicated the price per hundred. The term now serves as a measure of nail length and is abbreviated by the letter d.

perm. A measure of water vapor movement through a material (grains per square foot per hour per inch of mercury difference in vapor pressure).

pier. A column of masonry, usually rectangular in horizontal cross section, used to support other structural members.

pigment. A powdered solid in suitable degree of subdivision for use in paint or enamel.

pith. The small, soft core at the original center of a tree around which wood formation takes palce.

plasterboard. A term used to describe gypsum board.

plaster grounds. Strips of wood used as guides or strike-off edges around window and door openings and at the base of walls.

plate. Sill plate: a horizontal member anchored to a masonry wall. Sole plate: bottom horizontal member of a frame wall. Top plate: top horizontal member of a frame wall supporting ceiling joists, rafters or other members.

plough. To cut a lengthwise groove in a board or plank.

plumb. Exactly perpendicular; vertical.

ply. A term used to denote the number of thicknesses of layers of built-up roofing, felt, veneer in plywood, or layers finished pieces of such material.

plywood. A piece of wood made of three or more layers of veneer joined with glue and usually laid with the grain of adjoining plies at right angles. An odd number of plies are almost always used to provide balanced construction.

polyurethane. An oil modified urethane varnish which dries to a hard and tough clear finish.

pores. Wood cells of comparatively large diameter that have open cells and are set one above the other to form continuous tubes. The openings of the vessels on the surface of a piece of wood are referred to as pores.

primer. A special formulation that is applied to bare wood. A good primer seals the wood and provides a good adhesive base for the topcoat.

preservative. Any substance that, for a reasonable length of time, will prevent the action of wood-destroying fungi, borers of various kinds and similar destructive agents when the wood has been properly coated or impregnated with it.

putty. A type of cement usually made of whiting and boiled linseed oil that is beaten or kneaded to the consistency of dough. It is used in sealing glass in sash, filling small holes and crevices in wood and for similar purposes.

quarter round. A small molding that has the cross section of a quarter circle.

rabbet. A rectangular longitudinal groove cut in the corner edge of a board or plank.

radiant heating. A method of heating, usually consisting of forced hot water, with pipes in the floor, wall or ceiling or with electrically heated panels.

rafter. One of a series of structural members of a roof designed to support roof loads. The rafters of a flat roof are sometimes called roof joists.

rail. Cross members of panel doors or of a sash. Also the upper and lower members of a balustrade or staircase extending from one vertical support, such as a post, to another.

raw linseed oil. The crude product processed from flaxseed and usually without much subsequent treatment.

reducer. Paint thinner used for reducing the viscosity of various finishes. These are different thinners for different coatings such as lacquer thinner, mineral spirits, etc.

reflective insulation. Sheet material with one or both surfaces of comparatively low heat emissivity such as aluminum foil. When used in building construction, the surfaces face air spaces and reduce the radiation across the air space.

relative humidity. The amount of water vapor in the atmosphere expressed as a percentage of the maximum quantity that could be present at a given temperature. The actual amount of water vapor that can be held in space increases with the temperature.

resin. A natural resin is a nonvolatile solid or semisolid exudation from pine trees or other plants such as rosin. Resins are also synthetically made.

resorcinol glue. A glue that is high in both wet and dry strength and resistant to high temperatures. It is used for gluing lumber or assembly joints that must withstand severe service conditions.

rise. In stairs, the vertical height of a step or flight of stairs.

riser. Each of the vertical boards closing the spaces between the treads of stairways.

rubber emulsion paint. A paint that contains rubber or synthetic rubber dispersed in fine droplets in water.

run. In stairs, the net width of a step or the horizontal distance covered by a flight of stairs.

sapwood. The outer zone of wood that is next to the bark. In the living tree, it contains some living cells (the heartwood contains none) as well as dead and dying cells. In most species, it is lighter colored than the heartwood. In all species, it is lacking in decay resistance.

sash. A single light frame containing one or more lights of glass.

satin finish. A term used to describe a coating which is semiglossy.

saturated felt. A felt which is impregnated with asphalt and most commonly sold in rolled form.

scratch coat. The first coat of plaster which is scratched to form a bond for the second coat.

screed. A small strip of wood, usually the thickness of the plaster coat, used as a guide for plastering.

scribing. Fitting woodwork to an irregular surface. In moldings, cutting the end of one piece to fit the molded face of the other at an interior angle to replace a miter joint.

sealer. A finishing material, either clear or pigmented, that is usally applied directly over uncoated wood for the purpose of sealing the surface.

seasoning. Removing moisture from green wood in order to improve its serviceability.

semigloss paint or enamel. A paint or enamel made with a slight insufficiency of nonvolatile vehicle so that its coating, when dry, has some luster. It is between flat and high gloss.

shake. A thick, handsplit shingle that is resawed to form two shakes. They are usually edge-grained. Most often, they are used for rustic looking interior and exterior walls.

sheathing. The structural covering, usually wood boards or plywood, used over studs or rafters of a structure. Structural building board is normally used only as wall sheathing.

shellac. A transparent coating made by dissolving a resinous secretion of the lac bug—a scale insect that thrives in tropical countries such as India—in alcohol.

siding. The finish covering of the outside wall of a frame building. It can be made of horizontal weatherboards, vertical boards with battens, shingles or other material.

sill. The lowest member of the frame of a structure. It rests on the foundation and supports the floor joists or the uprights of the wall. The member forming the lower side of an opening such as a door sill, window sill, etc.

skin. A tough layer formed on the surface of a coating when left in an unsealed container and exposed to the air for some time. Skin is formed by oxidation or polymerization.

sleeper. Usually, a wood member embedded in concrete—as in a floor—that serves to support and to fasten subfloor or flooring.

soil cover (ground cover). A light covering of plastic film, roll roofing or similar material used over the soil in crawl spaces of buildings to minimize permeation of the area.

soil stack. A general term for the vertical main of a system of soil, waste or vent piping.

solid bridging. A solid member placed between adjacent floor joists near the center of the span to prevent joists from twisting.

solvent. The volatile part of a paint which is also the part that evaporates.

span. The distance between structural supports such as walls, columns, piers, beams, girders and trusses.

spot prime. To apply primer only to those areas in need of additional protection such as those areas that have been worn or scraped to bare wood and rusted areas which have been sanded.

stain. Any coating that changes the natural appearance of wood.

stile. An upright framing member in a panel door.

stool. A flat molding fitted over the window sill between jambs and contacting the bottom rail of the lower sash.

strip flooring. Wood flooring consisting of narrow, matched strips—hardwood or softwood.

stud. One of a series of slender wood or metal vertical supports placed as supporting members in walls or partitions.

subfloor. Boards or plywood laid on joists over which a finish floor is to be laid.

texture. A term used to describe surface characteristics.

thinner. Any material used to thin a coating.

thixotropy. The property of a coating which allows it to undergo a transformation from a partially gelled state to a liquid flowable state and then back to a partially gelled state due to agitation and subsequent rest. This property helps to create dripless coatings and is common in all latex coatings.

topcoat. The term used to describe the last coating applied.

touch-up. Repairing a coating in spots and not show color or glass differences.

turpentine. A distillate of coniferous trees, most commonly clear, and used as a thinner for oil paints and some varnishes.

undercoat. Usually the primer or first coat in a multicoat system.

under layment. A material placed under finish coverings, such as flooring or shingles, to provide a smooth, even surface for applying the finish.

urethane. A group of resins used in making certain varnishes and enamels. Dries very hard and stands up well to heavy abuse.

vapor barrier. Material used to retard the movement of water vapor into walls and prevent condensation in them. Usually considered as having a permanent value of less than 1.0. Applied separately over the warm side of exposed walls or as part of batt or blanket insulation.

varnish. A large class of clear coatings.

vehicle. The liquid portion of a coating generally classified as volatile or nonvolatile.

veneer. Thin sheets of wood made by rotary cutting or slicing of a log.

viscosity. The thickness or thinness of a liquid.

wainscoting. The lower 3 or 4 feet of an interior wall when lined with paneling or other material different from the rest of the wall.

water stain. A stain made by dissolving special dyes in water. It will usually raise the grain of the wood.

weathering. The wearing away of a film coating through the natural action of wind, sun, rain, etc.

wrinkling. Paint failure as evidenced by ridges and furrows on a dry paint film.

yellowing. The development of a yellow cast in a coating. It is quite common in some varnishes.

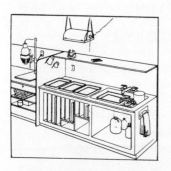

Appendix A
Suppliers,
Books & Magazines

In this appendix you will find a listing of sources of materials, tools, books and magazines for the major topics in this book. This information is offered to help you find equipment, supplies and sources of information that will aid you in not only setting up your workshop or studio, but to help with the work as well.

CANNING

Ball Corporation
Consumer Products Division
1509 South Macedonia Ave.
Muncie, IN. 47302

booklets on canning
Ball blue book $1
Ball freezer book 75 cents

University of California
Berkeley, CA 94720

booklet #2785
Drying Foods At Home;
includes plans for dehydrator

Garden Way
47 Maple Street
Burlington, VT 05401

gardening related
catalog; books
and plans

Kerr Glass Mfg. Co.
Consumer Products Divsion
Sand Springs, OK 74063

Kerr Home Canning &
Freezing Book—$1

Mirro Aluminum Co.
Manitowoc, WI 54220

information on
pressure canners

Oregon State University Extension Service Corvallis, OR	*booklet on how to build a* *portable electric* *food dehydrator*
U.S. Department of Agriculture Washington, D. C. 20250	*many booklets on food* *preservation*
Putting Food	The Stephen Greene Press Brattleboro, VT 05301

CERAMICS

A.D. Alpine Inc. 3051 Fujita St. Torrance, CA 90503	*kilns and ceramic equipment*
Amherst Potters Supply 44 McClellan Street Amherst, MA 01002	*ceramic supplies*
American Art Clay Co. 4717 West Sixteenth St. Indianapolis, IN 46222	*catalog of ceramic supplies*
Bluebird Manufacturing 100 Gregory Road Fort Collins, CO 80521	*ceramic supplies*
Kilns Supply & Service Corp. 39 Buckley Ave. Port Chester, NY 10573	*ceramics*
L & L Mfg. Co. P. O. Box 348 Chester, PA 19016	*ceramic supplies*
Sculpture House 38 E. 30th. St. New York, NY 10016	*ceramic supplies &* *equipment*

Standard Ceramic Supply Co.   *ceramic supplies*
P.O. Box 4435
Pittsburgh, PA 15205

Stewart Clay Company   *ceramic supplies*
133 Mulberry Street
New York, NY

Western Ceramics Supply Co.   *ceramic supplies*
1601 Howard St.
San Franciso, CA 94103

Jack D. Wolfe Co. Inc.   *ceramic supplies*
724 Meeker Street
Brooklyn, NY 11222

FLY TYING

All of the companies listed in this section offer catalogs or information.

The Angler's Supply House
Williamsport, PA 17701

Anglers Pro Shop
18 E. 23rd. St.
Lansdale, PA 19446

Dan Bailey Flies & Tackle
Livingston, MT 59047

Donegal
Box 979
Old Route 9W
Fort Montgomery, NY 10922

Fireside Angler
Melville, NY 11746

Fly Fishing Wholesalers
Missula, MT 59801

Fly Tyer Magazine
Box 1231
North Conway, NH 03860

Herters
RR 1
Waseca, MN 56093

McCarty's
P. O. Box 60101
Reno, NV 89506

Rangeley Region Sport Shop
P. O. Box 850
Rangeley, ME 04970

Reed Tackle
P. O. Box 1348
Fairfield, NJ 07006

The Rivergate
Route 9, Box 275
Cold Spring, NY 10516

Stackpole Books   *the best books on fly tying*
P. O. Box 1831
Harrisburg, PA 17105

Steckler-Tibor
P. O. Box 607
Stoneboro, PA 16153

Tackle Crafters   *spinning &*
14303 Robcaste Road   *rod-building supplies*
Phoenix, MD 21131

Windsor Fly Shop
348 N. 9th Street
Stroudsburg. PA 18360

GENERAL CRAFTS   *macrame supplies*

A.R.T. Studio
921 Oakton
Elk Grove Village, IL 60007

Arthur Brown & Bro. Inc.   *art & craft supplies*
2 W. 46th. St.
New York, NY 10036

Boin Art and Crafts   *general craft supplies*
87 Morris St.
Morristown, NJ 07960

Charrette Corporation   *art supplies*
31 Olympia Ave.
Woburn, MA 01801

Dick Blick Company   *general crafts*
P.O. Box 1267
Galesburg, IL 61401

Dorset Looms   *looms*
Woodin Road, RD 11
Clifton Park, NY 12065

Harrisville Designs   *looms & weaving supplies*
Harrisville, NH 13450

Hazel Pearson   *general crafts*
4128 Temple City Blvd.
Rosemead, CA 91770

E.E. Gilmore   *looms*
1032 N. Broadway
Stockton, CA 95205

Looms 'N Yarns   *looms & weaving supplies*
Box 460
Berea, OH 44017

The Mannings Creative Crafts   *general crafts, weaving*
R.D. #2
Berlin, PA 17316

Nasco Handcrafters   *general crafts*
901 Janesville Ave.
Fort Atkinson, WI 53538

Naturcraft Inc.   *general crafts*
2199 Bancroft Way
Berkeley, CA 94704

Light Impressions Corp.   *art supplies*
P.O. Box 3012   *framing materials*
Rochester, NY 14614

Pratt Tex Industries   *weaving supplies*
6501 Barberton Ave.
Cleveland, OH 44102

Peoria Arts & Craft Supplies   *general craft supplies*
1207 W. Main St.
Peoria, IL

Whittemore-Durgin Glass Co.   *stained glass supplies*
P.O. Box 2065 FR
Hanover, MA 02339

PHOTOGRAPHY

Calumet Photographic Inc.   *catalog*
1590 Touhy
Elk Grove, IL 60007

Eastman Kodak Company   *large selection of*
343 State St.   *publications on all*
Rochester, NY 14650   *aspects of photography*

Willoughby Peerless   *catalog—equipment &*
415 Lexington Ave.   *supplies for photographer*
New York, NY 10017

WOODWORKING

Constatine & Sons Inc.   *woodworking supplies*
2050 Eastchester Road   *and tools*
Bronx, NY 10461

Craftsman Wood Service Co. *hardwoods, hardware*
2727 S. Mary St.
Chicago, IL

Belsaw Machinery Co. *power equipment*
315 Westport Road
Box 593
Kansas City, MO 64141

Dremel *miniature power tools*
Division of Emerson Electric Co.
4915 21 St.
P. O. Box 518
Racine, WI 53406

Georgia-Pacific *plans, general information*
900 S. W. Fifth Ave.
Portland, OR 97204

Masonite Corporation *plans, general information*
Public Relations Dept.
1909 E. Cornell Drive
Chicago, IL 61614

Bob Morgan Woodworking Supplies *veneers*
1123 Bardstown Road
Louisville, KY 40204

The Princeton Company *tools for woodworkers*
P. O. Box 276
Princeton, MA 01541

Rockwell International *power tools*
Power Tool Division
Pittsburgh, PA 15208

Shopsmith Inc. *Shopsmith Mark V*
750 Center Drive
Vandalia, OH 45377

Skil Corporation *power tools*
5033 Elston Ave.
Chicago, IL

The Stanley Works
Advertising Services Dept.
New Britain, CT 06050

tools and much how-to information; booklets

U.S. Plywood
Champion Int. Corp.
1 Landmark Square
Stanford, CT 06901

plans, information

The Fine Tool Shops
20-28 Backus Ave.
Danbury, CT 06810

tools; catalog

Woodcraft Supply Corp.
313 Montvale Ave.
Woburn, MA 01888

tools; hardwoods

The Woodworkers Store
21801 Industrial Blvd.
Rogers, MN 55374

woodworking supplies

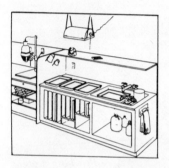

Appendix B
Underlayment
and Plywood
Paneling Charts

Table B-1. Subfloor Underlayment.

| Plywood Species Group | 2.4.1 | | Nail Size and Type | Nail Spacing (inches) | |
	Plywood Thickness (inches)	Maximum Spacing of Supports c to c (inches)		Panel Edges	Inter- mediate
Groups 1, 2, and 3	1-⅛	32(2 × joists)	8d ring-shank recommended or 10d common smooth-shank (if supports are well seasoned)	6	10
		48(4 × girders)		6	6

Table B-2. Combined Subfloor/Underlayment.

Plywood Grade(3)	Plywood Species Group	Maximum Support Spacing(1)(2)						Nail Spacing (inches)	
		16" o.c.		20" o.c.		24" o.c.			
		Panel Thickness	Deformed Shank Nail Size	Panel Thickness	Deformed Shank Nail Size	Panel Thickness	Deformed Shank Nail Size	Panel Edges	Inter-mediate
UNDERLAYMENT INT-APA (with interior or exterior glue) or UNDER-LAYMENT EXT-APA (C-C Plugged)	1	1/2"	6d	5/8"**	6d	3/4"***	6d	6	10
	2 & 3	5/8"*	6d	3/4"***	6d	7/8"	8d	6	10
	4	3/4"**	6d	7/8"	8d	1"	8d	6	10

*May be 19/32" **May be 23/32"

(1) Plywood edges shall be tongue-and-grooved, or supported with framing.

(2) In some nonresidential buildings, special conditions may impose heavy concentrated loads and heavy traffic requiring subfloor-underlayment constructions in excess of these minimums.

(3) For certain types of flooring such as wood block or terrazzo, sheathing grades of plywood may be used.

337

Table B-3. Minimum Stapling Schedule for Plywood.

Recommended Minimum Stapling Schedule For Plywood			All values are for 16 gauge galvanized wire staples having a minimum crown width of 3/8 inch.

A. Plywood wall sheathing/Without diagonal bracing

Plywood Thickness	Staple Leg Length	Spacing Around Entire Perimeter of Sheet	Spacing at Intermediate Members
5/16"	1-1/4"	4"	8"
3/8"	1-3/8"	4"	8"
1/2"	1-1/2"	4"	8"

B. Plywood roof sheathing

5/16"	1-1/4"	4"	8"
3/8"	1-3/8"	4"	8"
1/2"	1-1/2"	4"	8"

C. Plywood subfloors

1/2"	1-5/8"	4"	7"
5/8"	1-5/8"	2½"	4"

D. Plywood underlayment

1/4"·(1)	7/8"	3"	6" each way
3/8"	1-1/8"	3"	6" each way
1/2"	1-5/8"	3"	6" each way
5/8"	1-5/8"	3"	6" each way

E. Asphalt shingles to plywood/Staples to have crown width of 3/4" min.

5/16" and thicker	3/4"	According to shingle manufacturer.

(1)   18-gauge staples with 3/16 inch crown width may be used for 1/4 inch underlayment.

NOTE: The International Conference of Building Officials recognizes several types of special mechanical fasteners. They are covered in ICBO Report No. 2403.

Table B-4. Plywood Underlayment. For Maximum Stiffness, Place Grain Across Supports and End Joints Over Framing.

Plywood Grades and Species Group	Application	Minimum Plywood Thickness	Fastener Size (approx.) and Type (set nails 1/16")	Fastener Spacing (Inches)	
				Panel Edges	Inter-mediate
All Groups: UNDERLAYMENT INT-APA (with interior or exterior glue), or UNDERLAYMENT EXT-APA(3)	over plywood subfloor	1/4"	18 Ga. Staples or 3d ring-shank nails (1)(2)	3	6 each way
	over lumber sub-floor or other uneven surfaces	3/8"	16 Ga. Staples (1)	3	6 each way
			3d ring-shank nails (1)(2)	6	8 each way
Same Grades as above, but Group 1 or STRUC-TURAL I Only	over lumber floor up to 4" wide. Face grain must be perpendicular to boards.	1/4"	18 Ga. Staples or 3d ring-shank nails	3	6 each way

Table B-5. Interior Plywood Paneling.

Recommendations apply to all species groups.

Plywood Thickness[1] (inch)	Max. Support Spacing (inches)	Nail Size and Type	Nail Spacing (inches)	
			Panel Edges	Intermediate
1/4	16[2]	4d casing or finish	6	12
3/8	24	6d casing or finish	6	12

(1) Leave 1/32 inch spacing at all panel edge and end joints.
(2) Can be 20 inches if face grain of paneling is across supports.

Table B-6. Recommendations for Plywood Siding Direct to Studs.

Plywood Siding			Max. Stud Spacing (inches)		Nail Size (Use nonstaining box, siding or casing nails)	Nail Spacing (inches)	
Type	Description	Nominal Thickness (inches)	Face Grain Vertical	Face Grain Horizontal		Panel Edges	Intermediate
Panel Siding	MDO EXT-APA	19/32, 3/8	16	24	6d for panels ½" thick or less; 8d for thicker panels.	6	12
	MDO EXT-APA	1/2 & thicker	24	24			
	303–16 o.c. Siding EXT-APA (including T1-11)	5/16 & thicker	16	24			
	303–24 o.c. Siding EXT-APA	7/16 & thicker	24	24			
Lap Siding	MDO EXT-APA	19/32, 3/8	—	16	6d for siding 3/8" or less; 8d for thicker siding.	4" @ vertical butt joints; one nail per stud along bottom edge.	8" @ each stud, if siding wider than 12".
	MDO EXT-APA	1/2 & thicker	—	24			
	303–16 o.c. Siding EXT-APA	5/16, 19/32, or 3/8	—	16			
	303–16 o.c. Siding EXT-APA 303–24 o.c. Siding EXT-APA	7/16 & thicker	—	24			

Table B-7. Exterior Plywood Lap Siding Over Sheathing.

Recommendations apply to all species groups.

Plywood Siding		Nominal Thickness (inches)	Max. Stud Spacing (inches)		Nail Size (Use nonstaining box, siding or casing nails)	Nail Spacing (inches)	
Type	Description		Face Grain Vertical	Face Grain Horizontal		Panel Edges	Intermediate
Lap Siding	MDO EXT-APA	19/32 & 3/8	—	16[1]	6d for siding 3/8" thick or less; 8d for thicker siding. (2)	4" @ vertical butt joints; one nail per stud along bottom edge	8" @ each stud, if siding wider than 12"
		1/2 & thicker	—	24			
	303–16 o.c. Siding EXT-APA	5/16, 19/32, or 3/8	—	16[1]			
	303–16 o.c. Siding EXT-APA 303–24 o.c. Siding EXT-APA	7/16 & thicker	—	24			

(1) May be 24 inches with plywood or lumber sheathing.
(2) Use next larger nail size when sheathing is other than plywood or lumber, and nail only into framing.

342

Table B-8. Exterior Plywood Panel Siding Over Sheathing.

Recommendations apply to all species groups.

Plywood Siding			Max. Stud Spacing (inches)		Nail Size (Use nonstaining box, siding or casing nails)	Nail Spacing (inches)	
Type	Description	Nominal Thickness (inches)	Face Grain Vertical	Face Grain Horizontal		Panel Edges	Intermediate
	MDO EXT-APA	19/32 & 3/8	16[1]	24	6d for panels ½" thick or less;	6	12
		1/2 & thicker	24	24			
Panel Siding	303—16 o.c. Siding EXT-APA (including T1-11)	5/16 & thicker	16[1]	24	8d for thicker panels.		
	303—24 o.c. Siding EXT-APA	7/16 & thicker	24	24	(2)		

(1) May be 24 inches with 1/2 inch plywood, or lumber sheathing, if panel is also nailed 12 inches o.c. between studs, provided panel joints fall over studs.

(2) Use next larger nail size when sheathing (other than plywood or lumber) is thicker than 1/2 inch.

Table B-9. Plywood Subflooring Identification.

Panel Identification Index (1)(2)(3)	Plywood Thickness (inches)	Maximum Span (4) (inches)	Nail Size and Type (common)	Nail Spacing (inches) Panel Edges	Nail Spacing (inches) Intermediate
30/12	5/8	12 [5]	8d	6	10
32/16	1/2, 5/8	16 [6]	8d [7]	6	10
36/16	3/4	16 [6]	8d	6	10
42/20	5/8, 3/4, 7/8	20 [6]	8d	6	10
48/24	3/4, 7/8	24	8d	6	10
1-1/8" Gps 1 & 2	1-1/8	48	10d	6	6
1-1/4" Gps. 3 & 4	1-1/4	48	10d	6	6

(1) Applies to STRUCTURAL I and II grades, C-D Interior sheathing, and C-C Exterior grades only.

(2) Identification Index appears on all panels, except 1-1/8" and 1-1/4".

(3) Special conditions may impose heavy concentrated loads requiring subfloor construction in excess of these minimums.

(4) Spans limited to values shown because of possible effect of concentrated loads.

(5) May be 16" with 25/32" wood strip flooring at right angles to joists.

(6) May be 24" with 25/32" wood strip flooring at right angles to joists.

(7) 6d common nail permitted if plywood is 1/2".

Table B-10. Maximum Allowable Uniform Live Loads For Plywood Roof Decking. Five Pounds Per Square Foot Dead Load is Assumed. Live Load is Applied Load, Like Snow. Dead Load is the Weight of Plywood and Roofing.

Panel Identification Index	Plywood Thickness (inch)	Max. Span (inches)	Unsupported Edge—Max. Length (inches)(4)	Allowable Roof Loads (psf) (5) Spacing of Supports (inches center to center)									
				12	16	20	24	30	32	36	42	48	60
12/0	5/16	12	12	150									
16/0	5/16, 3/8	16	16	160	75								
20/0	5/16, 3/8	20	20	190	105	65							
24/0	3/8	24	20	250	140	95	50						
	1/2		24										
32/16	1/2, 5/8	32	28	385	215	150	95	50	40				
42/20	5/8, 3/4, 7/8	42	32		330	230	145	90	75	50	35		
48/24	3/4	48	36			300	190	120	105	65	45	35	
48/24(6)	7/8						225	125	105	75	55	40	
2·4·1	1-1/8	72	48				390	245	215	135	100	75	45
1-1/8 Group 1 & 2	1-1/8	72	48				305	195	170	105	75	55	35
1-1/4 Group 3 & 4	1-1/4	72	48				355	225	195	125	90	65	40

(1) These values apply for C-D INT-APA, C-C EXT-APA STRUCTURAL I and II C-D INT-APA and STRUCTURAL I and II C-C EXT-APA grades only. Plywood continuous over 2 or moe spans; grain of face plies across supports.

(2) Use 6d common smooth, ring-shank, or spiral-thread nails for 1/2 inch thick or less and 8d common smooth, ring-shank, or spiral-thread for plywood 1 inch thick or less. Use 8d ring-shank or spiral-thread or 10d common smooth-shank nails for 2-4-1, 1 1/8 inch and 1 1/2 inch panels. Space nails 6 inches at panel edges and 12 inches at intermediate supports, except that where spans are 48 inches or more, nails shall be 6 inches at all supports. Space panel ends 1/16 inch, and panel edges 1/8 inch. Where wet or humid conditions prevail, double these spacings.

(3) Special conditions, such as heavy concentrated loads, may require constructions in excess of these minimums.

(4) Provide adequate blocking, tongue-and-grooved edges or other suitable edge support such as Plyclips when spans exceed indicated value. Use two Plyclips for 48 inch or greater spans and one for lesser spans.

(5) Uniform load deflection limit: 1/180th span under live load plus dead load, 1/240th under live load only.

(6) Loads apply only to C-C EXT-APA, STRUCTURAL I C-D INT-APA, and STRUCTURAL I C-C EXT-APA.

Interior Type

Grade Designation (2)	Description and Most Common Uses	Typical Grade-trademarks	Face	Back	Inner plies	1/4	5/16	3/8	1/2	5/8	3/4
			Veneer Grade			**Most Common Thicknesses (inch) (3)**					
N-N, N-A, N-B INT-APA	Cabinet quality. For natural finish furniture, cabinet doors, built-ins, etc. Special order items.		N	N,A, or B	C						3/4
N-D-INT-APA	For natural finish paneling. Special order item.		N	D	D	1/4					
A-A INT-APA	For applications with both sides on view. Built-ins, cabinets, furniture and partitions. Smooth face; suitable for painting.		A	A	D	1/4		3/8	1/2	5/8	3/4
A-B INT-APA	Use where appearance of one side is less important but two smooth solid surfaces are necessary.		A	B	D	1/4		3/8	1/2	5/8	3/4
A-D INT-APA	Use where appearance of only one side is important. Paneling, built-ins, shelving, partitions, and flow racks.	A-D GROUP 2 INTERIOR P.S. 1-74 000	A	D	D	1/4		3/8	1/2	5/8	3/4
B-B INT-APA	Utility panel with two smooth sides. Permits circular plugs.		B	B	D	1/4		3/8	1/2	5/8	3/4
B-D INT-APA	Utility panel with one smooth side. Good for backing, sides of built-ins. Industry: shelving, slip sheets, separator boards and bins.	B-D GROUP 2 INTERIOR P.S. 1-74 000	B	D	D	1/4		3/8	1/2	5/8	3/4
DECORATIVE PANELS—APA	Rough-sawn, brushed, grooved, or striated faces. For paneling, interior accent walls, built-ins, counter facing, displays, and exhibits.		C or btr.	D	D		5/16	3/8	1/2	5/8	
PLYRON INT-APA	Hardboard face on both sides. For counter tops, shelving, cabinet doors, flooring. Faces tempered, untempered, smooth, or screened.				C & D				1/2	5/8	3/4
A-A EXT-APA	Use where appearance of both sides is important. Fences, built-ins, signs, boats, cabinets, commercial refrigerators, shipping containers, tote boxes, tanks, and ducts. (4)		A	A	C	1/4		3/8	1/2	5/8	3/4
A-B EXT-APA	Use where the appearance of one side is less important. (4)		A	B	C	1/4		3/8	1/2	5/8	3/4

Table B-11. Interior Plywood.

Table B-12. Exterior Plywood.

Exterior Type	Use	Grade stamp	Face	Back	Inner	1/4	3/8	1/2	5/8	3/4
A-C EXT-APA	Use where the appearance of only one side is important. Soffits, fences, structural uses, boxcar and truck lining, farm buildings. Tanks, trays, commercial refrigerators. (4)	A-C GROUP 2 EXTERIOR PS 1-74 000 (APA)	A	C	C	1/4	3/8	1/2	5/8	3/4
B-B EXT-APA	Utility panel with solid faces. (4)		B	B	C	1/4	3/8	1/2	5/8	3/4
B-C EXT-APA	Utility panel for farm service and work buildings, boxcar and truck lining, containers, tanks, agricultural equipment. Also as base for exterior coatings for walls, roofs. (4)	B-C GROUP 2 EXTERIOR PS 1-74 000 (APA)	B	C	C	1/4	3/8	1/2	5/8	3/4
HDO EXT-APA	High Density Overlay plywood. Has a hard, semi-opaque resin fiber overlay both faces. Abrasion resistant. For concrete forms, cabinets, counter tops, signs and tanks. (4)		A or B	A or B	C or C plgd		3/8	1/2	5/8	3/4
MDO EXT-APA	Medium Density Overlay with smooth, opaque, resin fiber overlay one or both panel faces. Highly recommended for siding and other out door applications, built-ins, signs, and displays. Ideal base for paint. (4)		B	B or C	C		3/8	1/2	5/8	3/4
303 SIDING EXT-APA	Proprietary plywood products for exterior siding, fencing, etc. Special surface treatment such as V-groove, channel groove, striated, brushed, rough sawn. (6)	303 SIDING 16 oc GROUP 2 EXTERIOR PS 1-74 000 (APA)	(5)	C	C		3/8	1/2	5/8	
T 1-11 EXT-APA	Special 303 panel having grooves 1/4'' deep, 3/8'' wide, spaced 4'' or 8'' o.c. Other spacing optional. Edges shiplapped. Available unsanded, textured, and MDO. (6)	303 SIDING 16 oc T 111 GROUP 2 EXTERIOR PS 1-74 000 (APA)	C or btr.	C	C				5/8	
PLYRON EXT-APA	Hardboard faces both sides, tempered, smooth or screened.				C			1/2	5/8	3/4
MARINE EXT-APA	Ideal for boat hulls. Made only with Douglas fir or western larch. Special solid jointed core construction. Subject to special limitations on core gaps and number of face repairs. Also available with HDO or MDO faces.		A or B	A or B	B	1/4	3/8	1/2	5/8	3/4

(1) Sanded both sides except where decorative or other surfaces specified.
(2) Available in Group 1, 2, 3, 4, or 5 unless otherwise noted.
(3) Standard 4x8 panel sizes, other sizes available.
(4) Also available in Structural I (all plies limited to Group 1 species) and Structural II (all plies limited to Group 1, 2, or 3 species).
(5) C or better for 5 plies. C Plugged or better for 3-ply panels.
(6) Stud spacing is shown on grade stamp.
(7) For finishing recommendations, see form V307.
(8) For strength properties of appearance grades, refer to "Plywood Design Specification," form Y510.

347

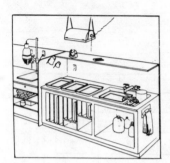

Appendix C
Nail Charts

Table C-1. Details of Common Nails.

PENNY SIZE	LENGTH (INCHES)	GAGE	NUMBER PER POUND
2	1	15	840
3	1¼	14	540
4	1½	12½	300
6	2	11½	160
8	2½	10¼	100
10	3	9	65
12	3¼	9	65
16	3½	8	45
20	4	6	30
30	4½	5	20
40	5	4	17
50	5¼	3	14
60	6	2	11

Table C-2. Nail-to-Plywood Thickness.

Plywood Thickness (inches)	Common Nail	Finish Nail
3/4	8d	8d
5/8	8d	8d
1/2	6d	6d
3/8	6d	4d

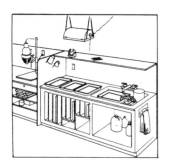

Appendix D

Wood Screws

Table D-1. Wood Screw Holes.

GAGE	SHANK DIAMETER (INCHES)	PILOT HOLE DIAMETER HARDWOODS	(INCHES) SOFTWOODS
2	0.086	3/64	—
3	0.099	1/16	—
4	0.112	1/16	—
5	0.125 (1/8)	5/64	1/16
6	0.138	5/64	1/16
7	0.151	3/32	1/16
8	0.164	3/32	5/64
10	0.177	7/64	3/32
12	0.216	1/8	7/64
14	0.242	9/64	7/64
16	0.268	5/32	9/64
18	0.294	3/16	9/64
20	0.320	13/64	11/64
24	0.372	7/32	3/16

Table D-2. Selecting Proper Screw Sizes.

Plywood Thickness	Screw Length	Screw Size	Drill Size for Shank
3/4 inch	1 1/2 inch	#8	11/64 inch
5/8	1 1/4	#8	11/64
1/2 inch	1 1/4 inch	#6	9/64 inch
3/8	1	#6	9/64
1/4	1	#4	7/64

Table D-3. Wood Screw Sizes and Drilling.

No.	SHANK DIA	SHANK HOLE		ANCHOR HOLE		LENGTH OF SCREW (inches) * ** ***																		
		HDWD	SFTWD	HDWD	SFTWD	1/4	3/8	1/2	5/8	3/4	7/8	1	1 1/4	1 1/2	1 3/4	2	2 1/4	2 1/2	2 3/4	3	3 1/2	4	4 1/2	5
0	1/16	1/16	** CP	1/32	** CP	×	×	×	×	×	×	×												
1	5/64	3/32	1/16	1/32	CP	×	×	×	×	×	×	×												
2	3/32	3/32	1/16	1/32	CP	×	×	×	×	×	×	×	×											
3	7/64	1/8	3/32	1/16	1/32	×	×	×	×	×	×	×	×											
4	1/8	1/8	3/32	1/16	1/32		×	×	×	×	×	×	×	×										
5	1/8	1/8	3/32	1/16	1/32		×	×	×	×	×	×	×	×										
6	9/64	5/32	1/8	3/32	1/16		×	×	×	×	×	×	×	×	×	×								
7	5/32	5/32	1/8	3/32	1/16		×	×	×	×	×	×	×	×	×	×								
8	11/64	3/16	5/32	3/32	1/16			×	×	×	×	×	×	×	×	×	×							
9	3/16	3/16	5/32	3/32	1/16			×	×	×	×	×	×	×	×	×	×	×						
10	13/64	7/32	3/16	1/8	3/32				×	×	×	×	×	×	×	×	×	×	×	×				
11	13/64	7/32	3/16	1/8	3/32				×	×	×	×	×	×	×	×	×	×	×	×				
12	7/32	7/32	3/16	1/8	3/32					×	×	×	×	×	×	×	×	×	×	×	×			
14	1/4	1/4	7/32	5/32	1/8							×	×	×	×	×	×	×	×	×	×	×		
16	9/32	5/16	1/4	5/32	5/32								×	×	×	×	×	×	×	×	×	×	×	
18	5/16	5/16	1/4	3/16	5/32									×	×	×	×	×	×	×	×	×	×	×
20	21/64	3/8	5/16	3/16	5/32											×	×	×	×	×	×	×	×	×
24	3/8	3/8	5/16	7/32	3/16													×	×	×	×	×	×	×

* Brass screws are measured differently.

** On soft woods, a centerpunch (CP) to mark point of entry is sufficient.

*** The length of flat-headed wood screws is measured from the top of the head to the tip of the point; for round-headed screws from the base of the head to the tip of the point.

Appendix E
Glue

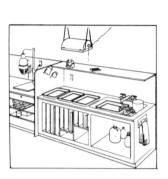

Table E-1. Glue Application Chart.

TYPE OF GLUE	DESCRIPTION	RECOMMENDED USE	PRECAUTIONS	HOW TO USE
UREA RESIN GLUE	Comes as powder to be mixed with water and used within 4 hours. Light colored. Very strong if joint fits well.	Good for general wood gluing. For work that must stand some exposure to dampness, but is not completely waterproof.	Needs well-fitted joints, tight clamping, and room temperature 70° or warmer. Some require heat to cure.	Make sure joint fits tightly. Mix glue and apply thin coat. Allow 16 hours drying time.
LIQUID RESIN (WHITE) GLUE	Comes ready to use at any temperature. Clean-working, quick setting. Strong enough for most work, though not quite so tough as urea resin glue.	Good for indoor furniture and cabinetwork. First choice for small jobs where tight clamping or good fit may be difficult.	Not sufficiently resistant to moisture for outdoor furniture or outdoor storage units.	Use at any temperature but preferably above 60°. Spread on both surfaces, clamp at once. Sets in 1½ hours.
RESORCINOL (WATERPROOF) GLUE	Comes as powder plus liquid, must be mixed each time used. Dark colored, very strong, completely waterproof.	This is the glue to use with Exterior type plywood for work to be exposed to extreme dampness. Good for farm buildings, boats.	Expense, trouble to mix and dark color make it unsuited to jobs where waterproof glue is not required. Needs good fit, tight clamping.	Use within 8 hours after mixing. Work at temperature above 70°. Apply thin coat to both surfaces; allow 16 hours drying time.

Appendix F
Paint

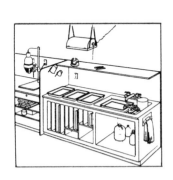

Table F-1. Interior Applications.

	TYPE OF FINISH*	RECOMMENDED FOR	APPLICATIONS
PAINT	Oil—flat paint, semigloss or gloss enamel	Medium Density Overlaid, regular plywood, striated, embossed.	Apply over stain-resistant primer recommended by manufacturer of topcoat.
	Latex emulsion	Regular and textured plywood, Medium Density Overlaid.	Apply over stain-resistant primer recommended by manufacturer of topcoat.
	Textured paints	Regular plywood, Medium Density Overlaid, Texture 1-11.	Use stain-resistant primer recommended by manufacturer of topcoat.
STAINS, SEALERS *Use only lead-free finishes		Regular plywood, textured.	Apply stains with companion sealer or over sealer separately applied. Follow with satin varnish or lacquer for increased durability. Where sealer alone is desired, use two coats.

Table F-2. Exterior Applications.

	TYPE OF FINISH	RECOMMENDED FOR	APPLICATION
PAINT	Acrylic Latex	Medium Density Overlaid, sanded, or 303 textured plywood.	Apply recommended non-staining primer plus two finish coats.
	Oil—Alkyd	Medium Density Overlaid only.	Apply with zinc-free primer, using two or three coats (including primer).
STAIN	Semi-transparent or penetrating stain	Unsanded plywood (303 textured plywood).	One or two-coat systems as recommended by the manufacturer.
	Opaque or highly pigmented stain	Unsanded plywood (303 textured plywood).	One or two-coat systems as recommended by the manufacturer.

Recent government restrictions on the use of lead and mercury compounds in finishes have resulted in some uncertainty regarding the performance of new paints and stains. In many cases, long-term performance information on the substitutes for lead and mercury is lacking, and results of tests in progress will not be available for some time. American Plywood Association finishing recommendations are based on experience with formulations made prior to the current restrictions. Consult supplier for interim recommendations.

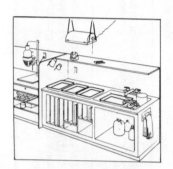

Appendix G
Concrete

Table G-1. Determining Thickness of Concrete Footings.

WEIGHT EXERTED UPON FOOTING	THICKNESS NEEDED
2,500 pounds	6″
3,500 pounds	7″
4,500 pounds	8″
5,500 pounds	9″
6,500 pounds (or more)	10″

Table G-2. Materials Needed for Concrete.

Mix Formula	Cement (bags)	Sand (cu. ft.)	Gravel (cu. ft.)
1:3:5	4½	15	22
1:3:4	5	15	20
1:2½:3½	6	15	21
1:2:3	7¼	14¼	21
1:2:2	8	16	16

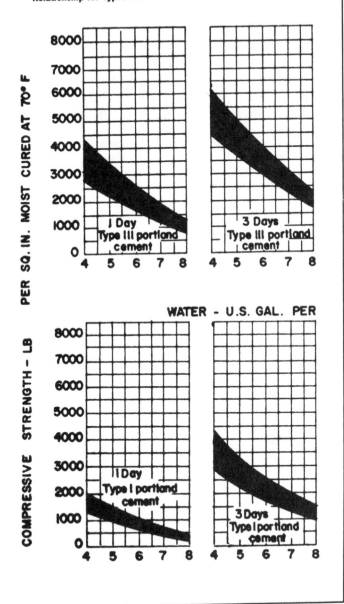

Age-Compressive Strength
Relationship for Types I and III Air-entrained Portland Cement.

WATER - U.S. GAL. PER

Age-Compressive Strength
Relationship for Types I and III Air-entrained Portland Cement.

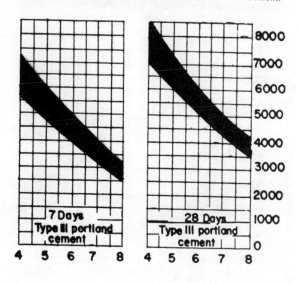

SACK OF CEMENT

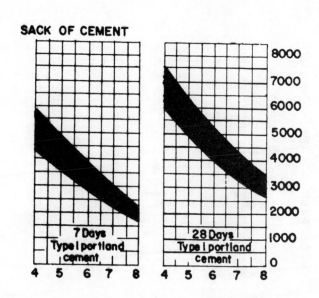

Age-Compressive Strength
Relationship for Types I and III Air-entrained Portland Cement.

(continued from previous page.)

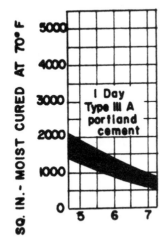

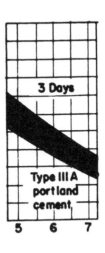

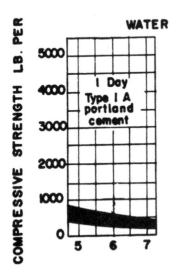

Age-Compressive Strength
Relationship for Types I and III Air-entrained Portland Cement.

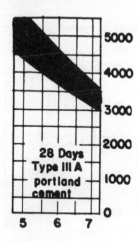

OF CEMENT

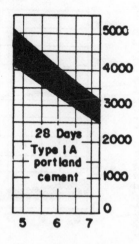

Appendix H
Working
Wood Joints

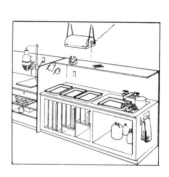

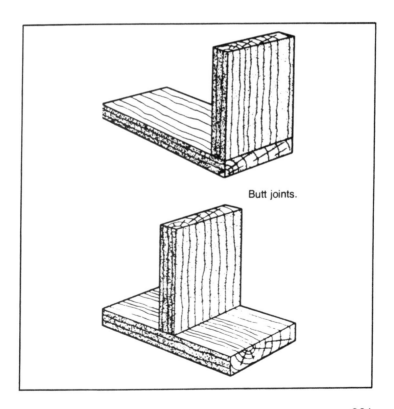

Butt joints.

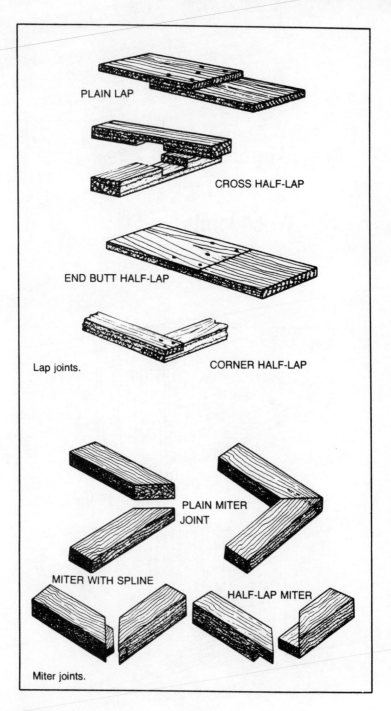

PLAIN LAP

CROSS HALF-LAP

END BUTT HALF-LAP

Lap joints.

CORNER HALF-LAP

PLAIN MITER
JOINT

MITER WITH SPLINE

HALF-LAP MITER

Miter joints.

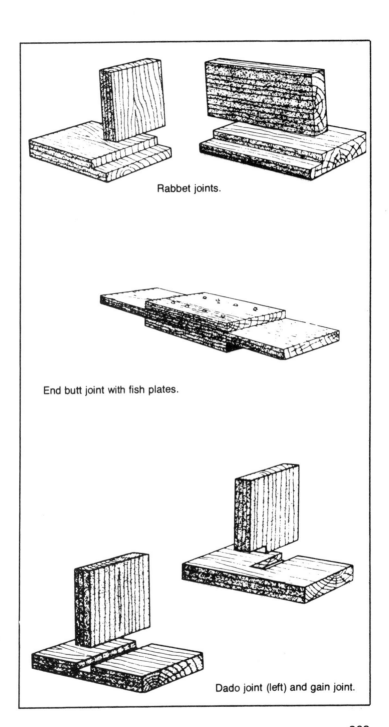

Rabbet joints.

End butt joint with fish plates.

Dado joint (left) and gain joint.

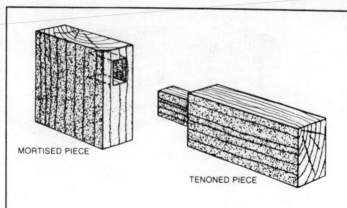

MORTISED PIECE

TENONED PIECE

BLIND MORTISE AND TENON JOINT

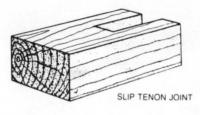

SLIP TENON JOINT

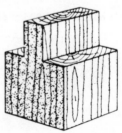

Mortise and tenon joints.

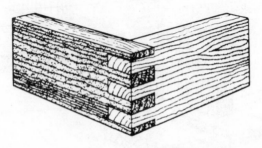

Box corner joint.

DOVETAIL JOINT

THROUGH SINGLE DOVETAIL

BLIND SINGLE DOVETAIL

THROUGH HALF-LAP SINGLE DOVETAIL

Dovetail joints.

PLAIN BUTT

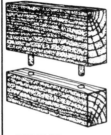

DOWELED

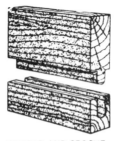

TONGUE AND GROOVE

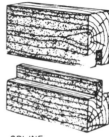

SPLINE

Edge joints.

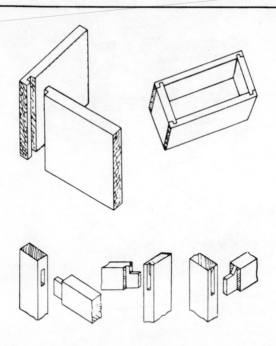

Stub, haunched and table-haunched mortise and tenon joint.

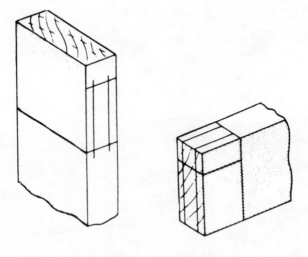

Layout of stub mortise-and-tenon joint.

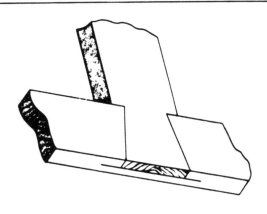

Dovetail half-lap joint.

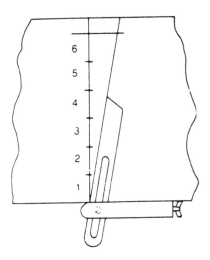

Laying out the 10² angle for the dovetail joint.

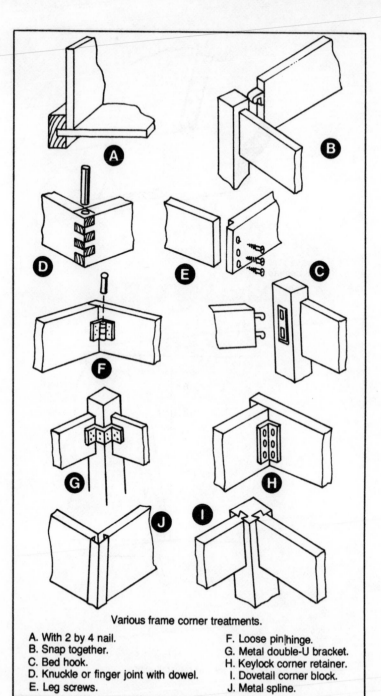

Various frame corner treatments.

A. With 2 by 4 nail.
B. Snap together.
C. Bed hook.
D. Knuckle or finger joint with dowel.
E. Leg screws.
F. Loose pin|hinge.
G. Metal double-U bracket.
H. Keylock corner retainer.
I. Dovetail corner block.
J. Metal spline.

Appendix I
Working Stresses
For Joists and
Rafters

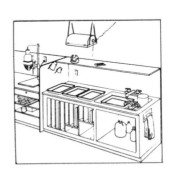

Table I-1. Allowable Spans for High Slope Rafters with a Slope over 3 at 12-30 Pounds per Square Foot Live Load.

DESIGN CRITERIA: Strength - 7 lbs. per sq. ft. dead load plus 30 lbs. per sq. ft. live load determines required fiber stress. Deflection - For 30 lbs. per sq. ft. live load. Limited to span in inches divided by 180. **RAFTERS:** Spans are measured along the horizontal projection and loads are considered as applied on the horizontal projection.

Allowable Extreme Fiber Stress in Bending, "F_b" (psi). (each cell: span / required E)

RAFTER SIZE (IN)	SPACING (IN)	500	600	700	800	900	1000	1100	1200	1300	1400	1500	1600	1700	1800	1900
2x4	12.0	5-3 / 0.27	5-9 / 0.36	6-3 / 0.45	6-8 / 0.55	7-1 / 0.66	7-5 / 0.77	7-9 / 0.89	8-2 / 1.02	8-6 / 1.15	8-9 / 1.28	9-1 / 1.42	9-5 / 1.57	9-8 / 1.72	10-0 / 1.87	10-3 / 2.03
	16.0	4-7 / 0.24	5-0 / 0.31	5-5 / 0.39	5-9 / 0.48	6-1 / 0.57	6-5 / 0.67	6-9 / 0.77	7-1 / 0.88	7-4 / 0.99	7-7 / 1.11	7-11 / 1.23	8-2 / 1.36	8-5 / 1.49	8-8 / 1.62	8-10 / 1.76
	24.0	3-9 / 0.19	4-1 / 0.25	4-5 / 0.32	4-8 / 0.39	5-0 / 0.47	5-3 / 0.55	5-6 / 0.63	5-9 / 0.72	6-0 / 0.81	6-3 / 0.91	6-5 / 1.01	6-8 / 1.11	6-10 / 1.21	7-1 / 1.32	7-3 / 1.43
2x6	12.0	8-3 / 0.27	9-1 / 0.36	9-9 / 0.45	10-5 / 0.55	11-1 / 0.66	11-8 / 0.77	12-3 / 0.89	12-9 / 1.02	13-4 / 1.15	13-10 / 1.28	14-4 / 1.42	14-9 / 1.57	15-3 / 1.72	15-8 / 1.87	16-1 / 2.03
	16.0	7-2 / 0.24	7-10 / 0.31	8-5 / 0.39	9-1 / 0.48	9-7 / 0.57	10-1 / 0.67	10-7 / 0.77	11-1 / 0.88	11-6 / 0.99	12-0 / 1.11	12-5 / 1.23	12-9 / 1.36	13-2 / 1.49	13-7 / 1.62	13-11 / 1.76
	24.0	5-10 / 0.19	6-5 / 0.25	6-11 / 0.32	7-5 / 0.39	7-10 / 0.47	8-3 / 0.55	8-8 / 0.63	9-1 / 0.72	9-5 / 0.81	9-9 / 0.91	10-1 / 1.01	10-5 / 1.11	10-9 / 1.21	11-1 / 1.32	11-5 / 1.43
2x8	12.0	10-11 / 0.27	11-11 / 0.36	12-10 / 0.45	13-9 / 0.55	14-7 / 0.66	15-5 / 0.77	16-2 / 0.89	16-10 / 1.02	17-7 / 1.15	18-2 / 1.28	18-10 / 1.42	19-6 / 1.57	20-1 / 1.72	20-8 / 1.87	21-3 / 2.03
	16.0	9-5 / 0.24	10-4 / 0.31	11-2 / 0.39	11-11 / 0.48	12-8 / 0.57	13-4 / 0.67	14-0 / 0.77	14-7 / 0.88	15-2 / 0.99	15-9 / 1.11	16-4 / 1.23	16-10 / 1.36	17-4 / 1.49	17-11 / 1.62	18-4 / 1.76
	24.0	7-8 / 0.19	8-5 / 0.25	9-1 / 0.32	9-9 / 0.39	10-4 / 0.47	10-11 / 0.55	11-5 / 0.63	11-11 / 0.72	12-5 / 0.81	12-10 / 0.91	13-4 / 1.01	13-9 / 1.11	14-2 / 1.21	14-7 / 1.32	15-0 / 1.43
2x10	12.0	13-11 / 0.27	15-2 / 0.36	16-5 / 0.45	17-7 / 0.55	18-7 / 0.66	19-8 / 0.77	20-7 / 0.89	21-6 / 1.02	22-5 / 1.15	23-3 / 1.28	24-1 / 1.42	24-10 / 1.57	25-7 / 1.72	26-4 / 1.87	27-1 / 2.03
	16.0	12-0 / 0.26	13-2 / 0.34	14-3 / 0.43	15-2 / 0.53	16-2 / 0.63	17-0 / 0.74	17-10 / 0.85	18-7 / 0.97	19-5 / 1.09	20-1 / 1.22	20-10 / 1.35	21-6 / 1.49	22-2 / 1.63	22-10 / 1.78	23-5 / 1.93
	24.0	9-10 / 0.19	10-9 / 0.25	11-7 / 0.32	12-5 / 0.39	13-2 / 0.47	13-11 / 0.55	14-7 / 0.63	15-2 / 0.72	15-10 / 0.81	16-5 / 0.91	17-0 / 1.01	17-7 / 1.11	18-1 / 1.21	18-7 / 1.32	19-2 / 1.43

[1] The required modulus of elasticity, E, in 1,000,000 pounds per square inch is shown below each span.

[2] Use single or repetitive member bending stress values (F_b) and modulus of elasticity values (E), from Table No. 25-A-1.

[3] For more comprehensive tables covering a broader range of bending stress values (F_b) and Modulus of Elasticity values (E), other spacing of members and other conditions of loading, see the Uniform Building Code.

[4] The spans in these tables are intended for use in covered structures or where moisture content in use does not exceed 19 percent.

Table I-2. Spacing of Douglas Fir or Southern Pine Posts for Wind Loads on Gable Roofed Buildings. The Design Bending Strength is 1500 Pounds per Square Inch (Courtesy of Northeast Regional Agricultural Engineering Service).

Post Size in × in[b]	Wind Load psf[c]	Wind Speed mph	Effective Building Height[a], feet 9.0	10.5	12.0	13.5	15.0	19.0
			Maximum Spacing[d], feet					
5.5×9.5	10	62	X	X	38.3	30.3	24.5	15.3
	12	68	X	X	31.9	25.2	20.4	12.8
	15	76	X	X	25.5	20.2	16.3	10.2
7.5×7.5	10	62	X	X	32.5	25.7	20.8	13.0
	12	68	X	35.4	27.1	21.4	17.4	10.8
	15	76	38.6	28.3	21.7	17.1	13.9	8.7
6.0×8.0	10	62	X	38.7	29.6	23.4	19.0	11.8
	12	68	X	32.3	24.7	19.5	15.8	9.8
	15	76	35.1	25.8	19.7	15.6	12.6	7.9
5.5×7.5[e]	10	62	X	31.2	23.9	18.9	15.3	9.5
	12	68	35.4	26.0	19.9	15.7	12.7	7.9
	15	76	28.3	20.8	15.9	12.6	10.2	6.3
6.0×6.0	10	62	29.6	21.8	16.7	13.2	10.7	6.6
	12	68	24.7	18.1	13.9	11.0	8.9	5.5
	15	76	19.7	14.5	11.1	8.8	7.1	4.4
5.5×5.5[e]	10	62	22.8	16.8	12.8	10.1	8.2	5.1
	12	68	19.0	14.0	10.7	8.4	6.8	4.3
	15	76	15.2	11.2	8.5	6.8	5.5	3.4
4.0×6.0	10	62	19.7	14.5	11.1	8.8	7.1	4.4
	12	68	16.5	12.1	9.3	7.3	5.9	3.7
	15	76	13.2	9.7	7.4	5.8	4.7	2.9
3.5×5.5[e]	10	62	14.5	10.7	8.2	6.5	5.2	3.3
	12	68	12.1	8.9	6.8	5.4	4.4	2.7
	15	76	9.7	5.4	5.4	4.3	3.5	2.2
4.0×4.0	10	62	8.8	6.4	4.9	3.9	3.2	2.0
	12	68	7.3	5.4	4.1	3.2	2.6	1.6
	15	76	5.8	4.3	3.2	2.6	2.1	1.3

[a]For roof slopes 4 in 12 or less the effective height is the vertical distance from grade level to the eave. For roof slopes greater than 4 in 12 the effective building height is the vertical distance from grade level to eave height plus half the roof height.

[b]The larger post dimension is in the same direction as the wind or parallel to the building width.

[c]In areas with 20 lb/sq. ft. (psf) wind loads (88 mph) use half the 10 psf spacing.

[d]Spacing greater than 20' not recommended.

[e]These sizes are commonly available in most areas.

Table I-3. Allowable Spans for High-Slope Rafters with a Slope over 3 at 12-30 Pounds per Square Foot Live Load.

DESIGN CRITERIA: Strength - 15 lbs. per sq. ft. dead load plus 30 lbs. per sq. ft. live load determines required fiber stress. Deflection - For 30 lbs. per sq. ft. live load. Limited to span in inches divided by 180. RAFTERS: Spans are measured along the horizontal projection and loads are considered as applied on the horizontal projection.

RAFTER SIZE	SPACING (IN)	Allowable Extreme Fiber Stress in Bending, "F_b" (psi)														
		500	600	700	800	900	1000	1100	1200	1300	1400	1500	1600	1700	1800	1900
2x4	12.0	4-9 / 0.20	5-3 / 0.27	5-8 / 0.34	6-0 / 0.41	6-5 / 0.49	6-9 / 0.58	7-1 / 0.67	7-5 / 0.76	7-8 / 0.86	8-0 / 0.96	8-3 / 1.06	8-6 / 1.17	8-9 / 1.28	9-0 / 1.39	9-3 / 1.51
	16.0	4-1 / 0.18	4-6 / 0.23	4-11 / 0.29	5-3 / 0.36	5-6 / 0.43	5-10 / 0.50	6-1 / 0.58	6-5 / 0.66	6-8 / 0.74	6-11 / 0.83	7-2 / 0.92	7-5 / 1.01	7-7 / 1.11	7-10 / 1.21	8-0 / 1.31
	24.0	3-4 / 0.14	3-8 / 0.19	4-0 / 0.24	4-3 / 0.29	4-6 / 0.35	4-9 / 0.41	5-0 / 0.47	5-3 / 0.54	5-5 / 0.61	5-8 / 0.68	5-10 / 0.75	6-0 / 0.83	6-3 / 0.90	6-5 / 0.99	6-7 / 1.07
2x6	12.0	7-6 / 0.20	8-2 / 0.27	8-10 / 0.34	9-6 / 0.41	10-0 / 0.49	10-7 / 0.58	11-1 / 0.67	11-7 / 0.76	12-1 / 0.86	12-6 / 0.96	13-0 / 1.06	13-5 / 1.17	13-10 / 1.28	14-2 / 1.39	14-7 / 1.51
	16.0	6-6 / 0.18	7-1 / 0.23	7-8 / 0.29	8-2 / 0.36	8-8 / 0.43	9-2 / 0.50	9-7 / 0.58	10-0 / 0.66	10-5 / 0.74	10-10 / 0.83	11-3 / 0.92	11-7 / 1.01	11-11 / 1.11	12-4 / 1.21	12-8 / 1.31
	24.0	5-4 / 0.14	5-10 / 0.19	6-3 / 0.24	6-8 / 0.29	7-1 / 0.35	7-6 / 0.41	7-10 / 0.47	8-2 / 0.54	8-6 / 0.61	8-10 / 0.68	9-2 / 0.75	9-6 / 0.83	9-9 / 0.90	10-0 / 0.99	10-4 / 1.07
2x8	12.0	9-10 / 0.20	10-10 / 0.27	11-8 / 0.34	12-6 / 0.41	13-3 / 0.49	13-11 / 0.58	14-8 / 0.67	15-3 / 0.76	15-11 / 0.86	16-6 / 0.96	17-1 / 1.06	17-8 / 1.17	18-2 / 1.28	18-9 / 1.39	19-3 / 1.51
	16.0	8-7 / 0.18	9-4 / 0.23	10-1 / 0.29	10-10 / 0.36	11-6 / 0.43	12-1 / 0.50	12-8 / 0.58	13-3 / 0.66	13-9 / 0.74	14-4 / 0.83	14-10 / 0.92	15-3 / 1.01	15-9 / 1.11	16-3 / 1.21	16-8 / 1.31
	24.0	7-0 / 0.14	7-8 / 0.19	8-3 / 0.24	8-10 / 0.29	9-4 / 0.35	9-10 / 0.41	10-4 / 0.47	10-10 / 0.54	11-3 / 0.61	11-8 / 0.68	12-1 / 0.75	12-6 / 0.83	12-10 / 0.90	13-3 / 0.99	13-7 / 1.07
2x10	12.0	12-7 / 0.20	13-9 / 0.27	14-11 / 0.34	15-11 / 0.41	16-11 / 0.49	17-10 / 0.58	18-8 / 0.67	19-6 / 0.76	20-4 / 0.86	21-1 / 0.96	21-10 / 1.06	22-6 / 1.17	23-3 / 1.28	23-11 / 1.39	24-6 / 1.51
	16.0	10-11 / 0.18	11-11 / 0.23	12-11 / 0.29	13-9 / 0.36	14-8 / 0.43	15-5 / 0.50	16-2 / 0.58	16-11 / 0.66	17-7 / 0.74	18-3 / 0.83	18-11 / 0.92	19-6 / 1.01	20-1 / 1.11	20-8 / 1.21	21-3 / 1.31
	24.0	8-11 / 0.14	9-9 / 0.19	10-6 / 0.24	11-3 / 0.29	11-11 / 0.35	12-7 / 0.41	13-2 / 0.47	13-9 / 0.54	14-4 / 0.61	14-11 / 0.68	15-5 / 0.75	15-11 / 0.83	16-5 / 0.90	16-11 / 0.99	17-4 / 1.07

[1] The required modulus of elasticity, E, in 1,000,000 pounds per square inch is shown below each span.

[2] Use single or repetitive member bending stress values (F_b) and modulus of elasticity values (E), from Table No. 25-A-1.

[3] For more comprehensive tables covering a broader range of bending stress values (F_b) and Modulus of Elasticity values (E), other spacing of members and other conditions of loading, see the Uniform Building Code.

[4] The spans in these tables are intended for use in covered structures or where moisture content in use does not exceed 19 percent.

Table I-4. Allowable Spans for High-Slope Rafters with a Slope over 3 at 12-20 Pounds per Square Foot Live Load.

DESIGN CRITERIA: Strength - 7 lbs. per sq. ft. dead load plus 20 lbs. per sq. ft. live load determines required fiber stress. Deflection - For 20 lbs. per sq. ft. live load. Limited to span in inches divided by 180. RAFTERS: Spans are measured along the horizontal projection and loads are considered as applied on the horizontal projection.

RAFTER SIZE (IN)	SPACING (IN)	Allowable Extreme Fiber Stress in Bending, "F_b" (psi).														
		500	600	700	800	900	1000	1100	1200	1300	1400	1500	1600	1700	1800	1900
2x4	12.0	6-2 0.29	6-9 0.38	7-3 0.49	7-9 0.59	8-3 0.71	8-8 0.83	9-1 0.96	9-6 1.09	9-11 1.23	10-3 1.37	10-8 1.52	11-0 1.68	11-4 1.84	11-8 2.00	12-0 2.17
	16.0	5-4 0.25	5-10 0.33	6-4 0.42	6-9 0.51	7-2 0.61	7-6 0.72	7-11 0.83	8-3 0.94	8-7 1.06	8-11 1.19	9-3 1.32	9-6 1.45	9-10 1.59	10-1 1.73	10-5 1.88
	24.0	4-4 0.21	4-9 0.27	5-2 0.34	5-6 0.42	5-10 0.50	6-2 0.59	6-5 0.68	6-9 0.77	7-0 0.87	7-3 0.97	7-6 1.08	7-9 1.19	8-0 1.30	8-3 1.41	8-6 1.53
2x6	12.0	9-8 0.29	10-7 0.38	11-5 0.49	12-3 0.59	13-0 0.71	13-8 0.83	14-4 0.96	15-0 1.09	15-7 1.23	16-2 1.37	16-9 1.52	17-3 1.68	17-10 1.84	18-4 2.00	18-10 2.17
	16.0	8-4 0.25	9-2 0.33	9-11 0.42	10-7 0.51	11-3 0.61	11-10 0.72	12-5 0.83	13-0 0.94	13-6 1.06	14-0 1.19	14-6 1.32	15-0 1.45	15-5 1.59	15-11 1.73	16-4 1.88
	24.0	6-10 0.21	7-6 0.27	8-1 0.34	8-8 0.42	9-2 0.50	9-8 0.59	10-2 0.68	10-7 0.77	11-0 0.87	11-5 0.97	11-10 1.08	12-3 1.19	12-7 1.30	13-0 1.41	13-4 1.53
2x8	12.0	12-9 0.29	13-11 0.38	15-1 0.49	16-1 0.59	17-1 0.71	18-0 0.83	18-11 0.96	19-9 1.09	20-6 1.23	21-4 1.37	22-1 1.52	22-9 1.68	23-6 1.84	24-2 2.00	24-10 2.17
	16.0	11-0 0.25	12-1 0.33	13-1 0.42	13-11 0.51	14-10 0.61	15-7 0.72	16-4 0.83	17-1 0.94	17-9 1.06	18-5 1.19	19-1 1.32	19-9 1.45	20-4 1.59	20-11 1.73	21-6 1.88
	24.0	9-0 0.21	9-10 0.27	10-8 0.34	11-5 0.42	12-1 0.50	12-9 0.59	13-4 0.68	13-11 0.77	14-6 0.87	15-1 0.97	15-7 1.08	16-1 1.19	16-7 1.30	17-1 1.41	17-7 1.53
2x10	12.0	16-3 0.29	17-10 0.38	19-3 0.49	20-7 0.59	21-10 0.71	23-0 0.83	24-1 0.96	25-2 1.09	26-2 1.23	27-2 1.37	28-2 1.52	29-1 1.68	30-0 1.84	30-10 2.00	31-8 2.17
	16.0	14-1 0.25	15-5 0.33	16-8 0.42	17-10 0.51	18-11 0.61	19-11 0.72	20-10 0.83	21-10 0.94	22-8 1.06	23-7 1.19	24-5 1.32	25-2 1.45	25-11 1.59	26-8 1.73	27-5 1.88
	24.0	11-6 0.21	12-7 0.27	13-7 0.34	14-6 0.42	15-5 0.50	16-3 0.59	17-1 0.68	17-10 0.77	18-6 0.87	19-3 0.97	19-11 1.08	20-7 1.19	21-2 1.30	21-10 1.41	22-5 1.53

[1] The required modulus of elasticity, E, in 1,000,000 pounds per square inch is shown below each span.

[2] Use single or repetitive member bending stress values (F_b) and modulus of elasticity values (E), from Table No. 25-A-1.

[3] For more comprehensive tables covering a broader range of bending stress values (F_b) and Modulus of Elasticity values (E), other spacing of members and other conditions of loading, see the Uniform Building Code.

[4] The spans in these tables are intended for use in covered structures or where moisture content in use does not exceed 19 percent.

Table I-5. Allowable Spans for Low-Slope Rafters with a Slope 3 in 12 or less at 30 Pounds per Square Foot Live Load.

DESIGN CRITERIA: Strength - 10 lbs. per sq. ft. dead load plus 30 lbs. per sq. ft. live load determines required fiber stress. Deflection - For 30 lbs. per sq. ft. live load. Limited to span in inches divided by 240. RAFTERS: Spans are measured along the horizontal projection and loads are considered as applied on the horizontal projection.

Values given as span (ft-in) / required modulus of elasticity E (in millions psi).

RAFTER SIZE	SPACING (IN)	Allowable Extreme Fiber Stress in Bending, "F_b" (psi).														
		500	600	700	800	900	1000	1100	1200	1300	1400	1500	1600	1700	1800	1900
2x6	12.0	7-11 / 0.32	8-8 / 0.43	9-5 / 0.54	10-0 / 0.66	10-8 / 0.78	11-3 / 0.92	11-9 / 1.06	12-4 / 1.21	12-10 / 1.36	13-3 / 1.52	13-9 / 1.69	14-2 / 1.86	14-8 / 2.04	15-1 / 2.22	15-6 / 2.41
	16.0	6-11 / 0.28	7-6 / 0.37	8-2 / 0.47	8-8 / 0.57	9-3 / 0.68	9-9 / 0.80	10-2 / 0.92	10-8 / 1.05	11-1 / 1.18	11-6 / 1.32	11-11 / 1.46	12-4 / 1.61	12-8 / 1.76	13-1 / 1.92	13-5 / 2.08
	24.0	5-7 / 0.23	6-2 / 0.30	6-8 / 0.38	7-1 / 0.46	7-6 / 0.55	7-11 / 0.65	8-4 / 0.75	8-8 / 0.85	9-1 / 0.96	9-5 / 1.08	9-9 / 1.19	10-0 / 1.31	10-4 / 1.44	10-8 / 1.57	10-11 / 1.70
2x8	12.0	10-6 / 0.32	11-6 / 0.43	12-5 / 0.54	13-3 / 0.66	14-0 / 0.78	14-10 / 0.92	15-6 / 1.06	16-3 / 1.21	16-10 / 1.36	17-6 / 1.52	18-2 / 1.69	18-9 / 1.86	19-4 / 2.04	19-10 / 2.22	20-5 / 2.41
	16.0	9-1 / 0.28	9-11 / 0.37	10-9 / 0.47	11-6 / 0.57	12-2 / 0.68	12-10 / 0.80	13-5 / 0.92	14-0 / 1.05	14-7 / 1.18	15-2 / 1.32	15-8 / 1.46	16-3 / 1.61	16-9 / 1.76	17-2 / 1.92	17-8 / 2.08
	24.0	7-5 / 0.23	8-1 / 0.30	8-9 / 0.38	9-4 / 0.46	9-11 / 0.55	10-6 / 0.65	11-0 / 0.75	11-6 / 0.85	11-11 / 0.96	12-5 / 1.08	12-10 / 1.19	13-3 / 1.31	13-8 / 1.44	14-0 / 1.57	14-5 / 1.70
2x10	12.0	13-4 / 0.32	14-8 / 0.43	15-10 / 0.54	16-11 / 0.66	17-11 / 0.78	18-11 / 0.92	19-10 / 1.06	20-8 / 1.21	21-6 / 1.36	22-4 / 1.52	23-2 / 1.69	23-11 / 1.86	24-7 / 2.04	25-4 / 2.22	26-0 / 2.41
	16.0	11-7 / 0.28	12-8 / 0.37	13-8 / 0.47	14-8 / 0.57	15-6 / 0.68	16-4 / 0.80	17-2 / 0.92	17-11 / 1.05	18-8 / 1.18	19-4 / 1.32	20-0 / 1.46	20-8 / 1.61	21-4 / 1.76	21-11 / 1.92	22-6 / 2.08
	24.0	9-5 / 0.23	10-4 / 0.30	11-2 / 0.38	11-11 / 0.46	12-8 / 0.55	13-4 / 0.65	14-0 / 0.75	14-8 / 0.85	15-3 / 0.96	15-10 / 1.08	16-4 / 1.19	16-11 / 1.31	17-5 / 1.44	17-11 / 1.57	18-5 / 1.70
2x12	12.0	16-3 / 0.32	17-9 / 0.43	19-3 / 0.54	20-6 / 0.66	21-9 / 0.78	23-0 / 0.92	24-1 / 1.06	25-2 / 1.21	26-2 / 1.36	27-2 / 1.52	28-2 / 1.69	29-1 / 1.86	29-11 / 2.04	30-10 / 2.22	31-8 / 2.41
	16.0	14-1 / 0.28	15-5 / 0.37	16-8 / 0.47	17-9 / 0.57	18-10 / 0.68	19-11 / 0.80	20-10 / 0.92	21-9 / 1.05	22-8 / 1.18	23-6 / 1.32	24-4 / 1.46	25-2 / 1.61	25-11 / 1.76	26-8 / 1.92	27-5 / 2.08
	24.0	11-6 / 0.23	12-7 / 0.30	13-7 / 0.38	14-6 / 0.46	15-5 / 0.55	16-3 / 0.65	17-0 / 0.75	17-9 / 0.85	18-6 / 0.96	19-3 / 1.08	19-11 / 1.19	20-6 / 1.31	21-2 / 1.44	21-9 / 1.57	22-5 / 1.70

[1] The required modulus of elasticity, E, in 1,000,000 pounds per square inch is shown below each span.

[2] Use single or repetitive member bending stress values (F_b) and modulus of elasticity values (E), from Table No. 25-A-1.

[3] For more comprehensive tables covering a broader range of bending stress values (F_b) and Modulus of Elasticity values (E), other spacing of members and other conditions of loading, see the Uniform Building Code.

[4] The spans in these tables are intended for use in covered structures or where moisture content in use does not exceed 19 percent.

Table I-6. Allowable Spans for High-Slope Rafters with a Slope over 3. These Figures are Based on 12-20 Pounds per Square Foot Live Load.

DESIGN CRITERIA: Strength - 15 lbs. per sq. ft. dead load plus 20 lbs. ner sq. ft. live load determines required fiber stress. Deflection - For 20 lbs. per sq. ft. live load. Limited to span in inches divided by 180. RAFTERS: Spans are measured along the horizontal projection and loads are considered as applied on the horizontal projection.

RAFTER SIZE / SPACING (IN)		500	600	700	800	900	1000	1100	1200	1300	1400	1500	1600	1700	1800	1900
		Allowable Extreme Fiber Stress in Bending, "F_b" (psi).														
2x4	12.0	5-5 / 0.20	5-11 / 0.26	6-5 / 0.33	6-10 / 0.40	7-3 / 0.48	7-8 / 0.56	8-0 / 0.65	8-4 / 0.74	8-8 / 0.83	9-0 / 0.93	9-4 / 1.03	9-8 / 1.14	9-11 / 1.24	10-3 / 1.36	10-6 / 1.47
	16.0	4-8 / 0.17	5-1 / 0.23	5-6 / 0.28	5-11 / 0.35	6-3 / 0.41	6-7 / 0.49	6-11 / 0.56	7-3 / 0.64	7-6 / 0.72	7-10 / 0.80	8-1 / 0.89	8-4 / 0.98	8-7 / 1.08	8-10 / 1.17	9-1 / 1.27
	24.0	3-10 / 0.14	4-2 / 0.18	4-6 / 0.23	4-10 / 0.28	5-1 / 0.34	5-5 / 0.40	5-8 / 0.46	5-11 / 0.52	6-2 / 0.59	6-5 / 0.66	6-7 / 0.73	6-10 / 0.80	7-0 / 0.88	7-3 / 0.96	7-5 / 1.04
2x6	12.0	8-6 / 0.20	9-4 / 0.26	10-0 / 0.33	10-9 / 0.40	11-5 / 0.48	12-0 / 0.56	12-7 / 0.65	13-2 / 0.74	13-8 / 0.83	14-2 / 0.93	14-8 / 1.03	15-2 / 1.14	15-8 / 1.24	16-1 / 1.36	16-7 / 1.47
	16.0	7-4 / 0.17	8-1 / 0.23	8-8 / 0.28	9-4 / 0.35	9-10 / 0.41	10-5 / 0.49	10-11 / 0.56	11-5 / 0.64	11-10 / 0.72	12-4 / 0.80	12-9 / 0.89	13-2 / 0.98	13-7 / 1.08	13-11 / 1.17	14-4 / 1.27
	24.0	6-0 / 0.14	6-7 / 0.18	7-1 / 0.23	7-7 / 0.28	8-1 / 0.34	8-6 / 0.40	8-11 / 0.46	9-4 / 0.52	9-8 / 0.59	10-0 / 0.66	10-5 / 0.73	10-9 / 0.80	11-1 / 0.88	11-5 / 0.96	11-8 / 1.04
2x8	12.0	11-2 / 0.20	12-3 / 0.26	13-3 / 0.33	14-2 / 0.40	15-0 / 0.48	15-10 / 0.56	16-7 / 0.65	17-4 / 0.74	18-0 / 0.83	18-9 / 0.93	19-5 / 1.03	20-0 / 1.14	20-8 / 1.24	21-3 / 1.36	21-10 / 1.47
	16.0	9-8 / 0.17	10-7 / 0.23	11-6 / 0.28	12-3 / 0.35	13-0 / 0.41	13-8 / 0.49	14-4 / 0.56	15-0 / 0.64	15-7 / 0.72	16-3 / 0.80	16-9 / 0.89	17-4 / 0.98	17-10 / 1.08	18-5 / 1.17	18-11 / 1.27
	24.0	7-11 / 0.14	8-8 / 0.18	9-4 / 0.23	10-0 / 0.28	10-7 / 0.34	11-2 / 0.40	11-9 / 0.46	12-3 / 0.52	12-9 / 0.59	13-3 / 0.66	13-8 / 0.73	14-2 / 0.80	14-7 / 0.88	15-0 / 0.96	15-5 / 1.04
2x10	12.0	14-3 / 0.20	15-8 / 0.26	16-11 / 0.33	18-1 / 0.40	19-2 / 0.48	20-2 / 0.56	21-2 / 0.65	22-1 / 0.74	23-0 / 0.83	23-11 / 0.93	24-9 / 1.03	25-6 / 1.14	26-4 / 1.24	27-1 / 1.36	27-10 / 1.47
	16.0	12-4 / 0.17	13-6 / 0.23	14-8 / 0.28	15-8 / 0.35	16-7 / 0.41	17-6 / 0.49	18-4 / 0.56	19-2 / 0.64	19-11 / 0.72	20-8 / 0.80	21-5 / 0.89	22-1 / 0.98	22-10 / 1.08	23-5 / 1.17	24-1 / 1.27
	24.0	10-1 / 0.14	11-1 / 0.18	11-11 / 0.23	12-9 / 0.28	13-6 / 0.34	14-3 / 0.40	15-0 / 0.46	15-8 / 0.52	16-3 / 0.59	16-11 / 0.66	17-6 / 0.73	18-1 / 0.80	18-7 / 0.88	19-2 / 0.96	19-8 / 1.04

[1] The required modulus of elasticity, E, in 1,000,000 pounds per square inch is shown below each span.

[2] Use single or repetitive member bending stress values (F_b) and modulus of elasticity values (E), from Table No. 25-A-1.

[3] For more comprehensive tables covering a broader range of bending stress values (F_b) and Modulus of Elasticity values (E), other spacing of members and other conditions of loading, see the Uniform Building Code.

[4] The spans in these tables are intended for use in covered structures or where moisture content in use does not exceed 19 percent.

Table I-7. Allowable Spans for Low-Slope or High-Slope Rafters at 30 Pounds per Square Foot Live Load.

DESIGN CRITERIA: Strength - 15 lbs. per sq. ft. dead load plus 30 lbs. per sq. ft. live load determines required fiber stress. Deflection - For 30 lbs. per sq. ft. live load. Limited to span in inches divided by 240. RAFTERS: Spans are measured along the horizontal projection and loads are considered as applied on the horizontal projection.

RAFTER SIZE (IN)	SPACING (IN)	Allowable Extreme Fiber Stress in Bending, "F_b" (psi).														
		500	600	700	800	900	1000	1100	1200	1300	1400	1500	1600	1700	1800	1900
2x6	12.0	7-6 / 0.27	8-2 / 0.36	8-10 / 0.45	9-6 / 0.55	10-0 / 0.66	10-7 / 0.77	11-1 / 0.89	11-7 / 1.01	12-1 / 1.14	12-6 / 1.28	13-0 / 1.41	13-5 / 1.56	13-10 / 1.71	14-2 / 1.86	14-7 / 2.02
	16.0	6-6 / 0.24	7-1 / 0.31	7-8 / 0.39	8-2 / 0.48	8-8 / 0.57	9-2 / 0.67	9-7 / 0.77	10-0 / 0.88	10-5 / 0.99	10-10 / 1.10	11-3 / 1.22	11-7 / 1.35	11-11 / 1.48	12-4 / 1.61	12-8 / 1.75
	24.0	5-4 / 0.19	5-10 / 0.25	6-3 / 0.32	6-8 / 0.39	7-1 / 0.46	7-6 / 0.54	7-10 / 0.63	8-2 / 0.72	8-6 / 0.81	8-10 / 0.90	9-2 / 1.00	9-6 / 1.10	9-9 / 1.21	10-0 / 1.31	10-4 / 1.43
2x8	12.0	9-10 / 0.27	10-10 / 0.36	11-8 / 0.45	12-6 / 0.55	13-3 / 0.66	13-11 / 0.77	14-8 / 0.89	15-3 / 1.01	15-11 / 1.14	16-6 / 1.28	17-1 / 1.41	17-8 / 1.56	18-2 / 1.71	18-9 / 1.86	19-3 / 2.02
	16.0	8-7 / 0.24	9-4 / 0.31	10-1 / 0.39	10-10 / 0.48	11-6 / 0.57	12-1 / 0.67	12-8 / 0.77	13-3 / 0.88	13-9 / 0.99	14-4 / 1.10	14-10 / 1.22	15-3 / 1.35	15-9 / 1.48	16-3 / 1.61	16-8 / 1.75
	24.0	7-0 / 0.19	7-8 / 0.25	8-3 / 0.32	8-10 / 0.39	9-4 / 0.46	9-10 / 0.54	10-4 / 0.63	10-10 / 0.72	11-3 / 0.81	11-8 / 0.90	12-1 / 1.00	12-6 / 1.10	12-10 / 1.21	13-3 / 1.31	13-7 / 1.43
2x10	12.0	12-7 / 0.27	13-9 / 0.36	14-11 / 0.45	15-11 / 0.55	16-11 / 0.66	17-10 / 0.77	18-8 / 0.89	19-6 / 1.01	20-4 / 1.14	21-1 / 1.28	21-10 / 1.41	22-6 / 1.56	23-3 / 1.71	23-11 / 1.86	24-6 / 2.02
	16.0	10-11 / 0.24	11-11 / 0.31	12-11 / 0.39	13-9 / 0.48	14-8 / 0.57	15-5 / 0.67	16-2 / 0.77	16-11 / 0.88	17-7 / 0.99	18-3 / 1.10	18-11 / 1.22	19-6 / 1.35	20-1 / 1.48	20-8 / 1.61	21-3 / 1.75
	24.0	8-11 / 0.19	9-9 / 0.25	10-6 / 0.32	11-3 / 0.39	11-11 / 0.46	12-7 / 0.54	13-2 / 0.63	13-9 / 0.72	14-4 / 0.81	14-11 / 0.90	15-5 / 1.00	15-11 / 1.10	16-5 / 1.21	16-11 / 1.31	17-4 / 1.43
2x12	12.0	15-4 / 0.27	16-9 / 0.36	18-1 / 0.45	19-4 / 0.55	20-6 / 0.66	21-8 / 0.77	22-8 / 0.89	23-9 / 1.01	24-8 / 1.14	25-7 / 1.28	26-6 / 1.41	27-5 / 1.56	28-3 / 1.71	29-1 / 1.86	29-10 / 2.02
	16.0	13-3 / 0.24	14-6 / 0.31	15-8 / 0.39	16-9 / 0.48	17-9 / 0.57	18-9 / 0.67	19-8 / 0.77	20-6 / 0.88	21-5 / 0.99	22-2 / 1.10	23-0 / 1.22	23-9 / 1.35	24-5 / 1.48	25-2 / 1.61	25-10 / 1.75
	24.0	10-10 / 0.19	11-10 / 0.25	12-10 / 0.32	13-8 / 0.39	14-6 / 0.46	15-4 / 0.54	16-1 / 0.63	16-9 / 0.72	17-5 / 0.81	18-1 / 0.90	18-9 / 1.00	19-4 / 1.10	20-0 / 1.21	20-6 / 1.31	21-1 / 1.43

1 The required modulus of elasticity, E, in 1,000,000 pounds per square inch is shown below each span.
2 Use single or repetitive member bending stress values (F_b) and modulus of elasticity values (E), from Table No. 25-A-I.
3 For more comprehensive tables covering a broader range of bending stress values (F_b) and Modulus of Elasticity values (E), other spacing of members and other conditions of loading, see the Uniform Building Code.
4 The spans in these tables are intended for use in covered structures or where moisture content in use does not exceed 19 percent.

Table I-8. Allowable Spans for Low-Slope Rafters with a Slope 3 in 12 or less at 30 Pounds per Square Foot Live Load.

DESIGN CRITERIA: Strength - 10 lbs. per sq. ft. dead load plus 20 lbs. per sq. ft. live load determines required fiber stress. Deflection - For 20 lbs. per sq. ft. live load. Limited to span in inches divided by 240. RAFTERS: Spans are measured along the horizontal projection and loads are considered as applied on the horizontal projection.

Allowable Extreme Fiber Stress in Bending, "F_b" (psi). (Each cell: span as feet-inches / required E in millions psi.)

RAFTER SIZE (IN)	SPACING (IN)	500	600	700	800	900	1000	1100	1200	1300	1400	1500	1600	1700	1800	1900
2x6	12.0	9-2 / 0.33	10-0 / 0.44	10-10 / 0.55	11-7 / 0.67	12-4 / 0.80	13-0 / 0.94	13-7 / 1.09	14-2 / 1.24	14-9 / 1.40	15-4 / 1.56	15-11 / 1.73	16-5 / 1.91	16-11 / 2.09	17-5 / 2.28	17-10 / 2.47
	16.0	7-11 / 0.29	8-8 / 0.38	9-5 / 0.48	10-0 / 0.58	10-8 / 0.70	11-3 / 0.82	11-9 / 0.94	12-4 / 1.07	12-10 / 1.21	13-3 / 1.35	13-9 / 1.50	14-2 / 1.65	14-8 / 1.81	15-1 / 1.97	15-6 / 2.14
	24.0	6-6 / 0.24	7-1 / 0.31	7-8 / 0.39	8-2 / 0.48	8-8 / 0.57	9-2 / 0.67	9-7 / 0.77	10-0 / 0.88	10-5 / 0.99	10-10 / 1.10	11-3 / 1.22	11-7 / 1.35	11-11 / 1.48	12-4 / 1.61	12-8 / 1.75
2x8	12.0	12-1 / 0.33	13-3 / 0.44	14-4 / 0.55	15-3 / 0.67	16-3 / 0.80	17-1 / 0.94	17-11 / 1.09	18-9 / 1.24	19-6 / 1.40	20-3 / 1.56	20-11 / 1.73	21-7 / 1.91	22-3 / 2.09	22-11 / 2.28	23-7 / 2.47
	16.0	10-6 / 0.29	11-6 / 0.38	12-5 / 0.48	13-3 / 0.58	14-0 / 0.70	14-10 / 0.82	15-6 / 0.94	16-3 / 1.07	16-10 / 1.21	17-6 / 1.35	18-2 / 1.50	18-9 / 1.65	19-4 / 1.81	19-10 / 1.97	20-5 / 2.14
	24.0	8-7 / 0.24	9-4 / 0.31	10-1 / 0.39	10-10 / 0.48	11-6 / 0.57	12-1 / 0.67	12-8 / 0.77	13-3 / 0.88	13-9 / 0.99	14-4 / 1.10	14-10 / 1.22	15-3 / 1.35	15-9 / 1.48	16-3 / 1.61	16-8 / 1.75
2x10	12.0	15-5 / 0.33	16-11 / 0.44	18-3 / 0.55	19-6 / 0.67	20-8 / 0.80	21-10 / 0.94	22-10 / 1.09	23-11 / 1.24	24-10 / 1.40	25-10 / 1.56	26-8 / 1.73	27-7 / 1.91	28-5 / 2.09	29-3 / 2.28	30-1 / 2.47
	16.0	13-4 / 0.29	14-8 / 0.38	15-10 / 0.48	16-11 / 0.58	17-11 / 0.70	18-11 / 0.82	19-10 / 0.94	20-8 / 1.07	21-6 / 1.21	22-4 / 1.35	23-2 / 1.50	23-11 / 1.65	24-7 / 1.81	25-4 / 1.97	26-0 / 2.14
	24.0	10-11 / 0.24	11-11 / 0.31	12-11 / 0.39	13-9 / 0.48	14-8 / 0.57	15-5 / 0.67	16-2 / 0.77	16-11 / 0.88	17-7 / 0.99	18-3 / 1.10	18-11 / 1.22	19-6 / 1.35	20-1 / 1.48	20-8 / 1.61	21-3 / 1.75
2x12	12.0	18-9 / 0.33	20-6 / 0.44	22-2 / 0.55	23-9 / 0.67	25-2 / 0.80	26-6 / 0.94	27-10 / 1.09	29-1 / 1.24	30-3 / 1.40	31-4 / 1.56	32-6 / 1.73	33-6 / 1.91	34-7 / 2.09	35-7 / 2.28	36-7 / 2.47
	16.0	16-3 / 0.29	17-9 / 0.38	19-3 / 0.48	20-6 / 0.58	21-9 / 0.70	23-0 / 0.82	24-1 / 0.94	25-2 / 1.07	26-2 / 1.21	27-2 / 1.35	28-2 / 1.50	29-1 / 1.65	29-11 / 1.81	30-10 / 1.97	31-8 / 2.14
	24.0	13-3 / 0.24	14-6 / 0.31	15-8 / 0.39	16-9 / 0.48	17-9 / 0.57	18-9 / 0.67	19-8 / 0.77	20-6 / 0.88	21-5 / 0.99	22-2 / 1.10	23-0 / 1.22	23-9 / 1.35	24-5 / 1.48	25-2 / 1.61	25-10 / 1.75

[1] The required modulus of elasticity, E, in 1,000,000 pounds per square inch is shown below each span.

[2] Use single or repetitive member bending stress values (F_b) and modulus of elasticity values (E), from Table No. 25-A-1.

[3] For more comprehensive tables covering a broader range of bending stress values (F_b) and Modulus of Elasticity values (E), other spacing of members and other conditions of loading, see the Uniform Building Code.

[4] The spans in these tables are intended for use in covered structures or where moisture content in use does not exceed 19 percent.

Table I-9. Allowable Spans for Ceiling Joists at 10 Pounds per Square Foot Live Load.

DESIGN CRITERIA: Deflection - For 10 lbs. per sq. ft. live load. Limited to span in inches divided by 240. Strength - Live load of 10 lbs. per sq. ft. plus dead load of 5 lbs. per sq. ft. determines required fiber stress value.

Joist Size (IN)	Spacing (IN)	Modulus of Elasticity, "E", in 1,000,000 psi													
		0.8	0.9	1.0	1.1	1.2	1.3	1.4	1.5	1.6	1.7	1.8	1.9	2.0	2.2
2x4	12.0	9-10 / 710	10-3 / 770	10-7 / 830	10-11 / 880	11-3 / 930	11-7 / 980	11-10 / 1030	12-2 / 1080	12-5 / 1130	12-8 / 1180	12-11 / 1220	13-2 / 1270	13-4 / 1310	13-9 / 1400
	16.0	8-11 / 780	9-4 / 850	9-8 / 910	9-11 / 970	10-3 / 1030	10-6 / 1080	10-9 / 1140	11-0 / 1190	11-3 / 1240	11-6 / 1290	11-9 / 1340	11-11 / 1390	12-2 / 1440	12-6 / 1540
	24.0	7-10 / 900	8-1 / 970	8-5 / 1040	8-8 / 1110	8-11 / 1170	9-2 / 1240	9-5 / 1300	9-8 / 1360	9-10 / 1420	10-0 / 1480	10-3 / 1540	10-5 / 1600	10-7 / 1650	10-11 / 1760
2x6	12.0	15-6 / 710	16-1 / 770	16-8 / 830	17-2 / 880	17-8 / 930	18-2 / 980	18-8 / 1030	19-1 / 1080	19-6 / 1130	19-11 / 1180	20-3 / 1220	20-8 / 1270	21-0 / 1310	21-8 / 1400
	16.0	14-1 / 780	14-7 / 850	15-2 / 910	15-7 / 970	16-1 / 1030	16-6 / 1080	16-11 / 1140	17-4 / 1190	17-8 / 1240	18-1 / 1290	18-5 / 1340	18-9 / 1390	19-1 / 1440	19-8 / 1540
	24.0	12-3 / 900	12-9 / 970	13-3 / 1040	13-8 / 1110	14-1 / 1170	14-5 / 1240	14-9 / 1300	15-2 / 1360	15-6 / 1420	15-9 / 1480	16-1 / 1540	16-4 / 1600	16-8 / 1650	17-2 / 1760
2x8	12.0	20-5 / 710	21-2 / 770	21-11 / 830	22-8 / 880	23-4 / 930	24-0 / 980	24-7 / 1030	25-2 / 1080	25-8 / 1130	26-2 / 1180	26-9 / 1220	27-2 / 1270	27-8 / 1310	28-7 / 1400
	16.0	18-6 / 780	19-3 / 850	19-11 / 910	20-7 / 970	21-2 / 1030	21-9 / 1080	22-4 / 1140	22-10 / 1190	23-4 / 1240	23-10 / 1290	24-3 / 1340	24-8 / 1390	25-2 / 1440	25-11 / 1540
	24.0	16-2 / 900	16-10 / 970	17-5 / 1040	18-0 / 1110	18-6 / 1170	19-0 / 1240	19-6 / 1300	19-11 / 1360	20-5 / 1420	20-10 / 1480	21-2 / 1540	21-7 / 1600	21-11 / 1650	22-8 / 1760
2x10	12.0	26-0 / 710	27-1 / 770	28-0 / 830	28-11 / 880	29-9 / 930	30-7 / 980	31-4 / 1030	32-1 / 1080	32-9 / 1130	33-5 / 1180	34-1 / 1220	34-8 / 1270	35-4 / 1310	36-5 / 1400
	16.0	23-8 / 780	24-7 / 850	25-5 / 910	26-3 / 970	27-1 / 1030	27-9 / 1080	28-6 / 1140	29-2 / 1190	29-9 / 1240	30-5 / 1290	31-0 / 1340	31-6 / 1390	32-1 / 1440	33-1 / 1540
	24.0	20-8 / 900	21-6 / 970	22-3 / 1040	22-11 / 1110	23-8 / 1170	24-3 / 1240	24-10 / 1300	25-5 / 1360	26-0 / 1420	26-6 / 1480	27-1 / 1540	27-6 / 1600	28-0 / 1650	28-1 / 1760

[1] The required extreme fiber stress in bending, F_b, in pounds per square inch is shown below each span.
[2] Use single or repetitive member bending stress values (F_b) and modulus of elasticity values (E), from Table No. 25-A-1.
[3] For more comprehensive tables covering a broader range of bending stress values (F_b) and Modulus of Elasticity values (E), other spacing of members and other conditions of loading, see the Uniform Building Code.
[4] The spans in these tables are intended for use in covered structures or where moisture content in use does not exceed 19 percent.

Index